Photo by Minor Studio

About the Author

Ellis Gibbs Arnall was, at the time of his election as Governor of Georgia in 1942, the youngest state chief executive. During his term in the gubernatorial chair and his preceding years as state Attorney General, Arnall became a colorful and commanding figure on the national scene as a spokesman for the enlightened South. He was a principal in Georgia's to-the-finish fight against the Ku Klux Klan, racial and religious intolerance, and back room politics, and he waged a successful battle against rate discrimination by railroads in southern states. His term as governor ended dramatically and on a high note in January, 1947, when he successfully opposed the attempt of Herman Talmadge to seize the chair as political heir to governor-elect Eugene Talmadge who died before inauguration.

Since leaving office, Mr. Arnall has practiced law in his native Newnan, Georgia, and in Atlanta. He has served as president of a Georgia insurance company, and he has travelled more than 75,000 miles during a lecture tour that has taken him to the small and large communities in 47 states. He is the author of *The Shore Dimly Seen,* a best-seller published in 1946 in which he gives his credo for the South; has written articles that have appeared in *The Atlantic, The Nation, The Yale Review* and other leading publications; and has frequently participated on such network radio programs as "Town Meeting of the Air," "Information, Please" and "The Chicago Round Table."

Mr. Arnall is married, and is the father of one son born in 1938, one daughter born in 1945.

WHAT THE PEOPLE WANT

By the Author of

THE SHORE DIMLY SEEN

ELLIS GIBBS ARNALL

WHAT THE PEOPLE WANT

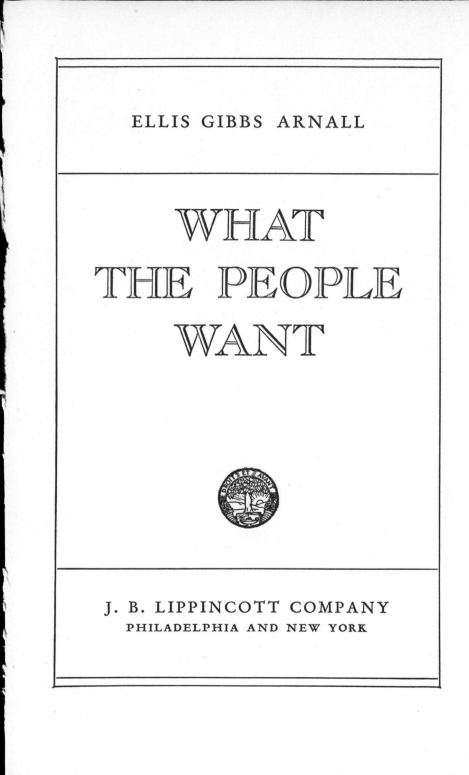

J. B. LIPPINCOTT COMPANY
PHILADELPHIA AND NEW YORK

To

MY MOTHER AND FATHER

who taught me

that freedom is more than a word

CONTENTS

WHAT THE PEOPLE WANT

O! thus be it ever when free men shall stand
Between their loved homes and wild war's desolation . . .
—FRANCIS SCOTT KEY

COMMON COUNTRY

Our Federal Union: it must be preserved.
—ANDREW JACKSON

1: COUNTER-REVOLUTION IN GEORGIA

The lock splintered with a crash and the mob poured into the outer office. My own door stood ajar, and I could see the montage of angry faces. A pathway opened in the crowd, and the young son of the dead Governor-elect of Georgia was led through the office on the arm of his chief adviser.

I remember that his face was ghastly pale, except for a scarlet spot at each cheekbone, and that his companion wore a smile of immeasurable elation. Behind them trailed the members of a committee of legislators.

They demanded of me the office of Governor of Georgia.

I refused to surrender that office to the pretender. Turning on his heel, the political manipulator who had engineered the midnight coup led his youthful puppet from the room. Then the mob started for the door, led by a giant professional wrestler who had been the strongarm man for the faction.

My executive secretary, P. T. McCutchen, Jr., and one of my aides, Thad Buchanan, barred their way. In the melee that followed,

Buchanan's jaw was broken. The door of the inner office was closed, as the mob, led by a carefully coached group of agitators, shrieked and cursed, overrunning the Capitol corridors.

I glanced at my watch. It was 2:30 A.M. on the morning of January 15, 1947. It was an historic hour, in a sense; it marked the first attempt in American history to seize the government of a sovereign Commonwealth by force.

We now could test in the United States whether Fascist techniques would work, or whether the political institutions of our country, especially the courts, could stand as a defense for constitutional government.

The background of the January putsch in Georgia involved many issues. In the campaign of 1946, Eugene Talmadge, three times elected as Governor of the State, sought a fourth term as the candidate of a coalition of political forces. His only defeat for Governor had come in 1942 when I had headed the anti-Talmadge ticket and academic freedom had been the principal campaign issue.

Eugene Talmadge was an individual of exceptional personal charm and a campaigner of unusual effectiveness, whose stock in trade was racial hate and class antipathy. As a candidate in every Georgia election except one since 1926, he had a strong personal following and a well-organized political machine. In addition, in 1946, he had the support of all reactionary interests in the State, especially those opposed to Georgia's efforts to readjust freight rates to eliminate discriminations against the South and West.

In the Democratic primary, whose choice is always elected in Georgia, he was opposed by James V. Carmichael, a young liberal business man with a good record as legislator and as operator of the enormous Bell Bomber plant, Georgia's largest wartime industrial establishment. There were two minor candidates in the race, also, whose combined vote of almost one hundred thousand affected the result.

Although Carmichael obtained a popular plurality, amassing over sixteen thousand more votes than Eugene Talmadge, the unique

"county unit system" used in Georgia for primary nominations resulted, because of the split vote for the minor entries, in a Talmadge
victory. The Georgia county unit system is modelled after the
Federal electoral system. The State Democratic Committee, which
had been named after my gubernatorial victory in 1942, certified
Eugene Talmadge as the party nominee, and in the November
general election he was duly elected.

Curiously, in that election there were several hundred votes cast
for Herman Talmadge, his youthful son, for Governor, as an independent. These votes came from counties thoroughly dominated by
the Talmadge organization, and subsequent investigation disclosed
numerous irregularities in them, especially in Telfair County, the
home of the Talmadges.

The reason for this mysterious campaign on behalf of the younger
man against his father became apparent soon, when the former
Governor's serious illness became known. In late December 1946,
he died.

The Georgia constitution, rewritten in 1945 and ratified by the people, provided that the Governor should retain office until the election
and qualification of his successor. Technically, under the constitution, I could remain in office for four years longer.

This was not the intent of the people, of course, and I had no
intention of doing so. I announced that as soon as the Lieutenant-
Governor, elected in 1946, had taken office, I would resign in his
favor. Almost simultaneously, there was an announcement that
Herman Talmadge would seek election by the General Assembly
of the State upon the curious basis that he had obtained 675 votes
in the general election and that the Assembly was authorized to
name a Governor from the two men obtaining the largest number
of votes who were still alive.

I did not participate in the maneuvers that preceded the session
of the General Assembly in mid-January. Even had I not known
that the efforts to prevent the "election" would be futile, I would not
have done so. The legislators met on January 14. Throughout the

day they wrangled over parliamentary questions. Soon after midnight, when the outer doors of the Governor's office were closed, they proceeded with their vote and the raid began.

Two or three thousand partisan followers of Herman Talmadge already had taken possession of the Capitol itself, and when he appeared on the arm of his principal adviser, they stormed into the offices.

Some of my friends had been concerned about my safety. A plan to mask an assassination under the general turmoil had been scented the day before. If it existed, and I was never wholly convinced, it originated with a group of gamblers, who were seeking to move into Georgia from the Florida resort area and who had invested heavily in a notorious Southeast Georgia politician identified with the putsch as one of its chief financial backers.

If such a plan existed, it never materialized. Many in the mob at the Capitol were intoxicated. Many were angry. All were excited. But except for a few seconds, when the Talmadge bodyguard led an assault on the inner Executive office, there was no danger.

In my recollection, the week that followed was a kaleidoscopic haze of action. On the day following the storming of the Capitol, I retained my private office and reception room. During the following night, the locks were changed surreptitiously, and I moved my office to the rotunda of the Capitol, until that space was seized by force. Then for several days the Executive Department of the State Government functioned from my law offices, 1406-1407 Candler Building, in the Georgia Capital City of Atlanta. Armed guards patrolled the Capitol. During this time the legislature debated a series of measures that would have established a political oligarchy in the State, disfranchising electors at the whim of a partisan committee, and placing complete control over government in the hands of the group that had seized power by force.

I directed Attorney-General Eugene Cook to bring an action in the courts for a declaratory judgment, to determine who was the lawful Governor of the State. Loyally, the Attorney-General brought

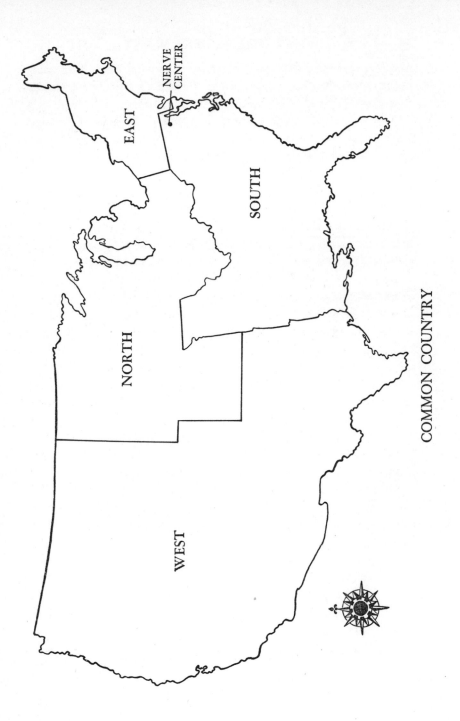

the suit, although he was threatened with impeachment and a measure was introduced in the Assembly to strip him of all authority.

As the week ended, Lieutenant-Governor M. E. Thompson, who had been my executive secretary and Revenue Commissioner, was enabled to take the oath of office. Immediately, I transmitted my resignation to the General Assembly and to the Secretary of State.

The next week, with the Capitol still in possession of the pretender and his usurping armed guards, it was necessary for me to leave Georgia for several weeks to fill a number of scheduled lecture engagements throughout the country.

Throughout Georgia there was intense popular indignation over the putsch. The newspapers of the State, which are preponderantly liberal, joined in the battle. But the matter would have to be determined by the courts of Georgia, and the case would test whether courts backed by public opinion could stand against armed men patrolling a State Capitol.

I thought they could.

2: THE TECHNIQUES OF FASCISM

Free institutions do not exist in a vacuum. They do not exist without a reason. They are expressions of the needs of men and women. Their purpose is to serve those needs, and they are affected by anything that affects the individual's liberty.

The free institutions of America are in danger today. That would be most alarming if they were not always in danger, if they had not been in danger ever since the establishment of the earliest colony in the New World.

Democracies rarely are overthrown by external forces. Even the transient Nazi triumph and the occupation of their countries by armed men could not destroy the essential liberty of the people of Norway and Denmark.

Democracies are destroyed from within. Historically, there seems to exist evidence that they die because men exchange freedom for what they mistake for security. Unhappily, they never obtain the security, and they lose the freedom.

The pattern of authoritarianism is always the same. Its economics may differ from time to time. The method of selecting the ruling caste may change from year to year; although always, as in the Russia of the last few years, there is an inevitable trend toward some kind of hereditary governing clique.

The distinguishing marks of the authoritarian government are the change of the operations of justice, and the erection of a police state. This was true in the Rome of the Flavian dynasty. It was true in the England of the Tudors. It was true of France in the era of the later Bourbons. It was true in Hohenzollern and Hitler Germany, in the Italy of Mussolini, in the Cuba of Machado, in the Spain of Franco, and in the Argentina of Peron. But always there is the substitution of force for debate.

Almost always, the dictators or oligarchs come into power through due process of law, or through methods that have a suggestion of legality. Henry VII rose from Earl of Richmond to the government of England by a convenient, if forcible, marriage to the daughter of Edward IV. Hitler, copying the techniques devised by the lesser Napoleon in his overthrow of the Second Republic in France, relied upon the plebiscite. Mussolini was the ostensible free choice of the Italian Parliament. Machado and Peron were victors in "legal" elections.

The technique of the authoritarian is to obtain power under the guise of legality, and then proceed relentlessly with the destruction of civil liberties and the subversion of free institutions. Once in power, he reasons most reasonably that law and order must be preserved; that all opponents of his corrupt, wasteful, and tyrannical regime are enemies of the state; that the best place for them is the salt mines, or the concentration camp, or the gallows. The last is most effective, since it obviates the possibility of escape; but it can be applied to only a limited number of opponents, so the great mass of citizens are simply deprived of their right to participate in government. That, too, is reasonable and wise, he reasons, since they need a period of tutelage and training before such rights and responsibilities can be trusted to them.

Tudors argued for the supremacy of the Crown, as the repository of all the national will. Stalinists, if I understand this particular deviation from Marxian socialism, urge a dictatorship of the party bureaucracy. The Nazis advocated a dictatorship of supermen, which they appointed themselves to be. All pointed out that they were trustees for all the people. Which, indeed, they were; and, not unlike occasional trustees in other fields, they were defaulters and embezzlers.

It may be argued that the people were silly to be duped in this fashion. The answer is that these events occurred in nations where freedom was not too well established, that force was employed skillfully, and that economic problems were so serious that many individuals felt that slavery was a better choice than hunger.

That was what made the application of similar techniques in Georgia so interesting. The seizure of Georgia's government might be described as an experiment to determine whether it can happen here.

The attempt was classic in design. There was the choice of a young pretender with hereditary claims. There was the usual plea of a specious legality. There was the ultimate resort to force, and the usual direct challenge to the public when the putsch had been accomplished.

I did not believe that the experiment with Fascist techniques would succeed in Georgia. I do not believe that such experiments will be successful elsewhere in America, whether upon a State or a national scale. But there is every likelihood that they will be attempted, again and again, as the American economy nears maturity, as we destroy our geographical frontiers and block those that might be created by an alert technology, and as we intensify the sense of outrage of the dispossessed.

The Georgia story, whether that of 1776 or of 1946, is the American

story. What impresses anyone most about the United States is less
the immense differences between sections, in their natural resources
and their economic development, than the startling similarity of one
American to another.

There are towns in Missouri and Kansas, in Michigan and Ohio,
that have a striking similarity to my native Newnan. The only
difference in the Court House square is that the monument, erected
sometime between 1885 and 1915, commemorates not the valor of
those men who wore gray uniforms at Shiloh and Chickamauga and
Manassas Junction and Fredericksburg, but the valor of those whose
uniforms were blue. There is another minor difference, to be noted
in some of these sections, and that is that, traditionally, until 1932
at any rate, the people voted for Republican candidates with the
same amazing regularity by which citizens of Newnan gave either
William Jennings Bryan or John W. Davis a thumping majority on
the Democratic ticket without a thought that Davis and Bryan stood
miles apart in their philosophies.

In American State government, in American rural development,
in community of exploitation, there is a homogeneity about that
three-quarters of the continental United States that comprises the
South and West. And the thinking of the other fourth differs little
in essentials.

That suggests that many problems of our country can be solved
by an examination of the successful experiments in one or another
section.

If Georgia can take the leg-irons off prisoners and abolish the
chaingang, Virginia can do likewise. If Michigan and Wisconsin
can point toward a solution of the problem of cutover timberland,
then Mississippi can learn from that example. If Georgia, where
only one farm home in thirty had electricity ten years ago, can point
to the electrification of more than a third of its rural homes, then
Missouri, where only one farmer in thirty-five has electricity, can do
as well. If Iowa can achieve so reasonable a balance between industry and agriculture that its average per capita income bears an

actual relationship to the income of average men and women, then forty-seven other States can learn something from Iowa.

3: COLONIES AND EXPLOITATION

Much of my excitement about our common country may seem naive. Newnan was a quiet, prosperous town where a few textile mills flourished and where the farmers of West Georgia came to market their crops and buy their supplies. I exchanged that quiet, unbroken except for a few trips with the high school football team, for the comparative chaos of college, and then for a small town law practice, and then for politics. Until I became Attorney-General of Georgia, I had hardly been outside the South. Until I became Governor of Georgia, I had had little occasion to think of the relationship between one section of our country and another.

To anyone living in the South, the problems of colonialism and exploitation are foremost. The occupation of the seceding Southern States was the longest military occupation in all modern history. The subsequent exploitation of the region was the cruelest in many generations. The tragedy of the era that began in 1865 and that did not end until 1933 is not only a Southern but an American tragedy. The waste and despoliation of Southern resources, both human and natural, was a national waste, as well as an oppression of a whole people.

Southern problems, and the problem of reorganizing the government of Georgia and modernizing its public services, occupied the thoughts of my friends in Newnan, and my friends in college, and my political associates. We thought of these questions as wholly local, or, at most, regional. It was not until my study of the freight rate discriminations against Southern industry gave me some insight into the parallel exploitation of the West that I discovered that Crédit Mobilier was a greater catastrophe to the West than Appomattox and the Force Bills were to the South.

The exploitation of the South and West has been a personal

tragedy for many Americans of those regions; but they have not been the only sufferers. The East was even harder hit by the depression of 1929. Its economy is disordered today. In its great cities are slums that rival the rural slums of the cotton belt or the Southwest. New York and Chicago and Detroit are tremendous. New York is making the hardest and most honest effort of any large city in the nation to solve the problem of housing and to ameliorate the tensions that arise from racial intolerance. Chicago seems inevitably destined to become the world's largest, and perhaps ugliest, city. Detroit is the center of America's industrial expansion, of its political and economic quacks, and of its hate cults.

Decentralization of industry and nation-wide prosperity are as important to the workers in the clothing industry in New York as to the cotton pickers of the Mississippi Delta. The welfare of the copper towns in the Mountain States is essential to the welfare of the automobile workers and automobile magnates of Detroit. The future of Chicago is inseverable from the future of the cattle lands of Texas and Florida. This is our common country.

No individual can cut himself clear of his roots and break his relationship with the earth from which he came. I shall always be the product of Newnan, of Georgia, of the South; possessing the viewpoint of one educated in a small town high school, a small college, a State university law school, and interested from boyhood in the techniques and practices of politics.

Political democracy, for those reasons, looms important in my eyes. Men must be free to think, to speak, to write, to choose for themselves their own governments and their own officials, and to enjoy individual liberty.

But it is impossible to have political freedom unless you have economic freedom. Political democracy demands economic democracy. Democracy must solve the problem of individual security, in order that we may have individual freedom.

Free men stand up for their rights best when they are not hungry and when they are not afraid.

4: There are three Manhattans

There are several Manhattans in the United States. Three of them interested me greatly on my trip around the nation.

One of them is an island, crowded with skyscrapers. One is a quiet community in Kansas, almost in the geographic center of our country. One of them is a bit of military terminology: the Manhattan District, with branch offices in Tennessee and on the Pacific Coast; it is engaged in the manufacture of fissionable materials and atomic bombs. The three have much in common.

A bomb from the third Manhattan could wipe out either of the others in something less than five seconds.

The incidental by-products of our experiments at Oak Ridge, however, might make life infinitely more comfortable in Manhattan, Kansas, where the winters are a little severe, or the cost of living much lower on the island Manhattan within sight of the Statue of Liberty in the harbor. The choice is one that the American people must make, among many other choices, within the next few years.

The use of uranium and plutonium to make bombs of terrific power has been discussed on every street corner in the United States. The destructive consequences of the warfare of the atomic age are realized by everyone. The fear engendered by the bomb is world wide.

Much less consideration is given to the use of fissionable materials as agents of peace, prosperity, comfort and security. Yet it should be possible to supersede fear with hope.

One of the most important battles of our generation was fought in the Congress of the United States over the issue of placing the atomic experiments in the hands of a civilian commission. The battle was only partly won; but, at least, it was not lost. There is still a possibility that the enormous resources of atomic energy may be saved for our people, as our public lands were not, as our oil fields were not, and as our hydroelectric potential has been saved only in part. At any rate, many products useful to the medical profession have been developed and are being distributed from Oak Ridge.

In theory, it is possible to utilize atomic energy to drive the wheels of industry and to provide electric power in any section of the country. Its use could enable us to process raw materials anywhere in America, without regard for the availability of coal, natural gas, or hydroelectric power. It might even permit the national transportation system to be reorganized on an incredibly efficient basis. It would unquestionably cause technological changes in industry even more radical than those that followed the invention of the steam engine.

It is not necessary to think of atomic power as a destructive force. It is a matter of choice. It is a matter in which the people must make the choice. It must not be made for them under the pretext that some one man, or ten men, or hundreds of men, are better able to make the choice.

That is an aspect of political democracy. It serves to demonstrate that it is impossible to have economic democracy without having political democracy, too.

The potentials of atomic power were developed by the Federal government. In the research, many scientists gave the people the benefit of their years of diligent work, their accumulated knowledge, their genius. The product belongs to all of the people, for their best use.

It would have been the greatest folly in national history to give over the control of atomic energy to a military-plus-monopoly bureaucracy. The sound sense of the people revolted at the thought.

The people are the best repository of their own destiny. Governments exist to carry out their collective will. Those governments that forget this, and that lose contact with the people, eventually cease to govern.

5: AMERICAN FAMILIES WANT HOMES

The four years that I served as Governor of Georgia had been crowded years. The State reorganized its government, rewriting its constitution on modern lines. The penal system was overhauled. The pardon racket was eliminated. Education was set free from political control, and the educational establishment was provided with enough money to operate efficiently. Better, though not adequate, provisions were made for public health. An attack was launched upon the transportation monopoly, which had strangled industrial development in the South. The State was freed from debt for the first time since 1838. Political democracy was realized, in a victorious fight against reaction to obtain elimination of the poll tax as a prerequisite for voting. The voting age was lowered to eighteen and no citizen was denied his vote by reason of race, color or creed.

As my term of office neared an end, there came invitations to make a number of talks in different parts of the country. I accepted them because they permitted me to see America; and to talk with Americans, as well as to talk to them.

When Lieutenant-Governor M. E. Thompson took the oath of office, enabling me to resign as Governor of Georgia, I started on this journey about the country which has carried me more than seventy-five thousand miles.

Most of all, I wanted to find out what things Americans thought were important, and what they expected from their government.

I found that all over America people are alike. They have the same hopes, ambitions and aspirations. They have the same problems; the same fears.

Their minds seemed centered on some topics that I am listing without any reference to the order of their importance: education, health, housing, the cost of living, jobs, taxation, monopoly, individual freedom, equal rights, racial and religious tolerance, the unity of our common country, and peace.

Next to peace, they talked most frequently of housing.

There are many factors in the creation of the housing shortage. Buildings became obsolete and uninhabitable and were not replaced during the war years. There are more people in the United States, and more family units, than a decade ago. There has been a shift of inhabitants from one part of the nation to another, and from the farm to the city. The larger cities have remained static, in some instances, while the medium-sized communities have grown rapidly.

Many of these items can be expressed statistically; but nobody can live in a statistic.

The plain truth is that we are not geared to the production of enough houses rapidly enough for those who could afford to buy houses, and that we have not yet solved the problem of providing homes for those who want to rent homes.

In the interval, instead of seeking a solution to the immediate problem of finding places for people to live in, we have debated endlessly upon the relative culpability of the workers who build houses and the material men who provide the brick and lumber and glass and hardware that go to make them. We have debated upon whether to subsidize the real estate operator or the renter, in setting up slum clearance projects. And, in an era of mass production in other fields, we have continued to build houses literally by hand.

Yet a great many Americans object that finding a place for people to live is not a legitimate function of the people acting through their government. Historically, of course, this is not so; from the days of colonization, government has helped in the matter of providing homes.

But the debate on housing goes off into some highly interesting bypaths. Senator Robert A. Taft, one of the most intellectually alert of the nation's conservatives, seems to believe that it is morally justified to subsidize housing for certain low-income groups, but that it is wrong to assist generally in solving the housing shortage. Moderate as is that view, it won for the Ohio Senator the designation of Communist, a rather inexact term applied to persons with whom one disagrees and for whom one has no reasonable answer. Mr. Taft has also been called a Fascist and many other things. Which is quite unjust, because Mr. Taft is an excellent American, with a political and social viewpoint precisely as honest and certainly as conservative as that of President Benjamin Harrison; and equally modern, as well.

Senator Taft is not a Communist. He is certainly not even what is commonly called a liberal. He is so intensely conservative, indeed, on all matters dealing with social and economic questions that, in a discussion I once had with him on a radio program, we found ourselves in agreement on only one thing: that his father, the President and Chief Justice of the United States, had been a courageous, able and public-spirited man. The employment of the name-calling against the Senator was because his opponent in the housing matter could not think up, at the moment, any argument against his proposed legislation, and instinctively felt that anyone who disagreed with his position must be something very bad, and again instinctively employed a name that he thought was very naughty.

Actually Senator Taft's proposals have a fundamental unsoundness. There is no reason why, if the government may with propriety assist in providing housing for the lower-income groups, the government may not assist in providing housing for anybody who needs a home. It ought not to be necessary for the government to do either in our free economy, if it is really free and truly competitive; but if there is an emergency, or if the freedom of enterprise has been affected by monopoly in some field, then the government has an obligation.

That does not mean that there should be opposition to proposals to subsidize housing for low-income groups during an emergency. But such subsidies should be reckoned as emergency expenditures to see that every American has a home that is clean and decent. But it is almost as wrong to subsidize housing for America's underprivileged as it was to subsidize the vast transportation monopoly, though the housing subsidy would be considerably less of a drain upon the public purse.

It seems to me that the approach to the housing problem must involve the coöperation of every unit of government. In many cities, restrictions are fantastic, creating local monopolies in building supplies. In many cities, inadequate authority exists for eradicating slums. No real attack has been made upon the problem of rural housing, although there are many hundreds of thousands of families that would like to return to agriculture if they could obtain reasonable comfort for themselves and their families.

What I saw around the United States convinced me that, while the Federal government could contribute tremendously toward solving the housing problem by vigorous enforcement of our monopoly statutes, by regulating labor abuses, and by helping to finance the program, the great obstacles lie within the communities themselves.

This suggests that we learned some of the wrong things from our experiences in the depression and recovery years. For generations, until 1933, the people of the United States had not thought of their Federal government as a useful tool to be utilized in an emergency; they sought too often for solutions on the local level of problems that were national in scope. Now the pendulum has swung too far in the other direction. Our State governments have become increasingly static, and lean on Washington for direction as well as for financial aid. In this process, they have starved their local self-government units, both of money and authority, until almost all cities and counties in the country have serious problems of finance and of autonomy.

In Georgia, we endeavored to cure one aspect of this by granting "home rule" to towns and counties, so that they could govern themselves to suit themselves, without having to come to the legislature for permission for the simplest change in their operations. The experiment looks promising; but it will require a good many years to restore the virility of local government.

The State governments are the weak spots in America today.

Many States are efficiently administered. There is less corruption in public affairs than in many generations. But there is more apathy. Public figures enjoy talking about "States' Rights" on holidays, but usually it turns out that the only "rights" to be exercised are those of delay. Unless State governments become more dynamic in the exercise of their rights, they will continue to lose them. This would be bad, for centralized government is no more to be desired than a centralized economy; either invites some form of authoritarian control.

Visiting over America, however, I saw little more enthusiasm for States' rights among political leaders than I saw enthusiasm for competitive free enterprise among certain types of business leaders.

6: BUREAUCRATS OF BIG BUSINESS

The bureaucracy of big business is one of the greatest threats to competitive free enterprise, whether public or private, in this country.

Obviously some large enterprises can be operated only by a bureaucracy; and some others, that have grown overlarge through the years, have developed bureaucratic systems that assuredly must rival pre-Revolutionary France both in inefficiency and nepotism.

Probably American Telephone and Telegraph has the most efficient bureaucratic arrangement; managerial and technical dominance is almost inevitable in the field of communications, for there is little difference between the operations of a postal enterprise and a communication system that operates over wires. United States Steel has a competent group of bureaucrats; but on the whole they have not done so well, since they started with absolute dominance in their field and have dropped in percentage of total production annually ever since.

The transportation companies perhaps present the example of the most complex, amazing, unaware, and irresponsible management in America. They are owned by the public; principally, I am assured almost daily, by a widow lady and her three orphan children. They are controlled by bankers; most of whom, again I am informed, do their travelling by yacht or private airplane. They were operated for many years by receivers appointed by various courts about the country, but most of them managed to pay out during the war years and now are in the hands of bureaucrats, who required an entire year or longer to make a ten per cent revision in their tariff schedules; at least they assured the Interstate Commerce Commission that they could not make those exceedingly difficult computations in any less time, and the commission, which knows them intimately, agreed.

However, there is an optimistic side to the picture. Ford and General Motors, two of the largest corporations in existence, have decentralized their internal government, and are decentralizing their production. Eventually they will have the status of enormous investment trusts, loosely supervising independent and integrated production units.

Even transportation shows some bright spots; or at least one. That bright spot is Robert R. Young, of Allegheny Corporation and the Chesapeake and Ohio Railroad.

When the State of Georgia decided that States' rights included the right to protect its citizens against unfair freight rate discriminations, a suit was filed in the United States Supreme Court against most of the major Eastern and Southern railroads, charging them with violation of the Sherman and Clayton Acts that prohibit conspiracies in restraint of trade. Chesapeake and Ohio was among the defendants, as were two other of the Young railroads, the Père Marquette and the Nickel Plate.

After the long preliminary skirmish, which ended with the Supreme Court accepting Georgia's view and setting the case for trial, Young filed a very startling answer for his railroads.

He said, in effect, that he was not conspiring against anybody or with anybody, and that C&O would be glad to handle freight on a competitive basis. He also quit the Association of American Railroads, and took some very independent attitudes about financing his line for the benefit of the stockholders instead of for the benefit of the investment bankers.

That led me to some very interesting conversations and correspondence with Bob Young.

Railroad timetables have been a source of much distress to Americans for generations. Their complexity is equalled only by the small type in which they are printed. It took me some weeks to understand fully the balance sheet of the State of Georgia, with its numerous departments and their various operational funds; I have never been able to master a timetable, and I have found difficulty in admitting my inadequacy to the train conductor, who has learned the schedule approximately by years of travel over the route. I always wait for some other troubled individual to make an inquiry and then strain to listen.

Soon after Young printed a rather startling advertisement, calling attention to the fact that a hog could cross America from coast to coast without changing cars but that a human passenger could not, and asking that something be done about it, I wrote him a letter about timetables.

A few weeks later, a new kind of timetable came to me from him. It consisted of a very simple card, with two rotating discs that showed the route of the Chesapeake and Ohio trains, eastbound or westbound. You could tell when your train left and when it would arrive.

A genius that can solve the timetable problem in a little over a month ought to be able to put transportation back into the field of competitive free enterprise in a few years.

Wherever Americans talk, they talk about the menace of monopoly. They fear it instinctively, and they know that it means an end to free enterprise.

7: NIGHT FLIGHT CONVERSATION

The American people want peace.

It has been the American dream, since the first colonist landed.

There are surface differences in the views of Americans about how peace can be obtained, but there is evidence that the average American understands the issue of peace better and feels it more deeply than many of those who are undertaking to lead him.

In the Middle West and in some of the Mountain States, there were more than traces of isolationist sentiment. But upon examination, it was easy to see that the isolationism of those Americans has been misrepresented in many ways. They have been quick enough to respond to human needs in Europe or China. Their sons have fought as valiantly as any in America's wars. Their isolationism was, in many ways, an expression of America's violent hatred for war and America's strong desire for peace. Many so-called isolationists, likewise, shared fully the view of the average American that any foreign policy that this country might evolve must be based upon moral values and upon the support of democratic governments everywhere in the world.

America lapsed into cynicism after World War One, because our leadership abandoned the fundamental American policy of open assistance to democracy. The shameful years between 1920 and 1932 saw freedom in retreat, because the world's greatest Republic did not adhere to its own doctrines in its foreign policy.

Today many Americans of the Henry Wallace philosophy appear to assume that there is no choice that our country can make except to accept the expansion by force of communism or the alliance of the United States with violent reaction throughout the world. They believe that we can save democracy by suspending its operations in those parts of the Balkans where we yet have a tenuous hold. Some other Americans believe we can save democracy by maintaining Franco in his tottering dictatorship, by acquiescing in Peron's infiltration of all the South American republics, and by basing our foreign policy upon military strategy instead of organizing our military strategy to carry out an independent and democratic policy.

The average American knows better than to accept either of these views, and his restiveness and uncertainty about our foreign policy take many forms. In the Middle West it is represented by a certain resurgence of isolationism. Among a considerable number of citizens it is resulting in a growing Anglophobia that refuses to recognize the grave plight of Britain or the honest effort that the Attlee government has made toward a solution of the Indian problem. Among many others, the failure to make a serious effort to solve the problem of those dispossessed by the Nazi hordes and driven into concentration camps, forced labor, or exile, has created a feeling that our foreign policy is again becoming one of expediency, such as sent the Marines into Nicaragua and provided loans to Mussolini's dictatorship.

The irrationality of the Anglo-American position toward Palestine has done much to produce this dissatisfaction. On the whole, however great the biting anguish of the Jewish community in America over the refusal to admit refugees and the herding of Hitler's victims back to the scenes of their agony, the vocative indignation has come largely from other Americans.

The merits of Zionism as a solution are not a subject of debate. There are many among the Hebrew congregations who do not sympathize with the aims of Zionism. But the simple fact, entirely irrefutable, is that a Jewish homeland was promised more than thirty years ago. The British mandate in Palestine was presumptively the forerunner of a Jewish state. The promise has been broken. The solemn pledge has been ignored.

One night, on a plane that was hurrying me east from a talk before a Michigan audience, I sat next to a young man who felt very strongly about the question of Palestine.

He recognized me—I suppose from the pictures that had been printed during the controversy over the Governorship in Georgia—

and began a conversation. It was just after Easter, and soon after the execution of Dov Gruner by the British.

"I'm glad you are making a fight in Georgia," he began, and I thanked him.

"But what can people do when there are no courts to which they can go?"

"There are usually courts in this country," I replied. "And the courts usually find a way to obtain justice."

"But when there are no courts?"

I told him I did not know; I supposed that then every man must protect his rights as best he could.

"I was thinking about Dov Gruner," he said. "It seems to me that they might have waited two or three days to hang him. Don't proconsuls usually arrange their executions for Good Friday?"

I sat silent. It was a long night flight, and I was tired from a very busy day.

"The next fellow in my squad was a Jew from the Bronx," he continued. "The kind that I guess a Kluxer would call a kike. He got killed in Italy. We got along all right, and he was always talking about hoping that after the war he could go to Tel Aviv."

"I'm sorry that your friend couldn't go home, for I suppose he thought of it as home," I answered. "Hanging Gruner probably was a mistake and unjust, but it is the kind of thing that happens when you have any kind of military occupation of a country. That doesn't justify it, of course. But military government concentrates on preserving order, and this results in instances of injustice for which you can never find anybody to blame. Except, of course, all of us."

"Do you know what he was reciting when they hanged him?"

I told him that I had not noticed that in the newspaper accounts, which had been very brief, but that it was undoubtedly one of the Psalms.

"Oh yes," he replied. "A very old hymn. We have a fine translation of it in the King James Bible that goes like this: 'My strength is dried up like a potsherd; and my tongue cleaveth to my jaws; and thou has brought me into the dust of death. For dogs have compassed me: the assembly of the wicked have inclosed me: they pierced my hands and my feet. I may tell all my bones: they look and stare upon me. They part my garments among them, and cast lots upon my vesture. But be not thou far from me, O Lord: O my strength, haste thee to help me. Deliver my soul from the sword; my darling from the power of the dog.'

"I think," he added, "that it is commonly called the Hymn of the Crucified Man."

We were silent the rest of the way into LaGuardia Field. Afterward, in the hotel, I looked up the text in a Gideon Bible. It is the Twenty-second Psalm.

The young man was very angry, and his story may have been apocryphal. But I shall never be wholly certain.

8: EXPERIMENTS IN CONSERVATION

The problem of obtaining freedom to make social experiments in this country, without endangering individual freedom, is uppermost in the minds of many people. You will find it best illustrated in the controversy over the Missouri Valley Authority, which is the major issue in some ten States, with populations of thirteen million.

There are some facts that are not in dispute. One is the need to extend navigation on this largest tributary of the Mississippi. Another is the need to promote conservation: land is being washed away at a terrific rate, jeopardizing the livelihood of 6,800,00 people. Electric rates in the area are high, by any standard; application of the same rates that apply in TVA territory would result in annual savings of $105,000,000. Every group demands that some agency of the Federal government assume the job, in one way or another.

There has been a resurrection of the power lobby that was so potent back in the evil old days when widows and orphans were investing their accumulated savings in Insull stocks under the appeal, indorsed by those in very high places in Washington, that it would mean two chickens in every pot. The lobby went into a certain retirement after the Federal Trade Commission exposures, the 1929 crash, and the obvious and enormous success of the Tennessee Valley Authority.

But many people see in the fight on the Missouri Valley Authority nothing more than the insidiously sinister maneuvers of power lobbyists. Doubtless, the lobbyists, who are presumably distinguished portly gentlemen much given to picking up tabs for influential people in expensive restaurants, and the propagandists, who are reputedly small, self-effacing people much given to picking up large checks for themselves in the inner offices of monopolistic magnates, have both been busy. It is comparatively easy to see what they have done in the way of creating false issues and erecting fine-sounding front organizations to fight MVA, which they like as little as they did TVA. Nevertheless, they are not the major factor in the fight, although they have capitalized on the local squabbles over water, over power sites and over navigation rights, with their usual cleverness.

MVA actually is a fight for decentralization, for regional independence. It is opposed most strongly by those doctrinaires, in and out of the government, who want to see government, industry, and political control in this country thoroughly centralized. It is opposed by some non-political bureaucrats, who share these beliefs and who do not want their power taken from them; these inhabit two rival offices, the Bureau of Reclamation and the offices of the Army Engineers. It is opposed by those monopolists who have exploited the colonial position of the Southern and Western States. Finally, it is opposed by those who find it possible to draw a distinction between an enormous Federal outlay, haphazard and uncoördinated, upon flood control and navigation, and a considerable Federal investment, under regional control, that will return cash dividends as well as social benefits; these argue that unless the government loses a great deal of money on the project, the project is Socialistic.

Centralized control over governmental agencies, like centralized control over a major industry, is monopoly, and monopoly always is dangerous to the liberty of the people. Moreover, Washington is a very long way from Cheyenne. If TVA had been managed from Washington instead of from Knoxville, Tennessee, it is unlikely that it would have been so successful a project.

There is no reason why the people should not use their government to perform any service that they need and wish. They have an unalienable right of endless experiment. But it would seem only logical and reasonable that they should select the governmental unit nearest to them that is able to perform the service. If it can be done by the local government, efficiently and cheaply, it is a local job. If it can be done by the State government, it is a State job. If it can best be done by a regional authority, one should be established. If it has to be done by the central government, then it belongs there.

The test is not some legal theory; the test is empirical. It would be as ridiculous to turn the job of cleaning the streets in America's thousands of municipalities over to the Federal government, as it would be to undertake the defense of the continent upon a local basis.

9: Our colonists are protesting

Centralization of government and of industrial control have a definite and close relationship with colonialism, and throughout the South, the Southwest, the Mountain States and the Pacific Coast areas, the talk of colonialism is heard with great frequency.

Sometimes it is coupled with enlivening discussions of monopoly, as when those in the West draw contrasts between the treatment accorded United States Steel, on the one hand, and Henry Kaiser, on the other, when it comes to matters of pouring Federal funds into wartime plants. Sometimes it is associated with discussions of freight rates.

So long had the freight rate issue been a standard subject of oratory by Southern politicians that there was rather intensive criticism of Georgia's action to break up the discriminations.

Not only did the overlords of transportation feel that the attack upon a system that charges approximately thirty-nine per cent more to move Southern goods to market than is charged for hauling manufactures of the favored imperial area, constituted an assault upon their vested rights, but many Southern politicians felt that their vested right in speeches deploring the condition was assailed. It was considered ill-mannered to attempt to break up a conspiracy that had existed since the middle of the previous century.

I had regarded the freight rate fight, initially, as a Southern affair. That was the result, no doubt, of having heard too many speeches on the subject. Actually, though the South's economy has been more seriously impaired by the discriminations than that of any other section, the Southwest and the Pacific Northwest suffer as acutely. The South has been drained longer, but not more relentlessly.

The military aspects of colonialism are receiving attention now. Strategists who observe that the USSR is locating much of its heavy industry on the other side of the Urals, and who witnessed the abrupt Russian decentralization in the face of the German onslaught, and who noted the redistribution of British wartime industry, and who consented, reluctantly, to the establishment of emergency plants in Utah, Georgia, Oregon and Texas, are urging more decentralization.

They recognize that an attack on the little strip of seacoast that runs from Baltimore to New York could have produced a paralysis such as the Japanese expected as a result of Pearl Harbor. They understand, after the delay that is inevitable to the professional military mind, that any "next war" may witness an attack upon industrial objectives instead of military concentrations. Even the enormous ground forces that they contemplate would be valueless under such circumstances. Unless factories making such essentials of war as shoes, buttons, typewriters, tires, pharmaceuticals, and truck bodies are dispersed around the country, the situation would be disastrous.

Obviously, the initial effort for national defense should be the termination of our domestic colonialism.

A more ready recognition of this fact may be expected from the Southern mind than from that of some other section. That does not arise from the South's position as an exploited colony; it arises from the South's practical experience eighty-odd years ago, when the Confederacy undertook to wage war without industries.

The organized militia of the South was much stronger than any force available in the Northern States. While the North possessed in Meade, Thomas, and Sheridan first-rate general officers, and in Sherman one of the great captains of any age, who knew not only how to define war but to wage it, the South had better officer material immediately available. But except in Virginia and Georgia, there were no industries with which to wage war.

If General Lee could not win a war without wagons, it is extremely unlikely that any present-day military man can win a war without trucks.

But no nation's economy should be reordered because of possible military expediency, any more than its political system should be altered in the interest of a readier discipline for wartime activities. Democracies are expected to wage war, when they must, in the most expensive, extravagant, wasteful and clumsy fashion that is possible; very likely it is desirable that this should be so.

Decentralization is essential to preserve political freedom and freedom for enterprise. In America, though not necessarily everywhere, the two are very closely associated. The present-day attacks on freedom of enterprise ought to scare the socks off any American.

That means free public enterprise as well as free private enterprise. Though there was an immense amount of pilfering and a greater amount of waste involved, for example, in the public enterprise that made possible the transcontinental railroads and most of the other units of transportation in the country, which were then given away to an incompetent private management with enormous subsidies attached, the country would never have expanded without the effort. The assault on free competitive enterprise by arbitrary arrogance, selfish labor leadership, greed, and a doctrine of scarcity can rob America of the full development of her potentialties. If the manufacturers of surreys, with or without fringe, had been permitted to halt the technological advances that made possible the automobile, the face of America would be different; though perhaps to the satisfaction of those who can find no parking places, and to the contentment of municipal officials who not only have lost the patronage involved in many street sweepers but who are much harried by the public's demand for a place to leave the family car. And the parents of teen-agers, no doubt, would welcome a moratorium on phonograph records.

The St. Lawrence Waterway, for example, represents something of a test between those who want the United States to become some kind of empire, with control located in the vulnerable East, and those who regard the United States as our common country.

When I appeared once, as the only Southern witness, before a Congressional committee, to urge construction of this needed link between the Great Lakes and the Atlantic, one representative expressed surprise that a Georgian should entertain any interest in a project so far removed from his State.

Immediately, of course, it makes little difference to the people of Newnan or Atlanta whether Chicago becomes the biggest city in the world. But it is important to every American that every section of America be permitted to expand normally and fruitfully.

Freedom of enterprise also means that valuable inventions, whether exceedingly involved as in the field of chemistry or quite simple, such as that which would provide us with better kitchen matches, shall not be suppressed. The patent laws were written to provide the inventor with a shield against thieves, not to arm monopolists with a sword against the public.

Freedom of enterprise means freedom for every section. In 1944, I predicted that the woollen industry would shift West and South, even in the face of the economic barriers erected through freight differentials. In 1947, on a visit to the Pacific Coast, an Oregon editor showed me a plaint from a Boston publication about the expansion of the Western woollen mills. He had saved the editorial for me, because it contained some splendid invective against me for attacking New England's hegemony in the textile field.

So deep is my sympathy with the multitudinous misfortunes of the Apleys and Pulhams and the other denizens of benighted Back Bay, the attack did not goad me into a minor interjection about "Massachusetts justice," which in the South is used as an equivalent for judicial lynching; nor into any gentle comment upon Bostonian literacy, which we speak of in Newnan as the verbal equivalent for book burning; nor even into a mild retort about the desecration of graveyards, which is acknowledgedly the favorite sport of those Boston intellectuals too energetically virile to express their inborn superiority by scrawling obscenities upon the walls of synagogues.

Instead, it was gratifying to see that the prophecy had been fulfilled, and that Americans were beginning to make cloth where they grew sheep, and thus save a haul of some eight thousand miles on the wool, the cloth, and the finished suits.

The industrialization in the West is strikingly interesting, because it is unlike anything else in America. The plants are new, more modern in design and more efficient than their counterparts elsewhere. The working force is the product of a new melting pot. You can find entering any factory gate on the Pacific Coast a cross section of America: sons of Basque shepherds come newly from Idaho; lanky plainsmen from Amarillo, Texas; Poles whose accent is that of Buffalo instead of Warsaw; cotton farmers from Burke County, Georgia; men from Maine, who speak French with more fluency than English and whose ancestors fled from Canada after Montcalm's defeat.

They are engaged in the American practice of going where they please within their common country, seeking opportunity, seeking satisfaction in their work, seeking the kind of home they wish.

They are trying, incidentally, to make this common country of ours into one nation. They are succeeding, in spite of adroit tampering with our economics, simply because the facts of geography are strongly against the exploiters who seek to retain the colonial system.

10: AN AWARENESS OF CIVIL RIGHTS

Throughout America there is to be found a sounder concept of civil rights than ever before, and a greater interest in individual liberty. This may seem, upon casual examination, to present a paradox, since Americans, especially of the older generation, are also concerned deeply about security in the economic sense.

But this seeming paradox rapidly dissolves itself. The quest for security, which sometimes assumes fantastic proportions and leads to political frauds such as the promise of fifty dollars every Friday or sixty dollars every Saturday from demagogic quacks, is an aftermath of the Great Depression.

In that period so many values, social as well as monetary, were shattered that many Americans have not recovered their sense of security. Vaguely, those citizens, whose life savings were swept away in the market crashes and real estate swindles and bank failures that marked the closing months of the 1920s, feel that they were defrauded and that their government had a part in the fraud. That feeling is widespread, although it is more vocative in California and Florida, perhaps, than in other States.

In a measure, it is true. The deliberate prostitution of the Federal government to a group of stock-jobbing swindlers was not precisely wholesome. The coalition of greed and bigotry that won the election of 1928 was a more debased one than that which won the election of 1872 or that which stole the election of 1876. It is true that foreign bonds of dubious value were sold to American investors with the blessings of those in Washington, and that the banking system was forced by the equivalent of government pressure into association with the thieves who dominated many enterprises, and that the collapse of our domestic economy was invited by the policies of that Great Engineer whose name has become a synonym for the era of human misery.

However, only among the doctrinaire extremists of Right or Left has this search for security taken the form of a willingness to surrender basic American concepts of liberty. The Ham-and-Eggers may be unreasonable, but they are not seeking to replace our form of government with something that promises security at the expense of freedom.

On the other hand, there has been no wholesale repetition of the outrages against civil liberties that followed the First World War. Instead of the horrors of the massacres in the coal mine areas, the bloody suppression of the IWW, and the Palmer Purge that did such damage to the reputation of the Wilson Administration and that contributed so heavily to the Democratic defeat of 1920—in spite of the liberal records of the party's nominees—there has been a burlesque show conducted by two interesting theatrical entrepreneurs. One employs the stage name of Thomas; the other is named Rankin and comes from the State once represented in Congress by L. Q. C. Lamar, Pat Harrison and John Sharp Williams.

I cite Lamar, Harrison and Williams, because Representative Rankin, at least previous to his actual experience with the wishes of the people of Mississippi in the election of 1947, appeared to believe that he represented their views authentically.

The reasons America has seen few serious assaults on civil liberties since the war are varied. For one thing, the government was very careful in its exercise of wartime powers. While the removal of American citizens of Japanese extraction from the West Coast represented a rather dangerous precedent, there were no such crimes against conscience as the Debs prosecution in World War One.

Moreover, the disclosures of Nazi methods served as an antidote. Americans realized that suppression of opinion was more dangerous than any opinion that could be expressed. They had only to look at the world about them to see the result of toying with ideas about a master race of supermen. They came to a realization that freedom is something that is dangerous to tamper with, and that each man's freedom is essential to the freedom of every man.

The libertarians had done a good job in the intervening years. Even if they did get their pants licked off them in 1928 politically, they aroused America to the menace of bigotry. They fought a great many losing fights between 1920 and the end of the Second World War, but they won their campaign to convince America that civil rights were important. So successful were they, indeed, that even in Boston there is a movement to permit people to read.

Finally, the economic conditions of 1946 and 1947 were less favorable to those who would like to attack the Bill of Rights. The sharp recession after the war boom, the 1920 "cotton depression" in the South, and the growing despair of Midwestern farmers created a condition where intolerance could flourish. Hunger is a mighty provoker of hatred.

Of these numerous factors, probably the most important and most valuable was the fight made by the libertarians. Some of them were conciliatory men, like Atlanta's Ashby Jones, who was a great preacher with that terrible meekness that the righteous ought always to have and so seldom possess. Some were adroit legalists, like Arthur Garfield Hays and Dudley Field Malone. Some were thundering prophets, like Heywood Broun of the great Sacco-Vanzetti columns. Most of them were quiet, unobtrusive folks: country editors, small town preachers and educators, lesser figures in the union movement, white-collar workers who had been shocked by the orgy of 1920.

They fought hard. They smashed hate organizations like the Ku Klux Klan through exposures that left the suckers, whose Klatocken had lined the wallets of Klagriffs and Kleagles and Kludds, gasping with disgust. They smashed a good many crooked politicians. They forced on America an awareness of the importance of civil liberties.

Political rights now are denied only infrequently to minority groups. The courts have adopted the doctrine advanced by Mr.

Justice Oliver Wendell Holmes that something more than conformity with technicalities is required to provide a fair trial. Religious groups seldom are subjected to attack.

But prejudice is not dead. There are more hate publications in the country than before the war. They are to be found in every section of America, pouring out their malicious falsehoods in the same old way. However, they seem duller and less zestful than in the past, as if the hate-mongers were weary now; or, perhaps, as if the suckers were more reluctant to part with their money in return for venom.

Prejudice can not be eradicated by legislation. Some of the end results of prejudice, of course, can come within the province of the law, since it is possible to guarantee freedom of speech, freedom of religion, the right to participate in government, and the right to speedy and impartial trials in courts of justice. It is impossible, however, to legislate understanding between men. That must be learned by the individual.

11: Those liberals in the South

Wherever I went in America, I was asked about the status of liberalism in the South.

I do not like the name-tag of liberal. Personally, I prefer to regard myself as a democrat, with a little d; though that, too, is inexact and cumbersome.

The enemy that must be combatted in America is authoritarianism, which is the same whether it wears a black shirt or a brown shirt or no shirt at all, and whether it stems from Right or Left, or whatever it promises in the way of dictatorship either by proletariat or by superman.

The antonym for authoritarianism is libertarianism. It is a word that has not deteriorated in meaning as has liberalism. It does not lend itself so readily to the vicious pun that "a liberal is somebody that is liberal with your money."

A libertarian believes in liberty, in the right of all the people to decide the destiny of their country, in the right of the individual to be secure in his property and his way of life.

It is necessary to be careful about words today. Their meanings change, with greater rapidity than the changes can be recorded in any dictionary.

Economy, for example, is a word that, with its derivatives, is to be found almost everywhere. All erudite writers lean heavily upon the adjective economic. They neglect to realize that it is not the all-embracing science that they suppose, but is actually the province of pots-and-pans.

Similarly, the words Fascist and Communist have been twisted from any semblance of meaning, as in the instance of the application of such words to Senator Taft.

Nationalist has changed in meaning, too. A century ago, the name was associated with movements to free subject people from tyranny. The great Garibaldi was an intense nationalist as well as a great Italian patriot and a great lover of freedom. So very intense was his nationalism that he fought for national freedom in South America, as well as in Italy, and his final battles were on behalf of the French against the Prussian invaders. A nationalist in those days meant a man who wanted every people to be free; he wanted the Austrian yoke lifted from the Czechs, and the Turkish yoke lifted from the Bulgars and Armenians and Greeks, and the Russian yoke lifted from the Finns, and the British yoke lifted from the Burmese, and the American yoke lifted from the people of the Philippines.

Then came Hitler and the National Socialists, who were neither Socialists nor Nationalists as the words had been understood. The Nazis and those who aped them in other lands gave nationalism a new meaning: instead of the nationalist desiring freedom for every nation, he desired that his nation plunder the world and reduce the citizens of other lands to slavery.

Poverty is another such word. Poverty was extolled, quite properly, by the saints; but the poverty of St. Francis of Assisi bore no striking resemblance to the poverty of a transients' camp in the fruit-packing country. Involuntary poverty is as wicked as involuntary servitude.

A sad fate has overtaken the word liberal. Its original political association was with the libertarian, mildly reformist party that, under the leadership of Campbell-Bannerman and Asquith, gave the British the most capable government it had enjoyed in generations. The British Liberals reasonably took the Centrist position, effecting economic changes when necessary but keeping in mind the essential fact that government is only an agent for the people, not an independent authority. This gave the England of 1912 a government that, if definitely to the Left of President Wilson's New Freedom, was only a hairsbreadth to the Right of President Roosevelt's New Deal.

But the term has been badly smeared today, somewhat by shrewd propaganda but rather more by its misuse by crackpots who utilize it to describe themselves, when they actually possess none of the libertarian beliefs that traditionally are associated with the body of liberal doctrine.

If the sincere liberals, who believe that freedom is as essential as food, seek or need a label, perhaps they had best revert to that of libertarian.

So, when I encountered the question about liberalism in the South, I always was forced into establishing some definitions before I could reply that those who believed in free government, responsive to the people, and in human dignity for every citizen, were doing all right. Alike in terms of political victories won and in influence in the shaping of public policies, they are making themselves heard.

This may seem paradoxical, in view of the victories of intensely conservative groups in some States and of perennial demagogues in others. But their virility is proved by the very intensity of the campaigns waged by reaction, usually financed by outside exploitative interests bent on maintaining a colonial system in the South and in keeping control of such things as transportation, oil, steel and sulphur.

If specific instances need to be cited, there are the 1944 victories of Lister Hill in Alabama and of Claude Pepper in Florida, against strong, popular and heavily financed opposition. There is Folsom's 1946 victory in Alabama. There is the defeat of "Cotton Ed" Smith in South Carolina, and the narrowness of the Senatorial victory of Texas' O'Daniel, and the fact that Eugene Talmadge, despite the backing of a coalition of powerful politicians and business interests and his own personal following, not only could muster no majority in Georgia in 1946, but ran second in popular votes in the party primary. Then there is Mississippi, which informed America that Mississippi shared America's opinion about Rankin rather than Rankin's opinion about Rankin.

These elections do not indicate that Alabama, Florida, Georgia, Mississippi, South Carolina or Texas are intense in their devotion either to Bourbons or demagogues, or utterly loyal to their out-of-state inter-meddlers. The myth of a reactionary South is a myth and nothing more.

It is a myth like the quadrennial Southern Revolt. In every Presidential year, the Democratic party faces a rebellion. In 1940 it took the form of a reported fight against the Third Term. In 1944 and 1948 it was to be rendered effective by having the Presidential electors of Texas and Virginia start the rebellion against the nominees of the National Convention.

There is dissatisfaction in the South about party affairs, always. The Southeast is unrepresented in the Cabinet, has not had a name on the national ticket in decades, and its political leaders are sensitive. A certain failure to comprehend the real nature of Southern problems may be successfully charged to Democratic leaders in the North and East. And the Bourbons naturally are stimulated to mock rebellion by their Republican affiliates. The Southern Revolt is a symptom of Southern resentment against being taken for granted and being misunderstood. It is a habit that has grown into a custom. It also, in part, is a struggle on the local level for party leadership; during the Roosevelt years, the Revolt always was led by reactionary stalwarts.

The 1948 Revolt, as those of 1940 and 1944, serves as propaganda for the Republican campaign. The local combat between reactionary and libertarian is more important.

Of course the reactionaries have an advantage in any Southern election. It requires money and organization to win political victories. Libertarians in the South seldom can raise much money, and they have neither ready-made organizations nor the services of skilled organizers.

Money is important in a campaign, especially when the people have to be told about the issues. In the Hill-Simpson contest in Alabama, it was estimated that Senator Hill's votes were developed at a campaign cost of twenty-four cents each, while the expenditures of his opponent averaged three dollars for each vote. In Georgia's 1946 race, the 317,000 votes for James V. Carmichael were obtained at a cost of a little below thirty cents each; his victorious opponent's votes cost almost two dollars. "Big Jim" Folsom, possibly because of the delightful novelty of his campaign and his tremendous personal gift of humor and his habit of seldom answering his campaign mail, won—spending fifteen cents per vote against more than two dollars.

That does not indicate that the opponents of reaction handle their money with greater skill. The relative economy is due chiefly to not having the money to spend, although a part is played by the fact that their money is raised and spent on the local level, while reactionary cash is sought on a national scale and spent by "practical politicians." Sometimes a "practical politician" commands a sizeable fee for his services in a campaign; and in three Southern States, at least, there are strong local machines that are kept together by the largess that gets distributed in major campaign years.

Since libertarian money comes from the people, and usually from people who can vote, it is arguable statistically that the reactionaries need at least a five-to-one margin in money in order to have a chance.

Reactionary forces always are organized; their opponents are never organized. If the reactionaries lose, their leaders are back in session within a week to plan the next campaign and to start building a reputation for the next candidate. Their partisan publications, which usually carry no advertising but somehow find a way to pay the printer very promptly, roll from the presses every week. In some States, notably Louisiana, Georgia and Texas, these publications have been effective media of propaganda, since they were built around the principal vote-getter's personality and were ghostwritten in a homey style.

However, the value of the personal propaganda organ was more than offset by an independent, courageous and libertarian local press. Georgia's weekly and daily papers are middle-of-the-road, and not ten per cent are either controlled or reactionary. North Carolina and Tennessee likewise have independent newspapers of enormous vitality, and while some Southern editors were played for suckers by the utility lobby, before the depression, the rural press of the region is exceptional for a lack of venal or time-serving members.

As in all other sections of America, the reactionaries of the South have the advantage of presenting a solid front, while their opponents fall victim to the vote-splitting technique. The prosperity, considerable influence, and notable reputation for silent wisdom of one Southeast Georgia politician can be attributed to having ever ready some available pseudo-liberal vote-splitter to broker to the reactionaries. He has his equivalent in every State of the South; each is prosperous, influential, and silent.

So it is necessary to say that there are four evident truths about the political aspects of Southern libertarianism:

Southern libertarians have no money to finance campaigns.

Southern libertarians have no organization to direct campaigns.

Southern libertarians have no discipline within campaigns.

But Southern libertarians win lots of campaigns: it is true that they lose many battles, but in the end they will win the war.

Reaction will be defeated in the South because of the South's tradition of liberty, which has deeper roots than almost anywhere else in America.

It is popular outside the South to deny this tradition exists or ever existed. Some wearers of the label "Southern liberal" are so self-conscious that they accept that fantasy of a Bourbon South, so that it is believed even in such cynical and inquiring quarters as might reject the better authenticated account of Jack and the Beanstalk.

There are horrible and disgusting and obnoxious things in the South that can be palliated neither by explanations nor outright lying. There are rural slums indescribable for squalor; there are outbursts of flaming violence, inspired by the combination of poverty, ignorance and demagoguery; but there are no Blue Ribbon juries in the South, and there has never been a *legal* lynching of the kind that makes "Massachusetts justice" a synonym for judicial murder in every civilized country from Uruguay to Czechoslovakia; nor does any Southern State ape Michigan and maintain a debtor's prison for youthful war veterans.

You can go back to the Founders, if you like. Or you can select James Jackson and Willie Jones and their peers, in the Jeffersonian era; or Forsyth and the Lamars and Kendall and the Blairs in Andrew Jackson's time. Or you can choose one of the Dark Ages of America, in the twilight of the McKinley Administration, and name Georgia's Bacon, who warned the United States of the evil implicit in our ruthlessly brutal subjugation of the Philippines; or Georgia's Hoke Smith, one of the fathers of national conservation. Or you can permit North Carolina to supply two names: Aycock, who gave his State the first modern State government in America, and Josephus Daniels, whose intelligent skill as a diplomat demonstrated that men of good will make better ambassadors than do tea-sipping career men or sabre-rattling, senile brass hats.

That tradition has not died in the South. It is not at the point of death now.

Southern libertarian idealism is inclined on occasion to explore ridiculous bypaths, because of those curious qualities of thought associated with the South's Gaelic ancestry. It is even inclined to meddlesomeness, because the ethical standards of the South are sometimes dogmatic rather than reasoned. But the standards are sound; the people of the South believe that stealing is wrong, that injustice is wrong, that cruelty is wrong; and campaign oratory does not overcome that ethical bias.

Since reaction is the offspring of theft's union with injustice, the South is against it, when the issue is clear. Only manipulation can save the reactionaries, when the people understand what the voting is about. When freedom of education was the issue in Georgia in 1942, the reactionaries took a bad beating. When getting the services for which they paid taxes was the issue in Alabama in 1946, the reactionaries took a bad beating. When progressive national legislation was the issue in Florida in 1944, the reactionaries took a bad beating. Reaction can win in the South only when its spokesmen can inject a false issue; probably that is the only time reaction can win anywhere in America, for that matter.

Reaction in the South, like reaction elsewhere in the United States, is usually very greatly aided by the over-niceness of its foes. Forgetting that it is exceedingly difficult to demonstrate statesmanship outside public office, the "liberal element" tends to an overserious attitude, and often condemns the men within their ranks who present lively and entertaining performances on the stump. Some of these question the good taste of Jim Folsom, because he illustrated his points from the platform by brandishing a commonplace and undignified kitchen-mop.

There is nothing in Mr. Jefferson's Declaration of Independence, nor in the Bill of Rights, nor in the constitutions of the fourteen Southern Commonwealths, that prohibits a libertarian from making his public addresses interesting or that requires him to speak to his constituents in the fashion of Ichabod Crane lecturing the more backward of his students.

While this applies especially to those making a fight for liberty in the South, it is applicable all over the nation. If the foes of reaction were not so frequently deadly serious, if they had the capacity for laughter that was possessed, for example, by George W. Norris and Fiorello LaGuardia when these turned their ebullient wits upon the foibles of stuffed-shirts, election results would be different many times.

12: ALL OF THE PEOPLE ALL OF THE TIME

It was early in 1947 that I set out on a speaking trip that carried me into every section of our common country. In large cities, in university towns, in communities that looked very much like Newnan but that were placed in the middle of the prairies or along the Mississippi and its tributaries or on the Pacific Coast, I talked with a great many Americans.

They differed very little in their thinking. They wanted a program of liberty and progress for our country. They wanted our country to be united, and the sectional barriers eliminated, and an equal opportunity for every citizen.

But they wanted it to be *their* program. They were unwilling to accept a ready-made concept of American policy, either foreign or domestic.

They were aware of many of the problems, displaying far more understanding for issues than many of their leaders seem to think possible, judging from the debates in Congress and the handouts of many administrators, who believe that the public must be fed pap.

Before many audiences, representative of many different segments of thinking, of many different income groups, and of many different sections of America, I made much the same talk. Always the same anecdotes, the same illustrations, the same appeals seemed to reach all of them. They felt much alike about opportunity; they wanted it for their children, and the boys and girls down the street, and for all other boys and girls in America. They wanted an orderly and peaceful world, where butter was not sacrificed for guns. They wanted a democratic world, in which every man's dignity was respected and every man's vote was counted. They wanted early solutions to our economic problems, so that production could catch up with the demand for the things that make life comfortable.

Most of them were frankly troubled about public affairs. They seemed to believe that there was a want of coherence and coördination in our policies, and that our domestic efforts did not coincide with our foreign efforts in every particular. They were a little tired of going blind; they wanted to be taken into the confidence of their leadership, and they were critical of Congressional leaders, playing for partisan reasons with the nation's economy, and of administrators who regarded all legitimate information on public questions as "top drawer secrets."

They wanted to write their own program for America.

The program that they wanted in Utah was not different from that asked in Ohio; Texans agreed with Californians. Manhattan, Kansas, not only had provided New York's Manhattan with its chronicler in Damon Runyon, but seemed to share the same ideas.

Evening after evening, after I had made my talk and answered the usual dozens of questions, I listened to what they had to say. They said it well, these club women, and business men, and college students, and small town teachers and ministers and lawyers and farmers and manufacturers. They were careful with their facts, for one thing; they were sincere in their emotions, for another; and they knew what they wanted.

They wanted, most of all, to be safe in their individual freedom, and they were willing to respect the freedom of others. They disagreed, sometimes, about immediate measures to carry out their objectives; but they agreed upon the objectives, and they were willing to experiment. They had a belief in trying again, in seeking something better, in expecting things to work out well in the end if courage and diligence are employed, and all those other naive, impractical, idealistic conceptions of citizenship and government and human relations that are essentially American, and that somehow work.

They had faith in other men, because they had faith in themselves.

They insisted that democracy had worked and could continue to work.

And as proof, they pointed to what was near them, to that part of America where they lived. Looking at America, one is compelled to agree that they are right.

NORTH

Yes, we'll rally round the flag, boys,
We'll rally once again,
Shouting the battle-cry of Freedom
—GEORGE FREDERICK ROOT

1: THE HOMELAND OF MRS. BABBITT

North is the section of the nation hardest to define. Despite the dissimilarity between the Mountain States, the Northwest and the Pacific Coast, all that vast area can be lumped together as West without wounding anyone's geographical pride or occasioning any misunderstanding. You may define South as a state of mind, or as the Confederate States, minus Texas or with Texas as you like. East is the area that owes fealty to Boston, with sprawling New York and Pennsylvania thrown in. But North is something else.

The New Englander, trying to explain to a Georgian where he lives, may assert that he is from the North; and the true North he is likely to call Middle West, assuming that Indians populate Chicago and that buffalo roam wild over uninhabited Iowa and Wisconsin.

To the Georgian, North is the Union Country, the place where the tough fighting men that followed General Sherman came from. It is not the East, but the great grain and industrial States that are in the middle of the nation and that lie above the borders of Kentucky and Missouri, where the War Between the States may properly be called a civil war.

When a Georgian speaks of a Northerner, he does not mean a Yankee. A Yankee comes from the vicinity of Boston, has a perpetual cold in the head, talks through his nose in the accents of the Cockney valet of an Oxford undergraduate, and has a patronizing manner and a perpetual ill-humor from bombarding his stomach with horrible food.

Twenty years or so ago, when Confederate veterans were still here to reminisce over the fraternal war that was so equally a mixture of chivalry and greed, they would say:

"We licked the tar out of the Yankees at Bull Run."

But they would also say:

"The Northerners fought like hell at Shiloh."

The North voted generally with Andrew Jackson. It was Douglas territory in the internal battles of the Democratic party, and its electoral votes all went either to Lincoln or Douglas in 1860. It wanted no slavery within its free economy, and it was nationalist in the Jacksonian sense.

The Northern States provided the fighting men who marched down against Vicksburg, who cut their way through Tennessee and into Georgia to burn Atlanta and desolate the area to the sea, who forced the capitulation of Joe Johnston's soldiers in the Carolinas. They were good fighting men, and no nonsense about it, these men from Illinois and Michigan, Wisconsin and Kansas, Indiana and Ohio. They won the war at Shiloh.

They were raucous and boisterous, and their war songs were offensive and no doubt they sang them as badly as their descendants sing at a luncheon club on ladies' day. When the war was over, they went back to their homes; the carpetbagger was not a Northerner, generally speaking. A great many of them voted for Horace Greeley, and more of them voted for Grover Cleveland. But they were not interested too much in politics, except when economic conditions disturbed them. They were interested in building cities that are a hodge-podge of solid comfort, tremendous industrial productiveness, and frequent bad taste. In normal times, they enjoy the highest standard of living in America for all comparable economic classes.

The Northerner has been ruthlessly satirized by expatriates who go East; he is as cruelly misrepresented in fiction as the average Southerner. His generic name, doubtless from some eponymous hero of the covered wagon era, is Babbitt. My own investigations have led me to a belief that the original George Babbitt was a mighty man of valor, like Paul Bunyan or John Henry or Steve Mestrovic: except that he laid out enormous subdivisions, building houses upon them in which there were almost uncounted bathrooms and no closet space. He also sang songs, the favorite being "My Wild Irish Rose," to the accompaniment of a badly tuned piano. He was incredibly sentimental and generous; the expression "to give away his shirt" being based on an episode in his middle years. He was also shrewd: having once been sold a wooden nutmeg by a visitor from Connecticut, he gilded it and resold it to the same gentleman at a considerably advanced price.

Often misguided by habit, he voted Republican: but in 1912, with tears streaming down his cheeks, he stormed up the aisles of the Colosseum singing "Onward, Christian Soldiers" and took his place beside the Colonel at Armageddon. If you tell him today that Warren Harding was not a great man, he is likely to snort his disagreement; but if you tell him that Calvin Coolidge was an able President, he will give you a look of incredulity that suggests that you hurry to your favorite psychiatrist. But he will not argue too much about it; for he is busy with making money, which he spends upon his wife and his children and upon pleasure and charity and poker and food. He is as hospitable as a Southerner, and as vain as Floridians and Californians disputing over climate, and so American that he is an easy subject for any form of satire that anyone cares to write.

I like Mr. Babbitt and I like his wife. The Little Lady, as Mrs. Babbitt is called by her husband, belongs to a good many civic organizations. I may add that she has been very happy since Carol Kennicott moved out of town and took her managing ways with her; and when I was travelling in those parts, I was glad both for Mrs. Babbitt and for myself, and shared with her the hope that the Kennicotts never move back to Main Street.

There are things about the section that I do not like, of course. Not the climate, however; at Ann Arbor, the sun was almost intolerably bright on the dry Michigan snow, and the land was as lovely —well, almost as lovely—as the hill country of North Georgia in autumn. Nor the people; like all the people everywhere, they are like people, like the people in Newnan, for instance. But there was, perhaps, throughout the section a trace of unawareness not shared by the rest of the country that made you want to paraphrase the sundial to them and say:

"It is darker than you think."

Yet it is hard to chide them about that, for their optimism and their courage is ebullient and contagious.

2: The Horatio Alger tradition lives

It is not mere geography that gives the North the right to be considered a single region. My inclusion of Texas and California in the West is open to obvious criticism, justified only by pointing out that these empires, with differences within their own borders as great as those that may be noted between Arkansas and Iowa, have to go somewhere. The linking of the Middle Atlantic States with New England into a very loosely integrated East is better sustained by an examination of economic facts.

The South can be defined as a state of mind. That also is true of the North. The area that Dr. Howard W. Odum calls the Middle States, together with some of the adjacent territory, has a homogeneity that is psychological rather than economic or ethnic. It has a common viewpoint, which may shift with the passage of the years in one or another particular but that retains a stable standard of values.

Though there are many large cities in the North, including those three sprawling monsters, Detroit, Chicago and Cleveland, these do not dominate its thought or its economy. The North is the section where the small city is the center of life, yet where farmers actually live on the farm instead of gathering in village communities.

The bitterer satirists who have pilloried the region, most of them wandering native sons whose attitude toward the region might be investigated profitably by some disciple of Dr. Sigmund Freud, as well as the gentler critics who remained at home, seem to have agreed upon a few criteria by which the North may be identified.

It is the area where caste is determined by economic status and therefore is the region where transition to another caste is easiest.

Its people are allied by family, rather than by clan as they are in the South.

It is the most comfortable section of the nation, by material standards, with a large middle class.

It is provincial without quaintness and thoroughly sold upon the Victorian precepts, the Alger tradition, and isolationism.

The bare statement of those truths about the North gives a defective picture of the region. Cleveland is a city with the same proportion of second-generation Americans as Boston, yet it remains that "city on a hill" that Tom Johnson visioned, easily the best managed metropolis in the nation and a center of culture and freedom devoid of racial tensions. Iowa presents the picture of the one American state with a perfectly balanced economy. Wisconsin represents one of the worst exploited States in the nation reorganizing its resources into a new prosperity that has lasted. There was a more intelligent approach to the problems of local government in the section than anywhere else in the nation.

It is necessary to examine a little more deeply into the reasons why the North is like that.

To begin with, it has none of the racial homogeneity of the South, where every white is kin to every other white in some degree. The North was settled by people from every section of America. Virginia and North Carolina contributed heavily to the settlement of Ohio, as did New England to that of Wisconsin and New York to that of Michigan. Illinois and Kansas were settled by families from the South as well as from the East. And upon these basic settlements of colonial stock there descended migrants from every part of Europe.

The Germans came in great number, especially after the crushing of democratic aspirations drove so many men of ability into exile in the middle of the nineteenth century. The Scandinavians came, and the Finns, and the Hungarians, and Slavs from Poland and the Balkans and the Ukraine. Cincinnati and St. Louis gave cordial reception to many Jewish families. The Irish reached every section. Before the War Between the States, the Negro community in Chicago was large, made up of relatively prosperous freedmen. The Italians arrived to help to build railroads, and remained as citizens. In the North, almost every strain that helps to make up America is to be found, and none can be said to predominate over another.

As a result, while racial tensions between whites and Negroes exist in some of the major urban centers, especially Chicago and Detroit where housing conditions have become intolerable, in the smaller cities there is no serious clash between different groups. Possibly it is advantageous to possess a Scandinavian name, if you wish to embark in politics in Minnesota; Olson and Stassen came from that stock, and no doubt their names did them no hurt; but Benson and Ball found the absence of Norse ancestry no very serious handicap in their campaigns. Wisconsin has a substantial group of German ancestry but the State's most famous political family, the LaFollettes, were original settlers with no trace of the Teuton in their lineage. While bloc-voting occurs here and there among national groups, the American melting pot has done its work admirably in most of the North. There may be a certain standardization about the product, especially in the middle-income groups, and you may have less affection for Mr. and Mrs. Babbitt than I hold, but you can not deny that the folks up North are Americans.

They are a little inclined to be nationalistic. Not in the sense into which the Nazis twisted the word, however, but in the perhaps equally mystic sense that the nationalists of the early nineteenth century understood it, when national freedom was so important and sacred a thing that men went from all corners of the globe to aid Garibaldi in his efforts to liberate Italy and when national freedom meant freedom within every land for all its people, and not conquest of one man's free country by some other nation.

It was that nationalism that led the men from the North to enlist in the Union Army in the sixties; yet they were never sympathetic with the Reconstruction policies, by almost the same process of reasoning. They were determinedly against secession, but never were they in favor of military rule for the South nor for the harsh policies of exploitation that were devised. Before the war they had been willing, in general, to settle the issue of slavery upon a local basis, although they wished no intrusion of slaveholders and slaves into their midst.

Out of their nationalism stems their isolationist sentiment. Despite many deep-rooted attachments to the old country, the people of the North want no part of Europe. They came to America of their free choice. They like the American way of life, and rather sensibly, at least so I think, feel that material comforts are a valuable part of freedom. They do not favor any American foreign policy that involves too close an association with any other nation. Their conception of an appropriate foreign policy seems to be one of unilateral action by the United States.

Until near the end of World War Two, isolationism perhaps was stimulated by a belief that war was distant from them; they may have had less consciousness of Europe than the people on the Atlantic Coast and less realization of Asia than those on the Pacific. But it is even more probable that they were simply too busy.

For the North is busy. It is the area of mass production. Its industrial establishments, its labor unions, its consumption of all products are on titanic scales. And if the people like money and the things it will buy, and have established their caste system about it, it is because money can be made there easily. The Horatio Alger tradition is not dead, as it is in the East.

Nor is the hostility between the city dweller and the farmer acute there, as it is in New York and New England. There is no such hostility against Chicago among the downstate farmers to compare with upstate New York's hatred of the metropolis. This is largely a matter of economics, however, and a demonstration that many social problems, once assumed to be emotional in basis, are actually matters of earning a livelihood. The farmers of the great grain States are prosperous; in general, they are more prosperous than the city folks. Their soil is good. Their buildings are neat and weather-tight and well painted. To them, the cities are trading centers, and the department store is a joy forever.

Neither war nor economic disaster has touched the North as they have the South or even the East. Sharp as were the depressions of 1896 and of 1929, these did not threaten the complete collapse of society as the latter did in the East, nor mortgage irretrievably for a generation the entire soil of the area as the former did in the South. Nor has the North known war upon its soil since the Indians were driven out, as the South knew it in 1861-65. Prosperity has had a chance to become deep-rooted in the region.

Governmentally, the North is interesting. Almost uniformly, its cities are well managed and interest in local affairs is high. The State governments, though often financed by regressive taxation, have a willingness to experiment that is seldom encountered elsewhere, but administration on the State level is seldom as efficient as on the municipal.

Politically there are many gradations of opinion in the various States of the North. South Dakota is one of the most conservative States in the nation, while North Dakota is one of the most liberal. Although the home of William Jennings Bryan and George W.

Norris as well as of Senator Kenneth Wherry, Nebraska is conservative except for a willingness to experiment in techniques of government, and has one of the worst tax systems in the nation. Ohio and Michigan also have regressive tax systems, with the former threatening to injure local self-government units eventually. Yet Michigan is one of the best administered of Northern States. The educational establishments of Iowa and Wisconsin might profitably be studied by all Americans.

The private school disease, which affects the East perniciously, is as absent in the North as in the South. In the medium-sized towns of the North, the high school is the center of community activity for young people, as in the South, and the type of intellectual snobbishness that the East affects is rejected. Somehow the North has reconciled a caste system based on income with some form of individual equalitarianism, at least among young people. And youth is esteemed in the North.

3: HEARTS FOR EVERYDAY USE

Late March is cold in Ohio, and I shivered a little as I climbed off the plane at the Greater Cincinnati airport and walked toward the station. A committee from the History Club of Hamilton was to meet me and drive me the remaining thirty-odd miles to their town.

I looked about for the committee, and a young man walked over to me and spoke pleasantly. It was my introduction to Joe Hirschhorn, who was eighteen and a senior in Hamilton High School and president of the History Club, and my host.

The lecture had been booked by my agent, and, somehow, I had expected the History Club to be a group of sedate elders. It now appeared that it was a high school organization.

"How does a high school club manage to pay its way and pay fees to the lecturers it invites?" I asked my young companion.

"We have the money. I have a check for you in my pocket now," he continued. "And we don't charge admission to our lectures."

"Then how do you do it?" I had heard of the amazing financial acumen of the people of the North, but I did not suspect that it extended to the senior class in high school.

"Every year, the seniors in the History Club provide a free lecture for the people in Hamilton," he explained. "You know those sales tax receipts that merchants give with every purchase in Ohio? Well, the purchaser is supposed to tear them up, but usually he just throws them down. The State will redeem them, for a nominal sum. So all year, the seniors pick them up, wherever they find them, and by March we have enough money to pay for one lecture that we think the people really would like to hear. We invited you this year."

Calculating the redemption rate of the receipts at a dollar a thousand, seniors of Hamilton High School had to collect more than a half-million of the tiny slips of paper.

We drove on to the town, and I was greeted by the class officers. The only Negro student among the seniors had been elected president; he was one of the school's athletic stars. The History Club was as serious a group as I met on my trip into forty-seven States; its members wanted to know about America, about the different sections of our common country, and about their place in its future.

In talking at Hamilton, I got away from the usual text of my talk to tell the people about Georgia's experiment with youth franchise. My native State has reduced the voting age to eighteen, and it has been useful in many ways. Young men and young women need an earlier introduction to the practical aspects of government; but, more important, government needs the voice of Joe Hirschhorn and his classmates, who have a sense of civic responsibility strong enough to induce them to collect over a half-million sales tax receipts to provide an evening of talk for their home town. It needs the sound emotions of young people, who do not use their hearts for dress-up wear only, regarding them as too good for everyday occasions.

4: CITIES AND MEN OF THE BUCKEYE STATE

There are more industries in Ohio than in any other State, and many splendid, robust, sprawling cities. Southern influences, often found in the North and seldom encountered in the East, are strong in parts of Ohio. The liberal tradition is strong there, also, though it is the State that provided America with Mark Hanna and Harry Daugherty. It also provided America with President Benjamin Harrison, the last responsible conservative to occupy the White House; and with Senator Allen G. Thurman and with Chief Justice William Howard Taft, a capable jurist who never became competent enough at politics to become a serviceable Chief Executive; and with James M. Cox, one of the most capable State administrators in the nation's history.

I liked urban Ohio. The cities have personalities. There is Delaware, dominated by Ohio Wesleyan; and Lorain, which sprawls on the riverside and lake front, where I watched them slice steel pipes at the American Tube and Foundry's giant plant with the ease with which the butcher slices salami; and Akron, where they make tires, using the fabric from Georgia and the natural rubber from the East Indies and the synthetic rubber from Texas. Canton and Toledo, I visited on days that were so cold that I wondered that the inhabitants did not hibernate like bears instead of swarming to work as usual. Then there is Cincinnati, which possesses the finest railroad station in America and the Taft family and an accent a little different from the rest of Ohio, compounded of the Kentucky variant of the Southern drawl and German accents. Columbus is composed of four cities, being at once the State capital, a college town, an industrial center, and a military establishment; the four communities seem to exist apart from each other, except in those years when the lobbyists representing pilfering interests congregate with the political leaders in the hotels on High Street as they have done since 1812.

Lorain represents an unusual civic development for a community with a normal population of fifty thousand. Possessing a remarkable geographical advantage as a manufacturing center, the community was developing speedily when the tornado of 1924 struck.

Instead of rebuilding haphazardly, Lorain undertook to develop a community pattern. Although essentially a workingman's town, with few pretentious homes, its streets are clean and the lilacs are beautiful in their season.

Lorain rejected the ghetto principle, when United States Steel imported foreign-born workers forty years ago. Tom Johnson had built a plant there, and was making a fortune by paying a fifty per cent higher wage to unskilled workers than anyone else. When he sold his plant, the monopolists stabilized wages, and native labor became scarce. But the imported Italians, Slovaks, Poles and Hungarians refused to be segregated, and today their children are good Ohio citizens.

Cincinnati is always fighting about local government and talking about the Tafts. The community's favorite citizen is Charles Phelps Taft, the brother of the Senator, and a strong advocate of the Charter group, which fights on better-than-even terms with the Republican organization. The Senator is well enough liked, but Cincinnati folks will often say that "Bob's stubborner than Charlie."

Cleveland is one of the most amazing cities in America. It is a fan-shaped sprawl of steel mills, factories, business districts and homes from the shore of Lake Erie along the twisting Cuyahoga River. It is a study in diversification of industry. Steel is made there, and almost everything that can be made from steel. Automobile parts and batteries are a considerable item in the freight it sends down the canal which Alfred Kelley induced the Ohio legislature to bring to the growing town of the 1850s.

For a while, Cleveland was the oil capital of the world, when John D. Rockefeller, borrowing Flagler's genius and Harkness' capital, was establishing his monopoly.

It is a town built by emigrants. Czechs, Slovakians, Germans, Hungarians, Irish, Rumanians, Greeks, Lithuanians, Poles came there to work in the steel mills. They made the community America's best ordered, best governed metropolis.

For me, Cleveland is dominated by the memories of two men. The first of these is Tom Johnson.

Johnson made his millions casually in steel and transportation and speculation. A great bluff man, the very model of the industrial barons of that day, he moved into Cleveland when he sold his steel plant at Lorain, and settled down to enjoy the life on Euclid Avenue, the Millionaire Row of that era, where Mark Hanna and the Standard Oil bosses had their homes.

The town belonged to Hanna in those days, and it wasn't much of a town in many ways. The parks had more signs saying "Keep off the Grass" than they had grass. The transportation system, dominated by Hanna, was inadequate, inefficient, and expensive, charging two fares wherever possible. Sometimes the garbage was collected, when anyone thought about it.

Johnson had to do something to keep busy. He had been a magnificent pirate in business, but was tired of that. He bought up a few of the streetcar lines to play with and a bunch of books to read. He cut fares on his lines and issued transfers, and read Henry George's books of economics, politics and social justice.

He became convinced that public enterprises, such as the transit system, should not be used to gouge the people, and, also, that they could be better run.

Hanna did not like interference. He bossed Cleveland. He bossed Ohio on the side. He was just preparing to install in the White House a singularly handsome ventriloquist's dummy through whom to boss the United States.

Johnson went into politics, and was elected Mayor, and made the worst transit system of any major city into one of the best. Hanna took time out from pulling the strings attached to the dummy labelled Major McKinley and went to Columbus to rig up a city charter for Cleveland and to grant perpetual franchises for all Cleveland's utilities. He lost to Johnson on the franchise fight, but he won

on the charter, and got a system by which government was placed
in the hands of a number of boards and the Mayor was stripped of
much of his authority. Johnson kept on getting elected Mayor, however, and dominated the scene until they finally beat him for his
sixth term.

By that time, he had made Cleveland a great city and a well-run
city. The conservatives kept their hands off for some years, but in
1924 they slipped in a city manager system, and for six years Cleveland went from bad to worse. But the Johnson tradition was strong,
and in 1930 Cleveland went back to popular government.

Johnson had a phrase, paraphrased from the Bible: "We'll make
Cleveland a city on a hill, whose light shall not be hid." He did,
and Cleveland has fine public services, and a fine park system, in
which each of its numerous racial groups has been allowed to plan
a park and dedicate it to one of its own national heroes; with one
limitation, the hero must not be a military man.

Cleveland is identified with another man. It was here that Eugene
Debs on September 14, 1918 looked squarely into the faces of the
jurors who had convicted him and of the judge who was about to
sentence him and delivered one of the most moving speeches in
American history.

"Years ago I recognized my kinship with all living beings, and
I made up my mind that I was not one bit better than the meanest
of earth," he began in a soft, quiet voice. "I said then, I say now,
that while there is a lower class, I am in it; while there is a criminal
element, I am of it; while there is a soul in prison, I am not free."

There was nothing in the background of the sixty-three-year-old
prisoner that can account for those singing words. His parents came
to Indiana from Alsace before the War Between the States. He
went to school, and helped organize the Brotherhood of Railroad
Firemen, and dabbled enough with Democratic politics to be city
clerk of Terre Haute and a member of the Indiana legislature. He
fought the Pullman Company's monopoly, and went to jail for doing so. He became a Socialist, though he never understood too

thoroughly the economic tenets of his party; and he made lectures over the country, and wrote pieces in magazines, and helped organize unions.

He knew about Prussian militarism from his father, and he hated it and criticized it. But when war came, he was against war; so they sent him to jail for saying so. He dominated the prison at Atlanta when he was there. The guards and the prisoners, alike, loved him. A million Americans voted for him for President in 1920, while he was in prison.

I have read a good many of his tracts and speeches. Most of them are somewhat dull. I have talked with a good many men who knew him, and not all of whom believed in his somewhat naive political and economic ideas; but all of them said he was a great man and a good man. Most of them said, too, that he was a very shy man.

So I suppose that on that day at Cleveland, as on occasions to other men, the flaming tongues of Pentecost descended upon him and he saw somewhere on the other side of the clouds a vision of a world made good, and he found the words that he needed there somehow.

Warren Harding gave him a pardon when he took office.

Around Marion, where he ran his paper, and around Lima, where he used to go fishing, there are people who will scrap with you about President Harding. The people who knew him liked him very much. Nobody thought him a great genius, or a first-class statesman, or even a pretty good politician; but few people blamed him for the debacle of his Administration.

Probably no President in American history ever had better intentions to govern well. A want of practical experience in government had led him to the belief that a strong Executive was undesirable under our party system, and that policy making should be left entirely to Congress. In addition, no President ever was saddled with such a Cabinet as that inflicted by the party leadership upon Warren Harding.

It is certain that Harry Daugherty was his preference for Attorney-General, and it is possible that Will Hays was also his choice.

The rest of the members were forced upon him, and four of them may be described as most unfortunate selections. Andrew Mellon contributed more to the wrecking of the American standard of living, to the undermining of free enterprise, and to the destruction of the national economy than any other single figure in American history. Albert Fall almost destroyed the people's belief in the basic integrity of our governmental system. Charles Evans Hughes fixed upon the country a foreign policy that robbed the United States of self-respect at home and prestige abroad. Herbert Hoover elevated the science of uttering platitudes to a degree of perfection not attained by either Henry Clay or William McKinley, and spent the eight years of the Harding-Coolidge period in seeking the Presidency; he is remembered for his military victory at Anacostia over the bonus marchers.

Warren Harding, himself, on the face of the official record and the judgment of those who knew him, was a gentle and considerate man. He was an intense believer in civil liberties, and his major contribution to his era was the ending of Mitchell Palmer's terror and the release of the wartime political prisoners. He did not share his successor's worship for Secretary of the Treasury Andrew Mellon, and the economic measures associated with the Mellon-Hoover leadership were not adopted while he was President.

Harding's failure in public life probably was due to a want of experience in administrative posts; his political experience had been limited to two terms in the Ohio legislature, and a term as Lieutenant-Governor, an honorary office in his State, and a term in the United States Senate. His want of skill as an administrator and his reliance on home State politicians for advice was unfortunate; these enabled a coterie of Cabinet and lesser officials and a legislative cabal to dominate the government at a time when a strong President was badly needed. However, he possessed both sounder judgment and sounder instincts than either of the Republican Presidents who followed him; for example, his handling of the postwar economic crisis

was more intelligent and realistic than the conduct of President
Hoover in the face of the 1929 collapse.

5: They buried him at Springfield

Illinois is divided into two parts: Chicago and downstate; but
while these disagree often politically, there is not the attitude of
hostility between them that divides New York.

Chicago is big, and when the Eastern politicians finally lose the
battle they are waging against the St. Lawrence Waterway, Chicago
will be bigger, the biggest city in the world. Everything about the
community is an exaggeration. It has the most beautiful residential
section in America, Lakeshore Drive; it has the worst slums in
America, Black Metropolis. It has one of the greatest universities
in the nation, perhaps the greatest; and more of its people read the
Tribune than any other newspaper. It has the major concentration
of railroads in the United States, and some of the worst passenger
stations ever built, dating, apparently, from the original settlement
of the community and escaping unscathed from the Fire. Its weather
is an exaggeration; it is either hot or cold in Chicago, never warm
or cool.

Chicago makes almost every product and distributes almost everything. Chicago is the ultimate destiny of all pigs and cows and
lambs. All the grain of America is sold there, usually several times
over on its Commodity Exchange. It is the biggest shopping center,
retail, in the country, if you count in its mail-order establishments,
and the second if you do not.

Except that it provided one of the few really bad school systems
in the North until the advent of Herold Hunt as their head, Chicago
has been a well-run community for some years. The Democratic
machine climbed into power when the people became disgusted
with the gang wars of the prohibition period. The Kelly organization has been more intelligent than most big city political groups,

and there have been no scandals and there has been a steady promotion for younger men, so that the machine stays alive.

Every visitor to Chicago is asked what he thinks about the *Tribune*. The *Tribune* is published by Colonel Robert R. McCormick and claims to be "The World's Greatest Newspaper"; but that may be discounted as a mild Chicago exaggeration. When they asked me what I thought about the *Tribune,* I could only express surprise that it had not moved from Chicago to the more compatible atmosphere of Boston, because it reads rather like the dirty little pamphlets produced by Brookline publishers.

The *Tribune* is a combination of glaring headlines, twisted stories, violent editorials, and a comic strip in which a moronic infant is subjected to a series of horrible adventures from which, unhappily, she always manages to escape. The comic strip, which the *Tribune* syndicates, also indulges in a deliberate blasphemy that would be shocking if it were not utterly pointless. I suspect the blasphemy to be an expression of the author's latent or active anti-Semitism, although it should be equally offensive to a member of any of the Christian denominations.

The *Tribune* is also anti-Russian and anti-British, as well as isolationist-nationalist, anti-Southern, anti-Eastern, and in general opposition to everything.

Chicago has Hearst, whose *American* once pressed the *Tribune* in circulation. Chicago also has the excellent Marshall Field paper, the *Sun-Times,* which operates around the clock. The *Daily News* is one of the best afternoon papers in America. But none of these approach the *Tribune* in circulation; and nobody in Chicago asked me what I thought of Hearst or Field or the *News.* Ford Hicks, who runs the National Lecture Bureau and who introduces me to people around Chicago when he books me there, ought to produce at least one friend who remembers the *News* of Victor Lawson's day.

The University of Chicago is undertaking an experiment in education. Its president, Robert Maynard Hutchins, is the outstanding critic of the specialists. He believes that men ought to know something except how to make and operate gadgets, whether the gadgets are better mousetraps or better atom bombs; he believes that learning to think is important. That, together with the fact that the University of Chicago dropped out of Big Ten football and does not subsidize athletics, is considered to be eccentric in some quarters.

Chicago does not dominate Illinois. There are many industrial communities throughout the State, like Moline, Rockford, and Kankakee, or Peoria, where tractors roll off the assembly line with breathtaking speed. Along the river there are many quiet, small towns, that probably have changed little since Mark Twain's day. Then there are the two towns rich in history: Quincy and Springfield.

Quincy is where a former Congressman named Lincoln staged one of his debates with Senator Stephen A. Douglas. The legislature elected Senators in those days, and the 1858 legislature was pretty solidly Democratic, and Senator Douglas won. It was at Quincy that Lincoln made his well-known prediction that a house divided cannot stand, and that America could not continue half-slave and half-free; every schoolboy is familiar with that phrase, but many have forgotten another of Lincoln's phrases on that day:

"As I would not be a slave, so I would not be a master."

Everything in Quincy recalls the Lincoln-Douglas debate, including the hotel, which bears their names and has their pictures in its lobby and on the paper matches that it distributes.

Springfield is a shrine for Lincoln. It is a busy town otherwise, but the memory of the Civil War President is impressed on every visitor. When I visited Springfield, as the guest of the Illinois Education Association in March 1946, I went to Lincoln's grave to place a wreath there.

It was not the first time that a Georgia Governor had done so. Eugene Talmadge, ten years before, had placed flowers at the tomb of the Emancipator. Lincoln essentially was a Southerner of Scotch-Irish descent and the South has a deep respect and affection for him.

At the time of my visit to Springfield, Georgia's historic freight rate suit, seeking to break the stranglehold of the transportation monopoly on the South, was nearing its climax. When they asked me to make a short talk beside Lincoln's grave, I could not help calling attention to his feeling that America was the common country of all Americans, and saying:

"I am glad to do homage to a great American who recognized the importance of fair treatment for all the people of our land. Just as he denied the possibility of a nation existing half-slave and half-free, he would deny today the possibility of a common country half-exploited and half-imperial. If he were here today, the South would find in this Kentucky man an able champion of its claims that America is the common country of all its people, and that economic justice is the right of every section as much as freedom is the right of every individual."

Everyone who writes a book of any kind on public affairs wishes to include a personal footnote on Lincoln. Mine will be brief.

The historians, the biographers and the novelists have made very extensive studies on Lincoln as statesman, military strategist, humanitarian, lover and husband. They have collected every anecdote, and can account for every moment of his waking or sleeping life from maturity. It seems to me that they have neglected one aspect of his many-faceted character: he was one of the most skillful men in our country's history at utilizing words as instruments of attack. The impact of his speeches and state papers was greater than of all the Union artillery in defeating Southern arms. The mastery of words was his chief political asset, and it became his most effective military weapon.

Some of the Lincoln hagiologists have attempted to divorce the man from his environment. He was the product of a Kentucky backwoods family, brought to manhood on the Illinois frontier, developing his personality in the small towns that still are to be found in Illinois, mainly clustering along the Great River, where there was time for talk and anecdotes and high jinks. The Union triumph came as a result of this understanding of the problem of the Border, which, except in the instance of Maryland, he handled with consummate skill. He could not have directed a successful war to preserve the Union without a knowledge, intimate and deep, of what moved the hearts and prompted the decisions of the people of Missouri, Southern Ohio, Tennessee, and Kentucky, who lived on farms or huddled in small towns along the riverbank.

Such a town is Elsah. It looks as if Tom Sawyer might have superintended fence-painting there in his boyhood. The community is the site of The Principia College, whose School of Government invited me to make a talk in March 1947.

The Principia College was moved to Elsah from St. Louis in 1935, seeking a quiet and secluded community for its campus. It found such a spot.

Elsah was a hundred years old when I visited it. Addison Greene and a group of woodchoppers settled the community in 1847, and made their living by selling fuel to the river steamboats. Elsah enjoyed a boom a decade later, when General James Semple acquired its site and offered a town lot to every person who would build a stone house. A distillery and two grist mills went up, and the village became a fairly important river port.

Then came the locomotive, and the decline of the great days on the river, and Elsah went quietly to sleep until Jay Gould's engineers came in 1888 with plans for spanning the Mississippi at that point. Gould was engaged in a battle with the proprietors of the only available span at St. Louis and was threatening to route his rails in another direction.

Gould's men even went through the farce of preparing grades and laying culverts. The owners of the St. Louis bridge did not dare to call his bluff. They capitulated, and Elsah's projected boom collapsed again.

But the community retained its charm, and the old homes are durable and comfortable. Change is slow there beside the river, and over the doorway of one of the filling stations a sign with very faded letters says: "Buggies made and repaired."

The Principia College looks like and has the atmosphere of all the small denominational colleges in America. It has a pleasant campus arranged like an English village, comfortable, neo-Gothic buildings, and a devoted faculty. It is exceptional only in that it is the only higher educational institution supported by the Church of Christ, Scientist. In consequence, its student body is drawn from almost every State in America, and from abroad as well.

The value of the small denominational school is very great. It is balanced against the enormous mass-production educational techniques of the State universities and the huge, heavily endowed private institutions. The quality of instruction usually is very high, and the emphasis upon the humanities is important in an age that has gone a little too far overboard in a devotion to gadgets, techniques and specialization.

The Christian Scientists are one of the smaller religious groups in the United States, numerically, although exceptionally influential. In some countries, they have been rigorously persecuted.

Freedom of religion is American in origin. It came into being in this country. It is the antithesis of tolerance, which, in a final analysis, involves the most contemptuous form of persecution: the denial of the importance of the dissident's belief and the effectuality of his individual efforts.

Freedom of religion was not obtained in America without a vigorous battle. It did not become nation wide until 1825, when the last of the New England States repealed its statute establishing a State church. It has been under assault time and again. As recently as 1928, a man's religious convictions were made an issue in a political campaign.

America is a country of minorities. Its governmental system of checks and balances, its elaborate constitutional provisions, the slowness of its governmental methods, were designed to maintain that condition. The only majority that can exist in a democracy is a temporary political majority, and its decisions must be limited to those spheres where collective action through government is appropriate.

The final battle for religious liberty has not been fought in this country. But the final word upon the subject has been written into the statutes of an American State. It was one of the three things that Thomas Jefferson regarded as important enough in his life's labor to include in his epitaph. It is not remembered often enough by all Americans, so I am going to quote it here, in full:

> "No man shall be compelled to frequent or support any religious worship, place, or ministry, whatsoever, nor shall be enforced, restrained, molested, or burthened in his body or goods, nor shall otherwise suffer on account of his religious opinions or belief; but all men shall be free to profess and by argument to maintain their opinions in matters of religion, and the same shall in no wise diminish, enlarge, or affect, their civil capacities. And the General Assembly shall not prescribe any religious test whatever, or confer any peculiar privileges or advantages on any sect or denomination, or pass any law requiring or authorizing any religious society, or the people of any district within this State, to levy on themselves, or others, any tax for the erection or repair of any house of public worship, or for the support of any church or ministry; but it shall be left free to every person to select his religious instructor, and to make for his support such private contract as he shall please."

6: Products of the Hoosier State

Indiana has much of the South about it in its manner of speech, and Evansville could be called a community half-Southern and half-German. Indiana is a prosperous State. The McCarran Committee, in that mammoth survey that demonstrated the relationship between rail rate discriminations and economic exploitation, found that Indiana had an almost perfect balance between its industry and its agriculture, and a well-sustained economy that minimized booms and depressions by the variety of its industrial products.

Indiana also is a State that loves politics, and produces authors who enjoy writing about politics as a sport. A charming sport it remained until the twenties, when a secret society gained control of its State government transiently. The Klan's power was broken, and its leader of that day is now a prisoner, described by some as a political prisoner whom no one dares to pardon or parole; and politics is a rougher sport than in the days when Tom Taggart played the game and Booth Tarkington wrote stories based on his term in the legislature.

Bloomington is an example of Indiana's diversification. The town has an immense furniture factory and has not less than seventeen enormous limestone quarries about its outskirts. It also has the University of Indiana, which possesses a football team coached by "Bo" McMillin, onetime chief of Centre College's Praying Colonels, and a president, Herman B Wells whose name is unique because he puts no period after the center initial; I never learned whether that B was like the S in President Truman's name or not.

The University of Indiana has memorials to two of its best loved alumni. As one enters the huge building that is the center of recreation and administration, the pride of Indiana in Wendell Willkie and Ernie Pyle is brought to one's attention immediately.

Ernie Pyle was one of America's great reporters, with a rare ear for the words that men use in everyday life. His accounts of the war were unlike any others. They dealt with the men themselves, and they attained a realism hardly ever encountered. He reminded Americans that it is not nations that fight, but men; it is not nations that die, but men; it is not nations that must make decisions, but citizens.

As an antidote for totalitarian nonsense, the stories that Ernie Pyle filed from the fronts that he visited, and the books that he wrote between times, are first rate. He insisted that bravery was a day-by-day characteristic of ordinary men, not some extraordinary outburst of transient emotions. With humor and pathos, he emphasized that the ordinary processes of living continue in the midst of war; that men sleep and eat and think even when machine guns are rattling and dive bombers are overhead.

Wendell Willkie was one of the extraordinary individuals of our day. Except for the nomination of Horace Greeley by the coalition of liberal Republicans and Democrats in 1872, the nomination of Willkie by the Republican convention in 1940 was the only selection by a major American party of a complete outsider to politics as its candidate in a national election.

Much of the Willkie charm was associated with his voice, which was wholly different from the cultivated master-of-ceremonies manner of speech affected on the radio by so many political speakers. It was sometimes a little harsh, the Willkie voice, but it had a remarkable ring of sincerity and a kind of folk-speech quality that attracted sympathy. It was a typical Indiana voice and way of speech, a legacy from his youth that stayed with him throughout his days, unaffected by New York or Washington. It was the kind of voice that is encountered often about Bloomington, where the merged Southern and New England language begins to shade off into the speech of the South Indiana hill country.

Wendell Willkie was undoubtedly a political accident. He received the 1940 nomination partly because of extremely skillful showmanship, but largely, I think, because the grass roots elements in the Republican party, which can not always be submerged by the adroit manipulators, rebelled against the various party hacks.

His nation-wide campaign bore a striking resemblance to that of William Jennings Bryan in 1896. He spoke everywhere, and he spoke his mind. The political realities were strong against his winning: he did not have unanimous and sincere party support; he was an outsider to the game of politics; he was running in a year when every good reason dictated the reëlection of the incumbent; he had Franklin Delano Roosevelt as an opponent.

The Willkie story, until day-after-election in November 1940, is a remarkable one and yet typically American. He was a brilliant and charming young man from what the East calls the Middle West. He had a good record at college, and began life as a mild radical in political viewpoint and an earnest believer in Woodrow Wilson's New Freedom and Woodrow Wilson's international co-operation.

He went into business, and selected a business in which charm and legal talent both pay dividends. Commonwealth and Southern was and is a great utility empire, erected during the boom years. It was rather more intelligently operated than many; it did not wreck its operating properties or indulge in the more wanton pyramiding of the Insull pattern, but its rates, especially in the South, were not modern in conception.

When the Tennessee Valley Authority was conceived, its prop-erties were directly affected. In that battle and the one over the proposal to require integration of holding company properties, Com-monwealth and Southern became the spearhead of the utilities' un-successful fight against the Roosevelt policies. Willkie fought well for his company, and after the battle, when Commonwealth and Southern faced many problems, including one of regaining popu-larity, Willkie became its head. Again he did an excellent job. Suddenly, in 1940, he emerged as a candidate for the Republican nomination for President, although his most recent political affilia-tions had been with the Democrats. He won the nomination, and while the statistics do not reveal the true closeness of the race, he gave President Roosevelt his one tough battle.

The defeat in 1940 well might have been the close of a career. Instead, it was the beginning of a life. In the four years that fol-lowed, Wendell Willkie made a profound impression upon Ameri-can thought. He set out upon an examination of himself, of the world about him, of the basic needs of the country, and of the well-springs of human emotions.

One World is an incredible autobiography, at once profound and naive. It is not the product of the skillful head of a great utility, not the product of a political leader. It is the work of an Indiana boy, who suddenly discovers himself and other men and realizes that they are akin, wherever they live. It is a confession of faith and an apologia for a way of life. It is the kind of book that only an American could write, I believe, because it has the kind of faith in the eventual good sense and good heart of men that is inseverable from the America that is clumsy in the solution of problems, generous in its concept of neighborliness, tenacious in its belief that things will be all right somehow, because men are all right.

I say that *One World* is autobiography, because, for all its narration of facts, it is the story of one man, and his momentous discovery that Earth is an extraordinary place because it is the home of many men, and that they have to get along together and respect each other's dignity as individuals, or all of them will perish, and Earth will become a burned-out cinder in a meaningless Universe.

That is an important discovery to make. It is one that every individual must make for himself, sooner or later, if there is to be any permanent peace for mankind. For peace is not obtainable by compacts between nations, but only by understanding between men.

In the years between 1940 and his death in 1944, Wendell Willkie expressed himself upon every phase of public affairs with a frankness unequalled in the history of American politics. About many measures that he advocated, about certain of his economic views, there is a great measure of disagreement; but that he endeavored to determine every issue for himself according to a single concept, there is no doubt. He examined every question in the light of one essential: "Is this policy consistent with the honor and dignity of the individual?"

There is a another monument to Wendell Willkie, in New York, where Freedom House is striving to secure a world peace built on a foundation of liberty for every individual.

Indiana is a State with many cities of medium size that seem, in most ways, to be overgrown small towns. Evansville, once a great port in the days of the steamboat traffic, remembers the showboats and the races between steamers. It still has a considerable volume of river freight, and its furniture factories maintain employment at a high level.

Evansville remembers its floods. These four disasters, in 1832, 1884, 1913 and 1937, caused enormous damage, and now the city is protected by a huge levee.

Evansville is partly Southern, and its accent is that of the South with a superimposition of German grammar. Much of the population descends from those who left Germany in the 1840s in search of liberty. Each year in a miniature German village that they have built, a *Volksfest* on the German model is staged, with magnificent singing by the Germania Mannerchor, a male chorus that is the community's pride.

South Bend has its industries, but the community is identified at a glance by the Golden Dome that rises above the University of Notre Dame, whose students are equally proud of their football squad, with its memories of Rockne and Gipp, and its representation of every American State on its campus.

Indianapolis has a speedway that provides the nation with its most spectacular single day of sport, and that provided Steve Hannagan with his start as a publicizer of everything from Miami Beach bathing beauties to Sun Valley ski enthusiasts—and, incidentally, Georgia's Coca-Cola.

Everywhere in Indiana there is a great pride in its host of authors. Conversations often begin: "Have you read?" The people buy books, too, which makes Indiana a very popular state with all those who write books or publish them.

7: GEOGRAPHICAL CENTER OF AMERICA

Kansas has been held up as an example of extreme peculiarity by many American writers. I was disappointed—not in Kansas, which I discovered had little the matter with it—to learn that it was not peculiar in any degree and quite like the rest of the United States.

It was unique in my travels only because it was the only State in which I encountered a bootlegger retailing his wares; but I have seen automobiles rather heavily laden in many States that I at least half-suspected were bearing to market the products of illegal distilleries in the hills.

I had been warned that Kansas was inherently allergic to Southern visitors, but this was not in evidence; on the contrary, there was the same cordial hospitality that all the rest of the grain belt provided; by way of welcome the Kansas legislators invited me to address them at Topeka. Nor did anyone mention John Brown of Osawatomie to me in Kansas, and the only individual who mentioned the disagreement between North and South was a faculty member of the University of Kansas at Lawrence, who said politely:

"My folks settled here just after the Civil War, but I believe you folks call it the War Between the States, don't you?"

New England provided most of the early settlers for Kansas, and even Vermont contributed its quota. But the New England strain has been supplemented by incursions of Swedes, Germans and Irish. Fewer of the Irish clung to the towns than in the other grain belt States, and there are almost as high a proportion of Irish settlers on the land as of any other emigrant group. Scattered here and there, small colonies of Mexicans can be found, having been brought in when the shortage of agricultural workers became acute. Their settlements, huddled along the railroad tracks, but always on the wrong side of them, seemed to be completely segregated from the life of the community where they lived.

Kansas produces much besides grain, including enormous quantities of livestock, and sunflowers that are an essential in poultry feed, a source of valuable oil and an emblem of former Governor Alf Landon, who carried Maine and Vermont as the Republican candidate for President in 1936.

Like the Border States, Kansas has every right to speak of the War Between the States as a civil war; it began in Kansas many years before the Secession Ordinance was passed by South Carolina's con-

vention. The ghastly battles between slaveowners, principally from
Missouri, and Free Staters from New England and Ohio, gave the
name Bleeding Kansas to the territory, and gave Charles Sumner of
Massachusetts occasion for some of his most fervid oratory.

Kansas, geographically, is the very center of the continental United
States, and Manhattan is the center of the State and of the nation.

Manhattan lies within a circle of low hills. Like most grain belt
cities, it is large in area for its population. The main street has eight
traffic lanes and is shaded by magnificent elms. Every house has
elbow room, and many of them are built of native limestone.

There are so many trees that it would be hard to find Manhattan
from the air, except for a few downtown buildings and the spires of
its eighteen churches, which seem to represent almost every religious
creed in America.

Predominantly, the community is a market town. The small industries of Manhattan derive from the farms or serve them, consist-
ing of hatcheries, creameries, two packing plants, and a manufacturer of egg crates. The biggest single industry is Kansas State
College, which had forty-five hundred students before the war and
half as many again today, so that the campus population is about
half that of the town itself. Until he joined the staff of UNESCO,
the college was headed by Milton Eisenhower, who was rather better known than his brother, General Dwight Eisenhower, when
war came.

Manhattan and its college offer a summary of American history in
their own. The town and school, founded in 1859 as Bluemont
College, are almost coexistent. For as late as 1854, the Kaw Indians
had a village at the mouth of the Blue River. Missouri slaveholders,
hopeful of establishing Kansas as a slave State, planted a settlement
near the Indian village. The New England Emigrant Aid Society
gave its help to a group of Free Staters, who set up another village,
which they called Boston. A year later, a boatload of citizens came
from Ohio and built a third community. They outnumbered the

other two groups, and the name they gave to their village was adopted.

Bluemont College was taken over by the State of Kansas after a few years of operation, and became Kansas State College, devoted primarily to agriculture. The State Agricultural Experiment Station was located near the campus and became an important center in developing new farm techniques.

In 1934, Manhattan buzzed with the story of a student strike over compulsory military training. Officially at least, the strikers numbered but three, and claimed to be conscientious objectors. Kansas legislators turned stern, and today students who object to drill can obtain their educations elsewhere.

I have described Manhattan and its history in some detail for two reasons. First, because the history of its settlement, disagreement, coalescence into homogeneity, disgust with war after the bitter aftermath of 1918, and concentration upon production in its educational establishment, has a parallel everywhere in America. Second, because of the two other Manhattans that immediately enter my mind by association.

Manhattan, Kansas, located in the center of America, once might well have considered itself invulnerable from attack. That was before the new geography, which involves distances through the air instead of upon the sea and the land. Manhattan, Kansas, today is as open to attack as any other community in the United States. It is as much in danger of the products of the Manhattan District as the Manhattan Island at the mouth of the Hudson. There is no more isolation for any part of America or any part of the world.

That means a new boundary for America. Our marches no longer are the two oceans, nor are the Rhine or the Elbe. They are not physical at all, but ideological. Unless democracy can be made to work, not only in America but everywhere, there is no defense against the ineluctable destruction of civilization and, perhaps, of mankind.

Manhattan, Kansas, has pleasant, broad, tree-shaded streets, where young people stroll in the evening. It is almost an epitome of the comfortable life that liberty evokes. I should dislike very much to see it blotted out.

8: BREAKFAST FOODS AND AUTOMOBILES

While I was Governor of Georgia, the State of Michigan returned to the Georgia Capitol a number of Confederate battleflags that had been taken during Sherman's March to the Sea. The action was not only generous and typically American, but it was significant: the most intensely Union state, perhaps, of them all had decided to forget the fratricidal struggle.

Michigan contributed many of the men who marched through Georgia with Sherman, and two Michigan boys were among the last casualties of the War Between the States. A monument at Jefferson Davis Park, in Irwin County, Georgia, remembers that Corporal John Hines, of Company E, and Private John Rupert, of Company C, both of the Fourth Michigan Cavalry, were shot in the darkness of May 10, 1865, by other Union soldiers from neighboring Wisconsin. All were part of the force that took prisoner the President of the Confederate States of America.

Michigan is the State of Lewis Cass, that tough old friend of Andrew Jackson and one of the stoutest of Union men and a first-rate democrat, whether you use a capital or a little d; for he hated disunity, Whigs, the Bank of the United States, the Know Nothings, intolerance, monarchy, Calhoun, Clay, McDuffie, Garrison, and people who were self-important, all with apparently equal intensity; had he been willing to compromise with a few of them, he might have been President of the United States.

Michigan is also the State where automobiles are made; three-fifths of all the automotive equipment of the world is manufactured there, and important though Pontiac, Flint, and Lansing and other Michigan cities are in the making of cars, most of them are sold "f.o.b. Detroit."

Michigan is sharply divided into the Upper Peninsula and the Lower Peninsula, and the division is occupational, temperamental, political, and puzzling to any outsiders. The Upper Peninsula is populated almost wholly by Republicans, who have never voted otherwise except in 1912 and, perhaps, in 1932 under the misapprehension that the Colonel was running again. That political fact is well known to every Democrat, while every Southerner is aware that Michigan has an almost infinite number of lakes and that the hardy inhabitants fish through the ice in the winter months, comfortable within small, well-heated houses that they erect on the frozen surface. It is a current belief in Michigan that Florida is populated almost entirely by retired Michigan citizens, just as it is thought in Iowa that California is an Iowa colony.

Ann Arbor is one of the most attractive college towns in America, just as the University of Michigan is one of the best of the State institutions and one of the biggest. In the winter, under a heavy blanket of snow, Ann Arbor looks like a Christmas card; the busses run every half-hour to Willow Run, where they made planes during the war and where Henry Kaiser is building automobiles at a terrific rate in a one-man assault on the Big Three's dominance in motor production.

Battle Creek is divided by a war between the manufacturers of breakfast foods. There is a Post Tavern and there is a Kellogg Inn, and both are delightful, though the guest undoubtedly must go through agonies at mealtime, fearful that he might order the wrong cereal.

Grand Rapids is identified with furniture in the public mind, and actually is the site of extremely diversified manufacturers, of one of the most interesting Ladies' Literary Clubs that I encountered as a lecturer, and of a large bloc of Democratic votes. Mount Pleasant, the State oil capital, has an interesting small college as well as refineries.

Lansing is dominated as a manufacturing center by the enormous Oldsmobile plant, educationally by Michigan State College's magnificent campus, and architecturally by the collection of buildings housing the State government. On the State level, it is probable that Michigan is the best managed of the heavily populated Northern States. Its tax system is clumsy rather than regressive, but it produces the money to permit exceptional State services, the best highway system in the nation, and a splendid educational establishment.

Detroit was founded by Antoine de la Mothe Cadillac, who gives his name to an automobile and to the Book-Cadillac Hotel, the finest in the nation, where you can amaze and amuse yourself by looking south at Canada, our neighbor to the north. Detroit is the automobile capital of the world, but it is my misfortune to have seen less of it than of any of America's large cities. In March 1947, my first lecturing visit, I heard much about the town from visitors who came to see me at my hotel, but my spare moments were devoted to an appearance on a local chit-chat radio program.

I found that I had been co-starred with Miss Gypsy Rose Lee who also was touring Michigan, though whether as a lecturer or otherwise, I can not say; Miss Lee is a competitor as an author, and I have no doubt that she is an engaging lecturer, for she worsted me in argument over whether women's clothes were designed for practicability. She said that they were.

On my next visit to Detroit, late that fall, I met the only individual I have encountered whose surname is that of my home town, and I was so surprised that I failed to get his Christian name into my notes.

Mr. Newnan told me of passing through Newnan in the early hours of morning as he was travelling south for the winter, and of asking the attendant at the filling station about the origin of the city's name. He was informed that the founder and name-giver was honored by a statue on the Court House square. But Mr. Newnan was disappointed to discover that, as is usual on Court House squares in the South, the only monument was to the valor of the soldiers of the Confederacy. When he called on me, he still wanted to know how Newnan got its name, so I supplied him with what few facts I possessed about the valor and patriotism of General Daniel Newnan.

So again I did not get to examine Detroit.

But Detroiters tell me that, before the assembly line came into being, it was the most beautiful town in the world, or at least in America. It was intentionally that way; its Chamber of Commerce had a slogan: "The Most Beautiful City in America." It was justified, they said, by the magnificently broad, tree-shaded streets, by the charm of its Georgian mansions, by the dignity of its plan of thoroughfares, which was an adaptation of L'Enfants' plan for Washington. It was a city of homes, leading American communities in its population group in residences occupied by their owners.

Today it is a city of automobile owners. There is one car for every five persons, and if you leave taxicabs out of the count, to eliminate Washington's leadership, it has more cars per capita than any other place in the world.

Almost every passenger car in America, prior to the postwar trend toward decentralized assembly plants, was made within two hundred and fifty miles of Detroit. The arrival of the automobile plants made Detroit the fourth city in America in size, and the most bizarre melting pot of the nation. It also superimposed a gridiron pattern upon the radial streets laid out according to the plan for a beautiful community, so that when the factories disgorge their workers the result is an unequalled traffic snarl. The public transportation facilities are undeveloped; experts in Detroit traffic say that there will never be a demand for expanded services, because everybody owns a car. The transit lines are publicly owned, having been acquired by the city while James Couzens was Mayor, and are efficiently operated, but they serve no such proportion of the public as those of any other metropolitan center.

Detroit has a housing problem, considerable racial tension, a need for expanded frontiers and unification to eliminate the two cities that it encloses: Highland Park, the earlier domain of Ford Motor

Company, and Hamtramck, a community with French names for its streets and a population almost wholly Polish.

Detroit's demand for man-power to produce automobiles has attracted population from every source. It has a larger Southern-born population than Birmingham, Alabama. It has more Poles than Poznan, and only two cities of the Ukraine have more Ukrainians. There are 120,000 Negro citizens, 126,000 Germans, and America's largest colonies of Bulgarians and Yugoslavians.

Three notable Mayors have served the city. Hazen S. Pingree fought the monopolies during his ten-year term that started in 1890, forced gas rates down and provided a municipal lighting system. When the depression hit in 1896, he invented work relief and turned vacant lots into potato patches for the unemployed. James Couzens, in the interval between liquidating his holdings in Ford Motor and becoming one of the most useful members the United States Senate ever acquired, served four years, being elected in 1919. He encountered the "normalcy panic" and also turned to public works plans to spur employment.

Detroit's greatest Mayor was Frank Murphy. He was chosen in 1930, after a bitter recall election had ousted the pseudo-reform administration that had turned Detroit over to the racketeers. Murphy inherited the depression, which struck Detroit like a tornado. No industrial center in the nation was affected so profoundly; industrial unemployment was complete. Mayor Murphy spent a million dollars a month, no small sum from any municipal budget, on his relief program, which continued until President Roosevelt took office and Federal Emergency Relief Administration undertook the task of feeding Detroit's hungry.

Michigan promoted Frank Murphy to the Governorship, and his career in Lansing was equally great. His subsequent career took him to the Philippines as High Commissioner, into the Cabinet as Attorney-General, where he made the most impressive record since the incumbency of Knox, if not of Taney, and to the Supreme Court.

Michigan regards Mr. Justice Murphy as its greatest citizen. Of all the men in American politics, he appears to have the fewest detractors. His simplicity, integrity, sympathy and warmth of character made him beloved as few men in public life. On the bench, he has been remarkable. Not a lawyer's lawyer like Oliver Wendell Holmes or Hugo Black, nor an economist's lawyer like Louis D. Brandeis, he is a great judge because he is interested primarily in justice and believes that the purpose of the courts of America is to provide justice for every citizen.

Michigan has produced some notable political figures, from the day of Chase Osborn, who broke the old machine and forced progressive measures upon his fellow-Republicans, to Senator Arthur Vandenburg. But one of the State's Congressmen, Clare Hoffman, is as misrepresentative of Michigan as John Rankin is of Mississippi or Alvin E. O'Konski of Wisconsin, which demonstrates that demagoguery is not regional and that hate and prejudice respect the boundary lines of none of the States.

9: CENTURY OF THE COMMON MAN

Iowa is one of the States that the McCarran Committee found had a sound and well-rounded economy. In the East and the South, Iowa is thought of as a great agricultural State, with a minimum of manufactures. Actually, the State has a very great industrial production, closely identified with the region that produces America's grain. Des Moines is a great industrial center, manufacturing a large part of the machines that have revolutionized grain production. Almost every Iowa community boasts a degree of industrialization, and small business is prosperous.

The approach to agricultural problems seemed to me remarkably intelligent and realistic. At Ames, where Iowa State College is located, I encountered several Georgians, and men from other Southern States, who had been offered a chance for experimenting and teaching. Iowa has promoted consistently a scientific approach to agricultural problems. It has sought grains and grasses adapted to its soil and its climate, and has reaped an enormous reward in consequence.

The farms are so perfectly arranged that, from the air, the entire agricultural region resembles an endless chequer-board.

Politically, Iowa is conservative, except in acute depressions. Its conservatism does not follow the pattern of South Dakota, however, probably the most reactionary of Northern States. Nor is it as variable as that of Nebraska. It is the conservatism of a well-adjusted and prosperous State, with a minimum of economic problems and with a stability of income almost unequalled in the nation. Its conservatism is the conservatism of contentment, which has nothing much to do with ideologies.

Iowa business men are alert. Indeed, Northern business men seemed to me to be more aware of their problems and more progressive in their methods than those of the East or South or West. One of the most intelligent cost-accounting systems that I have encountered was that of the Hotel Montrose in Cedar Rapids. Tony Saverelli, one of Father Flanagan's products of Boys Town, had installed simply operated controls by which items of demand and of profit and loss on the menus could be checked hourly. The Rath Packing Company at Waterloo is one of the nation's finest and most efficient. The same efficiency marks the State University at Iowa City and the machine shops at Davenport. Council Bluffs and Sioux City are progressive and expanding.

In Des Moines one evening I had dinner with Jake More, Chairman of the Democratic Central Committee of Iowa, who drove in from his home at Harlan to talk with me. After dinner, he accompanied me to the session of the Iowa State Education Convention, where I spoke. Then I went with him to the party headquarters in the Fort Des Moines Hotel, for more conversation, chiefly about politics. More is personable, charming, and an effective organizer, and I always enjoy exchanging political views with him.

On the wall in the headquarters hung pictures of Franklin Roosevelt and Harry Truman and Henry A. Wallace. Naturally our talk drifted to the three men, participants in political events of unusual drama. I asked him about Henry Wallace, and his relationship with Iowa Democrats after his resignation from the Truman Cabinet.

"Wallace isn't a resident of Iowa any longer," he told me. "He has transferred his legal residence to New York. He has a great many friends, but there are many people who do not understand his present course. For that matter, he has something of a gift for being not understood."

We talked about the Democratic party's future in the grain belt for a while and parted; he to drive back to Harlan; and I to go to bed, and remember the circumstances of my acquaintanceship with Henry Agard Wallace.

In 1944, President Roosevelt had permitted me to announce to the press his rather reluctant agreement to accept a fourth term. At the time, Vice President Wallace was in China upon a delicate and confidential war mission. The President told me, in direct words, that he desired that Wallace be nominated again, and I promised him that the Georgia delegation would vote for the Iowa man, whom I had never met.

Later that day, I called at the Vice President's office and talked with Harold Young, an amiable and able Texan with whom I had crossed swords in the Gallogly extradition case when I spent two hectic weeks in Austin seeking the youth's return to a Georgia prison. I told Young frankly that a good many influences were seeking to halt the Wallace renomination, but that the President wished him renominated. Young subsequently met Wallace on the Pacific Coast and the renomination campaign got under way. The Gallup and other polls began to show strong support for Wallace. On the eve of the convention, FDR left Washington for the Pacific.

In the interval, I met Henry Wallace, and was impressed by his courage, simplicity, sincerity and intense shyness. Indeed, when we met again at Chicago, I urged him to accompany me to visit some delegations on the first evening of the convention. He declined, observing that he did not want to appear to be trying to influence delegates by personal contact, which seemed strange politics indeed to a Georgia politician accustomed to rather direct approaches to vote-getting.

He talked a little of the speech that he would make seconding the Roosevelt nomination, and observed that he hoped that his statement: "The poll tax must go" would not embarrass me, since Georgia had not then removed that obstacle to a free franchise. I assured him that it would not, and that while I hoped the tax would be removed by State action, inevitably voting would become free all over America.

The next night at the convention, had Chairman Samuel D. Jackson permitted the members to vote for a Vice President immediately after the President's acceptance speech by radio, Wallace undoubtedly would have won. The following day, it was different. At his request, I seconded Wallace's nomination and Georgia voted for Wallace on both ballots, in keeping with my pledge to FDR.

Soon after the convention, Henry Wallace was my guest at the Executive Mansion in Atlanta, and showed me a telegram from the President, saying: "Please tell Ilo not to make any plans for leaving Washington in January." Ilo is Mrs. Wallace. A little later, the President wrote me requesting that I come to Washington to see him.

President Roosevelt, showing more animation than on my previous visit, began with his usual grace to talk about my speeches for the party in Oklahoma and Missouri and Minnesota, and his hope that I had not been disappointed about the Wallace results.

"As a matter of fact," the President said, "I had no idea that Wallace would get as many delegates as he did. When my train stopped at Chicago during the convention I was told that under no circumstances could Wallace receive the nomination. Then I wrote the note about Harry Truman and Bill Douglas being acceptable on the ticket."

"Well, that's water over the dam, Mr. President. Truman is a good man and we've got to win," I responded.

I called attention to the unusual value of the personal campaign Henry Wallace was making for the Roosevelt-Truman ticket, and observed that I thought he should be offered any place in the administration that he would accept.

"He can have any place that he would like in the Cabinet, except the place of Cordell Hull," President Roosevelt replied. "Henry is a great friend, the most loyal man I know."

He asked me to talk with Wallace about it, and I went over to the Vice President's office. He expressed a wish to have the post of Secretary of Commerce, primarily to attempt to make that agency an effective vehicle to help small business and individual enterprise in the postwar period that would be such a test of the dynamic qualities of the American theory.

"You are making a mistake in taking it," I told him, in effect. "If you reënter government, you will be held responsible for general policies that you will not help to shape. Today, you are somewhat of a political martyr; a symbol; you are enormously popular with the people, who regard you as the country's leading independent and non-conformist. If you go back, you will have to give up some of the strength of your personal views."

"Agriculture and labor have improved their status, and I think the average small business man will need help after the war is over," he replied. "I think the Commerce Department will give me a good platform to express my views about those needs and to do something that is needed."

I returned to the White House, and told the President that Wallace would accept the Commerce post.

"But I assume that you will not wish to evict Jesse Jones," I added. President Roosevelt shook his head.

"Not at all," he said, "I was planning to get rid of Jesse anyway."

Wallace was to get a foretaste of future political attacks when the fight developed over his confirmation. Then came Roosevelt's death, and the request by President Truman that Wallace remain in the Cabinet.

It is a commentary upon the spontaneous gentleness of Henry Wallace that he won the quick respect and regard of Robert Hannegan, who as the friend of Senator Truman and the Chairman of the party, had been the engineer of Wallace's defeat at Chicago. Hannegan, himself a cheerful, energetic professional in politics, held few animosities. Indeed, I strongly suspect that he joined Attorney-General Tom Clark as one of the prompters of President Truman's tender to me of the office of Solicitor-General, the job all lawyers dream of holding, and which I declined only because I felt an obligation to complete my term as Governor of Georgia. In my subsequent meetings with Hannegan, he never alluded to our conversation at the convention, in which he told me that the President "really wants Truman" and in which I replied that the President had told me his preference and would have to tell me that he had changed his mind were I to change my position.

Even after Henry Wallace's speech on foreign policy at Madison Square Garden and his resignation from the Cabinet, it is quite probable that Hannegan might have kept him within the party fold if he had not quit politics. Wallace might well have decided to make his fight for liberalism within the Democratic party instead of forming a third party if the consequences had been presented to him effectively.

He will find, I believe, that the third-party venture is a mistake. There have been numerous fractional parties, ranging in importance from the Know-Nothings, who sought to capitalize on hatred, to the Socialists, who never expected to win. Of all such ventures, only the Free Soilers, the Populists, and the Progressives of 1912 and 1924 have polled important numbers of votes, and only the first of these grew into a major party. I believe that liberals can fight more effectively within the major party that, traditionally, welcomes them, than they can outside.

But, the Wallace insurgency reminds the leaders of the Democratic party that they can win elections only by claiming the support of liberals.

Henry Wallace expressed that truth with forceful bluntness in his great Chicago speech seconding the fourth Roosevelt nomination:

"The Democratic party cannot long survive as a conservative party. The Republican party has a monopoly on the conservative brains and the conservative dollars."

For a shy individual, with a very genuine and sometimes rather terrible meekness, Henry Wallace has a marvelous capacity for stirring up a storm. He is a pamphleteer of parts and an author of distinction. He is one of the great empirical scientists of our time, who has contributed more, probably, to the actual wealth of the grain States than any other man of this generation. He is an astute business man. He demonstrated in the Cabinet that he was a competent administrator. He is generous, humane, unresentful, without malice; but wherever he goes, there is a fight.

With many of his views on domestic policies, I find myself in strong accord; he speaks for an economy of abundance, for full employment, for the American belief that the individual is entitled to a chance to have a life of comfort and security by his own effort; for the Century of the Common Man.

With his foreign views, I disagree. Acknowledging his wisdom in foreseeing the inevitability of a clash with fascism as early as 1934, and his intelligence in providing, through the "ever-normal granary" for the feeding of the nation in emergency, and his early grasp of the acute need for stockpiling rubber, quinine and rare metals when procurement officials stupidly spent their time arguing over the size of the offices they were to occupy, I still think his views on foreign policy are erroneous. While his criticisms of incipient American imperialism are trenchant, they lose their force through a failure to see the menace of Russian imperialism. No thoughtful American can desire our country to set out on a program of world dominance; but no prudent American can wish to leave us helpless before the menace of world dominance by some totalitarian state or ideology. Imperialism is bad everywhere, and must be fought everywhere.

But, before Henry Wallace made his foreign policy speech at Madison Square Garden, the United States had no foreign policy. His criticism stung somebody into action, and a policy was evolved.

Perhaps that is his function in America today: to sting somebody into action, to state a thesis that may be full of error but that challenges to action.

In Iowa, they accept his independence philosophically. The Wallace men are like that, they say. John Wallace, who came to this country, was an insurgent. And the Henrys who descended from him, three of them, all have been. Insurgency and independence and love of liberty is in the veins of these Scotch-Irish, as it was in William Wallace, the ancient chief of their clan, who defied all that England's Edward might bring against him, and went to the scaffold as bold as a lion. William Wallace died, but Bruce and his gillies crushed Edward's son and his horsemen at Bannockburn.

At heart, always, Henry Wallace has been a democrat, with a little d. I hope he stays a Democrat, within the party; or comes back to the fold after his experiment. But within or without, he is a man of courage and honesty, and his criticisms are worth weighing.

10: THE RIGHTEOUS IN REBELLION

Nebraska presents an enigma. It is the State in which Kenneth S. Wherry succeeded George W. Norris in the United States Senate. It produced William Jennings Bryan, who dominated Democratic politics for decades, and made his brother, Charles, Governor in the middle of the Harding-Coolidge cycle. It has experimented boldly and intelligently with its State government, and has excellent administrative techniques, and one of the most faulty tax systems of any Commonwealth.

Norris is one of America's great heroes. His career covered the years of readjustment in American life. His integrity of purpose made him one of the great fighters for freedom in national history.

From the day that he broke the power of Uncle Joe Cannon, czar and speaker of the national House of Representatives, to his retirement from the United States Senate more than thirty years later, he was tireless and often misunderstood, even by those who regarded him with affection and admiration.

He was one of the great critics of the Treaty of Versailles, and obtained thereby a reputation as an isolationist. Few have taken the trouble to search out his criticisms of the Treaty or to contrast his motives with those of Brandegee, Lodge and Penrose, with whom he shared hardly a single thought. His speech, examining the British and American repudiation of obligations to China in turning over the Shantung Peninsula to the Japanese for exploitation, ranks with Sumner's denunciation of the Grant Administration's plunderings in the Caribbean and with Bacon's solemn rebuke against our wholly ignoble Philippine policy. He uttered a warning against the inevitability of a clash with Japanese imperialism then that Americans should have heeded.

It is impossible, of course, to estimate how the course of history might have been changed had not the United States, beginning in 1918, supported actively the Japanese aspirations at the expense of a democratic and constitutional regime in China. It is unprofitable, except as the kind of intellectual game in which Winston Churchill engaged in his celebrated essay, "If Lee Had Not Won at Gettysburg," to consider the question again today. But the fact remains that George Norris challenged in 1918 any compromise; he was critical of the American imperialism of the Coolidge-Hoover era, with its use of American Marines to suppress republican institutions in Nicaragua; he was the earliest, next to Franklin D. Roosevelt, of all men in high public life to sense the direct menace to America of the Fascist coalition.

George Norris believed in freedom for people in Nebraska. He believed in freedom for men in Fengtien, Framingham, Frederiksted or Friedek. He believed in freedom for corn growers, coolies, and cotton picking tenant-farmers. He believed that the freedom of each of them was, somehow, inextricably involved with the freedom of all of them.

He believed that the people had a right to experiment with their government and to utilize it for their good, in any way they saw fit. One of the ways that he thought reasonable and proper was the conversion of a wasteland into a land of plenty. Nebraska might, with propriety and pride, place a plaque upon the theatre in which George Norris spoke, with none to introduce him, in his campaign of 1918, when he defended his beliefs and his record. But they need no monument to George Norris in Tennessee.

Every blade of grass that grows on hillsides that once were barren and water washed speaks in memory of his patience. Every throbbing dynamo of the vast hydroelectric system of the Tennessee Valley Authority is engaged endlessly in a lyric in his praise. Thousands of farm families that knew want and that now know plenty can testify that this quiet man from a small Nebraska town was a great friend, when they needed a friend. The South is indebted to him, as it is indebted to few; the nation is indebted to him for reminding it that America belongs to all its citizens, and that every clod of earth that makes it up is a part of the heritage of every American, whether he lives in Idaho or Nebraska, Tennessee or Maine.

Although Norris possessed an adroit wit and the gift of deft satire, which occasionally stung such smug gentlemen as President Coolidge and Vice President Dawes, his two greatest resources were patience and facts. He began his fight for the Tennessee Valley modestly, in the days of the Harding Administration, by saving Muscle Shoals for the people. He studied the problems of water power, the facts of erosion, the question of a yardstick by which to measure the efficiency of privately operated utilities. His fight went on for a dozen years before it bore fruit, and then TVA came into being.

His sympathies always were with the underdog: with the farmers who had mortgaged acres, with the workers who had no security against unemployment, with the aged whose savings had been swept away in the depression. He believed that society could help its members, and that democratic processes could solve the economic and political problems of the nation.

If North Dakota is boldly experimental in the field of government's responsibilities, and if South Dakota is timid, Wisconsin has somehow found the middle ground. And if George Norris belongs to the whole nation, Wisconsin as a modern State belongs to Robert M. LaFollette.

When he emerged on the political horizon, just at the turn of the century, Wisconsin was dominated economically by exploiters and politically by absentee bosses. Few States in the Union had poorer public services or a bleaker outlook.

The Wisconsin that exists today is largely the product of the political skill of LaFollette and his great ability at making State government a useful and energizing force for the people. That he was sometimes wrong-headed and stubborn is unquestionable. He was hurt bitterly when his ill-health, T. R.'s ambitions, and the manipulations of politicians who time and again had joined GOP stalwarts in rejecting the Wisconsin Idea, permitted the progressive movement to fall into the hands of the Beveridge-Munsey-Perkins cabal. He was oppressed by political loneliness at times; Washington in the era of normalcy was not cordial.

But the fight to win Wisconsin was a good fight and a great fight, and the result was a great State; and the campaign of 1924 was as gallant as that which sent Rosinante's rider on his way to tilt with windmills that might—in the noble words that Rostand imagined for Cyrano—toss one into the mire of life and lift one toward the stars.

The LaFollette dynasty temporarily is in defeat in Wisconsin. The loss was Wisconsin's and the nation's when Robert M. LaFollette, Jr., after a career of unusual promise that included sincere and effective fighting for civil liberties and liberal legislation, was defeated for reëlection to the United States Senate. But the sound institutions of Wisconsin, its intelligent evaluation of public questions, and its honest government are monuments to "Fighting Bob" and his courage. He never took a step backward, and he never ceased to fight.

Wisconsin is diversified. The exploiters stripped much of the timberland and helped to create an erosion problem of considerable seriousness. But agriculture is effectively balanced by manufacturing, so that even the gigantic dairy farming enterprises do not lead to an overdependence on a single source of revenue.

A great part of America's farm equipment is manufactured in Wisconsin, together with such specialities as bathtubs and fountain pens. Parker Pen, at Janesville, sent me a quite ornate combination with the impressive name of "Magic Wand Desk Set" after an appearance on *Information, Please!* Milwaukee produced Hildegarde, and is the center of the brewing industry; it also has excellent municipal government, long dominated by Dan Hoan, patriarch of Wisconsin Socialists. Eau Claire, a city that was as beautiful as its name under a heavy blanket of snow when I saw it, is a prosperous example of diversification. Madison is dominated by the offices of the State government, but is an important business center as well as State capital and home of the University of Wisconsin.

Next-door Minnesota is boldly experimental in government. St. Paul, where the impressive Capitol is located, and Minneapolis, are twin cities that merge on their outskirts. They do not like to be identified as a single metropolitan area, however. They are important as manufacturing, publishing and marketing centers. General Mills at Minneapolis is the best known converter of grains in the nation, with a gigantic plant. Hubert Humphries, Minneapolis' Mayor, is a specimen of college professor turned politician, and one of the ablest young progressive leaders in the North.

Minnesota's political pattern is unique. The Democrats of the State effected a merger with the Farmer-Labor party, dominated by memories of Olson, and the organization bears the joint name of the groups.

The Minneapolis district provided an almost unique Congressman in William Gallagher, a veteran street sweeper. On election night, it had been thought that he had lost; but with a battered stub of pencil, Gallagher totalled up the votes himself, uncovering an error of ten thousand in the tabulation, and went into office. Moreover, he made a great Congressman and was deeply beloved by the people of his district.

Minnesota also possesses the last remains of the world's genuine Communists, the Trotskyites so hated by the Stalinists. Insignificant in numbers, although influential in one or two labor groups in St. Paul and Minneapolis, they continue to advocate world revolution on the Lenin-Trotsky pattern and to nominate candidates for their Workers party. Rochester has made a name for Minnesota in affairs medical by reason of the brothers Mayo, who demonstrated that the mousetrap theory still works.

11: WITHOUT CROOKED WEIGHTS AND MEASURES

Wherever I went in the Northern States, I talked quite freely about the problem of equal opportunity for the people of every section and about the need for ending colonialism. There were no dissenting voices anywhere. The people of that section, including most of their business and industrial leaders, have a feeling of confidence in their own ability to get along without using crooked weights and measures. They have achieved their economic position very largely through hard work and the utilization of their resources, which, in general, they never permitted to be exploited.

They had no brief for monopoly, and, with their own industry already decentralized to a considerable extent, they understood the advantages of an economy based upon diversification of enterprise.

In the North, I found something that was almost wholly lacking in the East: responsible conservatives, with a sense of society's obligation to its members and an understanding of government's place in human affairs. If the Republican party is not to go the way of its Federalist and Whig predecessors, it must shake off its Eastern control and accept the leadership of the conservatives from the lake and grain belt States.

As a Democrat and a Democratic politician, I would regret to see such intelligent action on the part of the leaders of the rival party. As an American, I can not help hoping that it happens, though I do not think it is likely that the Eastern monopolists and stock-riggers will give up their control in what once was the party of Lincoln; for it has been the one weakness of the American system of government that no responsible conservative party has ever existed, except upon State and local levels.

The Northern States may provide such a national party, one of these days, if Mr. and Mrs. Babbitt get around to it. And if they can't find room for their ideas of good government within the Republican party, perhaps they can be converted into good Democrats, after all.

EAST

These are the Three Principles of the People:
The people shall own;
The people shall control;
The people shall enjoy.
—SUN YAT-SEN

1: CROWDED AGAINST THE ATLANTIC

In America there exists many a paradox; the East is one. There is a concentration of wealth there, such as no other region of the world has known. There are the largest industrial installations in existence. There are the tallest buildings, and some of the worst slums, and the only wholly agricultural State in the Union, and the melting pot of a hundred tribes of men, and the widest variety of political and economic concepts to be found in America.

If any section of the country serves as an example of the immediate need for decentralization of industry, the East so serves. If the inevitable deterioration of a society based on exploitation needs to be studied at first hand, the East will supply the needed data. If the magnificence of man's daring, in visioning the ways in which he might adapt the world to his dreams, is to be seen on display, the East provides that, too.

Here are to be found barns painted with ancient, abstract symbols to ward off the spells of malignant charm-makers. Here are to be found architectural and engineering triumphs unrivalled in the world. Here are some of the worst slums in the nation, more pitiful than the rural slums of the South, or the transient camps of the Pacific Coast and Mountain States, or the hovels that infest the wrong side of the river in San Antonio: they are more pitiful, because they tell of deterioration of an empire that endured for hardly more than three-quarters of a century.

The East is, roughly, made up of the New England States, together with New York, Pennsylvania, New Jersey, and Delaware. It is not homogeneous. Much of the beautiful rolling countryside of Pennsylvania is indistinguishable from Virginia. Delaware, divided sharply between industry and farming, has little in common with New England and much in common with Maryland. The hill people of Vermont resemble rather the more-prosperous mountaineers of Georgia and Tennessee than they do the denizens of Boston or the citizens of Buffalo or Trenton.

What unites the East is its favored position in American government. Since 1794, the East has enjoyed a very considerable subsidy from the remainder of the country, first through the fiscal schemes of Hamilton, then through the operation of the tariff, and finally through the freight rate differentials that restrained production in other sections.

Historically, the capital of the East is Boston. New York and Philadelphia are bigger, but Boston is in many ways dominant. New York is compelled, by its handling of so large a share of American trade, to lay aside its insularity and assume an attitude of interest in the entire nation. Philadelphia, itself in part a victim of the freight rate differentials and supine in the hands of a political oligarchy that has reigned for seventy years or more, is somnolent, decaying, and pleasant, with the nation's principal shrine and the most famous department store as its attractions. Boston is the center of exploitation, with its dominance of manufacturing enterprises throughout New England, its control of coördinated and non-competitive subsidiaries in the South and West, and its financial eminence through generations of money-lending.

The East is more acutely provincial than the rest of the United States, and more diverse in its makeup. There are divisions of the population into ethnic and racial groups, such as are almost unknown in that part of the North called the Middle West by most Americans but simply known as "the west" to the Brahmins in New England. Although the French Canadian residents of New England have been there as long, or longer, than the Germans of Cincinnati, or the Czechs of Chicago, or the Swedes of Minnesota, they have not been absorbed into the population. Nor have the Slavs of the rich Connecticut Valley, nor even the Irish of Boston.

The racial strains in New England are hardly more diverse than those in the Southeast, where, except for the Negro, every group was absorbed, so that only in family traditions do Huguenots, Salzburgers, Highlanders, Irish, Scotch, English, and Spanish exist.

This astounded me as much, I think, as anything else to be found in the East. It is characteristic, however, of any area that is the center of an empire and that permits the settlers of subject races to enter only on the understanding that they live apart. Only in New York, a city of many races and creeds and languages, does the East present any resemblance to the rest of America in its larger centers. Its small towns, however, are much like other small towns in America, because, actually, all small towns in our common country bear a startling resemblance to one another in atmosphere and tradition.

Illustrative of the conditions in the urban East is the situation in Boston. The Irish are to be found everywhere in America. Almost everywhere they were met, as are all refugee groups, by a certain coldness that thawed in a few years and permitted their absorption into the community. In many of the larger cities of the country, the Irish genius for laughter fitted so well into the politics of the community that they achieved leadership in public affairs.

In Boston, they obtained that leadership otherwise, by breaking out of the ghetto into which they had been confined. In Boston, alone in America, are the Gaels vindictive and intolerant. The Christian Front is as much a part of Boston as the Watch and Ward Society. Persecution sustained by the Irish emigrants fostered a bitterness of spirit that endures. The power that they seized from the coupon-clippers who dominate the industrial East has not made them aware of America; it has only made them aware that economically they are impotent and that, no matter what the individual's attainments, the barrier between them and the Brahmins is insurmountable.

The illness that pervades Boston, an illness somewhat like that which must have swept over ancient Rome in its day, is quite different from the illness that currently affects New York.

There may be a certain tawdriness today about Times Square, though one well may doubt that there ever existed the dreamland that O. Henry invented in his hotel room. There may be squalor in Harlem and in the walk-up, cold-water "old-law tenements." But New York is at work on its problems, intelligently and warmheartedly.

From Baltimore to Boston, crowded against the Atlantic, are industrial plants that employ enormous numbers of Americans, produce enormous quantities of goods, and provide enormous profits. Some of these industries happen to be where they are because the skilled workers are available there and nowhere else. Some of them are there because of the availability, decades ago, of raw materials or water power. Some owe their existence almost entirely to the discriminations developed against other sections.

There is considerable evidence of decadence in the East. I do not mean this in the sense employed by the Chicago *Tribune,* for the decay is physical and is implicit in geography and is not the result of any effeteness on the part of the people themselves. It is due to the collision of a myth with a fact.

Distribution has become enormously costly in this country. It is no longer practical to manufacture consumers' goods in areas that do not possess raw materials. The double-haul is too expensive.

Moreover, there are so many obsolescent plants in the East that need rebuilding completely to compete with newer and more efficient installations elsewhere. New England is losing its position in the textile industry not because of decreased efficiency on the part of workers but because its mills have not been modernized.

There is an inevitable readjustment taking place, however. The boom-depression cycle of the 1920s made profound changes in the thinking of the East, where a more complex society felt a more serious collapse than was felt in the agrarian regions. The readjustment has not been comfortable, and the discomfort has been increased by the inadequate revenues of municipalities. New York's vast metropolitan area is at the mercy of upstate politicians in the matter of revenues, for example; and in Philadelphia those who could and should pay taxes apparently decline to do so. As a result, public services frequently have been impaired and the progress of the section has been retarded.

Throughout the East is to be found a greater concern with foreign affairs than elsewhere, even on the Pacific Coast; a great majority of the people in this section know the necessity of America's moving more actively into international affairs. The extreme vulnerability of the congested industrial centers, recognized by every inhabitant, no doubt accounts for this phenomenon, although the importance of Europe in the eyes of the East always has been great.

The most encouraging signs in the East are the political independence of the people and their willingness to adapt their economy intelligently to changing conditions in spite of the intense conservatism of part of their financial leadership. The most disquieting sign is the development of a caste system that is unhealthy.

In many parts of the region, this has resulted in an elaborate, expensive and essentially dangerous duplication of educational facilities. The private school flourishes, at the expense of the State-supported common schools. These private schools apparently vary much in quality. They range from the very excellent older endowed institutions, that owe their solvency to the patronage of aristocratic families and their virility to a broad and decently administered scholarship system, to nasty little snob schools that flaunt advertisements asserting that they cater to "select clientele only."

As a result, except for the Negro schools in the South and those for Mexicans and Filipinos in the Southwest and on the Pacific Coast, the public educational facilities of the East are the worst in America.

If I take the liberty of discussing conditions in the East with a certain candor and quite without reticence, it is because the problems of our common country are common problems. Americans have a right to discuss any section of their country freely. The South has profited a great deal from the generous criticism by others. Occasionally this criticism may seem to have been a little less than constructive, and once in a while lacking in sympathy; but it has been valuable nonetheless to the Southern mind and it has stimulated a good many improvements in Southern institutions.

The want of health in the East is serious to every American, no matter where he lives. The immense economic waste in our imperial system is costly to the resident of the Northwest or the Southeast, precisely as it will prove ultimately ruinous to the citizens of the supposedly favored area.

2: Host to men from many lands

Philadelphia is typical of the disorganization of the large urban centers of the region.

The ownership of the city is non-resident. The water supply comes from the streams where the sewage is poured and tastes indescribably of the heavy chlorination necessary to render it safe. The government of the municipality is lethargic and dominated by the oldest political machine in the nation. The slums are less crowded and less filthy than those of Chicago or New York or Detroit, but more distressing in their slow decay. In a city dominated by monopoly, competition was until recently to be found in the telephone system, the most unlikely place of all.

Yet there is a charm to Philadelphia unmatched among the great cities of the nation. So much of the history of the world has been written there that the memory of the past hovers over the community.

One of the great revolutions was born in Philadelphia; and one of the great revolutionary documents, certainly the shortest, was written there.

Its writing rounded out that chain of coincidence in history that began when a bell-founder, selecting an inscription for his product, soon to be hung in Philadelphia's Statehouse, chose from Leviticus the words:

"Proclaim liberty throughout all the Land unto all the inhabitants thereof."

For not only did Thomas Jefferson write in Philadelphia his Declaration of Independence, which freed some thirteen million Americans, and listen to the Liberty Bell summon the citizens to hear it read to the public for the first time, but in Philadelphia was written the document that began the freedom of three hundred million citizens of another continent. Here Dr. Sun Yat-sen wrote "The Three Principles of the People."

How it came to be written is one of the great stories of the enduring quality of the struggle for freedom.

The years of battle against the tyranny imposed upon China in the name of its shadowy Emperor by the Dowager Empress had taken their toll of Dr. Sun. He had been kidnapped in London, probably with the connivance of the British Foreign Office, and had been saved from death there only by the miracle of aroused public opinion. He had seen the first republican uprising on Chinese soil crushed relentlessly. He had witnessed the apathy of the Western nations to his pleas for liberty, and their connivance with meretricious quacks who promised a mild reform in the name of the tyrant. His health was almost broken; his courage was shaken; his funds were exhausted; and he sat in mean lodgings in Philadelphia brooding over the fate of his people.

The history of mankind does not belong exclusively to the great names and the great leaders. If anywhere is preserved the name of the visitor who came to Dr. Sun in the darkness of a rain-swept Philadelphia night, I have not been able to find it. He was a laundryman; and he had with him two hundred silver dollars, the savings of ten years of hard work. He handed them to the Provisional President of the Republic of China in his garret Capitol, and went his way, and disappeared into oblivion to join Bruce's piper, and Nelson's signalman, and Marion's bugler.

A few weeks later, Dr. Sun was in San Francisco. The real revolution was organized. The Republic of China became a fact. But before he left Philadelphia, with his writing brush, upon a card no bigger than a calling card, he wrote his great manifesto. It required fewer than a score of characters to tell the people of China his dream of the good world that men could have, if they wished.

He wrote:

> "These are the Three Principles of the People:
> The people shall own;
> The people shall control;
> The people shall enjoy."

In twelve words, Sun Yat-sen summarized the Declaration of Independence.

It is not sufficient that the people shall own their natural resources. It is not sufficient that they shall control that which they own, together with their political destinies. It is necessary that they shall enjoy the fruits of their ownership and their effort. It is necessary that they possess the unalienable right to the pursuit of happiness; without that right, the rights to life and liberty are incomplete and valueless.

The things that are wrong with democracy are almost innumerable, and many of them are in evidence in Philadelphia. Democracy is clumsy and very often highly inefficient. Democracy is wasteful of material things. Democracy often results in obtaining stupid or corrupt or crackpot leaders in government. Trains can be made to run on time in a democracy only by the application of economic pressure on the people who own the railroads; a simple directive from The Boss will not suffice. Democracy starts magnificent public works, like Philadelphia's eight million dollar subway tunnel, and then walks off and forgets about the enterprise.

Of course, some of those same things affect authoritarian governments, also. But they can be exempt, theoretically, from almost all the ailments of democracy, and can proceed with the utmost efficiency. They have but one thing wrong with them, and that is that they are founded completely upon untruth.

Always, of course, it is a currently fashionable untruth, the untruth-before-last that transiently seems so wholly satisfying. For a great many centuries, the untruth was metaphysical; since Hegel's time it has been mechanistic and material. The Roman brand of authoritarianism was justified upon the grounds that the Divine Emperor was united in mystical wedlock to Dea Roma, the presiding divinity of the Empire. Such a wholly rational and reasonable view ultimately was supplanted, some thousand years later, by that which held that the subnormal clockmaker, Louis XVI, was absolute monarch by Divine Right, his family having been selected by God to govern France when his ancestors were Counts of Paris.

This equally reasonable and righteous opinion appears to have been rejected by the Nazis, whose Fuehrer was a self-appointed superman. A superman may be defined as one who has a suitable number of concentration camps at his disposal and the coöperation of the General Staff.

Communist philosophy depends, apparently, upon the errors in mathematics, biology and physics that gained currency in the nineteenth century. The Universe is a great clock that nobody wound up; everything proceeds, according to the Hegelian formula of dilution, by a series of reactions; time and space may be measured by minutes and inches, and human desires may be measured in terms of food supply.

The arrival upon the scene of Einstein and Whitehead, with their troublesome theories, has been the great disaster for communism. The wholly mechanistic Universe that is a necessary axiom in their materialistic metaphysic does not seem to exist; instead, something infinitely more complicated and, paradoxically, a great deal simpler is in its place. The Earth may not be the center of the Universe, which may have either no center or an infinite number of centers; but Man reëmerges as somewhat more important and less expendable.

The fallacy of authoritarianism was always implicit in the subtlety of its logic, which always rested upon some unproven hypothesis that, eventually, was disproved. For there is something not at all ignoble about Man's sense of his importance; it is something more than a sense of self-esteem; it is a vision and the fulfillment of a vision; and that vision is the vision of a world in which ownership and control culminate in enjoyment.

Fundamentally, the basic authoritarian heresy is that some men are better than others, or stronger than others, or endowed with some special quality of rulership. About this fundamental heresy is assembled a series of findings of pseudo-science that demonstrates the especial fitness of the group of bullies in power for exercising power. It is neither more nor less fantastic to believe that Domitian was mystically wedded to Dea Roma, or that the imbecile descendant of Hugh Capet was endowed with a supernatural heritage, than it is to believe that the wardens of Buchenwald were supermen, or that the bureaucrats that fawn about the Kremlin are honest trustees for the proletariat, or that the preposterous myth named Private Management can bring the good world when it stages its projected Managerial Revolution.

Quaint as the rhetoric may seem, and as hackneyed as the assertion that the simpler aspects of arithmetic require but a single demonstration for absolute verification, the paper read at Independence Hall was right when it declared that certain truths were self-evident, including, unhappily for the authoritarians, this one:

"That all men are created equal, that they are endowed by their Creator with certain unalienable Rights."

It is a strange thing that Philadelphia, steeped in the libertarian tradition from the days of its founding, and still one of the most humane and pleasant cities of the nation, should have a slovenly and reactionary municipal government. There have been periods when its government was slovenly, reactionary, and corrupt as well. Yet the pattern of its bad government was always negative even in its theft; its political bosses were almost always amusing; and were menaces only to the purses and health of the citizens, never seeking to interfere seriously with the freedom of Philadelphia's folk.

Of course the crooked-boss-with-heart-of-gold is a legend, like the happy bandit. Not Robin Hood but Dillinger is the suitable comparison, for all the charm of Fouquet and Walpole abroad, or Burr and Hanna who were American grown. But I have never visited Pennsylvania without recalling with sympathetic pleasure the myths that have been erected about that most priceless of political buccaneers, Matt Quay. Alone among the masters of that art, Quay was in the game for excitement rather than money or power, and possessed a naive integrity that compensated for many of his lapses from complete rectitude.

As I took a plane from Philadelphia for Pittsburgh one afternoon, and watched the colossal statue of William Penn atop the City Hall dwindle, I thought about some of the tales about old Matt Quay.

How, for example, he outsmarted the Democrats of New York, not without cunning themselves in rigging elections, by having a quiet census of Manhattan taken on the eve of the 1888 election and threatening to challenge the "floating" voters at the polls; with the result that Benjamin Harrison, a rugged Puritan and hardly the type to qualify as a crony of Matt Quay, became President although he ran behind in popular votes.

Or how, when the great Mark Hanna bestowed the Federal

patronage for Mississippi on one of his best delegate-providers, so that shortly the widow of a Confederate veteran, who had been kind to Quay when he lay wounded near Vicksburg, lost a job as post-mistress, Old Matt stalked into the presence of President McKinley to remind that affable spouter of soft-soap that Pennsylvania could and would stage a rebellion in the 1900 Republican convention, unless. Mr. McKinley unlessed with celerity, without waiting to get permission from Hanna.

Or how he provided Pennsylvania with an honest Governor, one of the best in its history, in the person of his distant cousin, Samuel W. Pennypacker. They complained to him that his candidate was unreasonably opposed to larceny, did the boys in the ring; but he glared them down with the remark: "You'd be honest, too, with a name like that."

Or how, as he lay dying, he advised corpulent Boise Penrose, whom he had tutored carefully in the gentle art of manipulating politics, to put the Quay seat in the United States Senate on the auction block. Because of this advice, Philander C. Knox, an ardent trust-buster, was surprised to find himself elected instantly to the place by a trust-controlled legislature; the monopolists paid more than a million, it was said, to get him out of Theodore Roosevelt's Cabinet.

Pennsylvania is a complex State. Once the literal keystone of the Democratic party, it became the backbone of Republicanism, al-though it rebelled in 1912 to vote for Colonel Roosevelt. It is one of the richest agricultural States of the East and yet it is crowded with industrial communities like Allentown, Johnstown, and York, which are enormously important in America's economy and yet are little known.

It is in the East, yet not quite of the East; for the colonial East was predominantly English, as the colonial South was predomi-nantly Scotch, while Pennsylvania was host to men from many lands, but especially to the Germans. As in Virginia and the Caro-linas, a large part of its people came to these shores as indentured servants; and the Revolution was a civil war, with the back country strongly against the Tories of Philadelphia, as well as something of a class struggle. Neither of Pennsylvania's greatest statesmen, Dr. Franklin and Gallatin, was regarded as quite respectable by the ruling caste of their State.

Philadelphia is not dominant in Pennsylvania; it is not the titular capital, for that is Harrisburg; nor the actual capital, which is Pittsburgh. For even the magnificently indifferent rich who live on the Main Line and draw their wealth from Philadelphia real estate and mortgages, and the even more indifferent and much richer who live in other suburbs of Penn's city, are pawns in the hands of the dominant family of Pittsburgh.

The Mellons are quiet bosses, who permit others the privilege of looking like rulers. That is why Philadelphians challenge the assertion that Mellon brains and Mellon wealth control the Republican politics of the State. For Philadelphia furnishes a great bloc of the Republican votes, and succeeded once temporarily in sending its garbage-contractor, William S. Vare, to the United States Senate. There is also Joseph Grundy, Bristol textile manufacturer, writer of the Smoot-Hawley tariff measure, amateur historian, and enemy of the child labor laws, who is spoken of reverently in Republican circles as Mr. Grundy, with the same inflection that Memphis' Beale Street uses in speaking of Mr. Crump. There is also Joseph Newton Pew, Jr., more irreverently called Mr. Money Bags, who is one of the Sun Oil Pews, with sidelines in shipping and publishing; he is the main contributor to Republican war chests, with estimated gifts of a million dollars in the ten years that followed 1934.

The Mellons smile on the titular bosses, although they permitted James J. Davis to whip the socks off Mr. Grundy for the Senate in 1930. But whenever there is an actual test of power, the Mellons suavely demonstrate that their influence is supreme. Philadelphia politicians indignantly deny that this is so, but in Washington the party leaders know better. They know that Pittsburgh is the Pennsylvania capital, and that the State is dominated by a man who died

some years ago, bequeathing to Washington a magnificent building
by way of monument and to the nation a wrecked economy by way
of remembrance. Pennsylvania, except when it rebels and votes
Democratic, is safely in the hands of the Mellons, where Andrew
W. Mellon, Secretary of the Treasury under Harding, Coolidge and
Hoover, placed it.

Although Pittsburgh is the nation's principal steel center, and
therefore very like Youngstown or Birmingham externally, it also is
the center of the Mellon empire, which includes the Aluminum Corporation of America, the archetype of American trusts. The Mellon
interests control also a few banks, an oil company or two, a few
subsidiary enterprises in other lines such as light metals, power, and
electricity, and, perhaps, a few Canadian enterprises in the same
fields. But although it was not the foundation of the family's enormous fortune, aluminum is the mainstay of the Mellon empire and
is the most complete monopoly of its kind in America.

The story of the Aluminum Corporation of America has been re-
told many times. It is a story that is not as discreditable as that of
some of the other monopolies; the Mellons took a chance on a new
process for producing the light metal, and they did not swindle the
inventor of the process. On the other hand, it is a story of the use of
patents to prevent competition, and of the use of political power to
attain ends, and of exploitation of workers and of natural resources.

It is also the story of personal government, for seven years, of the
United States by a man who was wholly untrained in public affairs
and untalented for public life. Andrew W. Mellon bossed the Republican party from Warren Harding's death until his resignation
from the Hoover Cabinet. He was responsible for the ridiculous
financial measures adopted. These measures in turn were largely
responsible for the outrageous strangling of foreign commerce, for
the Wall Street boom and collapse, for the broken economy of the
agricultural regions, and for the government becoming the bill-col-
lector for sinister, crooked bankers.

He was an honest man. Depositors in his institutions did not lose their money in crashes, for he and his associates did not make speculative loans nor wild investments. He simply believed that those who possessed financial resources should run the nation, and he was not skillful enough in government nor aware enough as a judge of human nature to distinguish between one policy and another, or one financier and another.

He left a great part of his fortune to establish at Washington a magnificent museum of the arts. While it was being built, hungry veterans sold apples across the street.

Because scarcity is the life of monopoly and because you can not wage a war without adequate supplies of light metals, the Aluminum Corporation of America was one of the major bottlenecks of national defense during World War Two. The Federal government had to erect more plants speedily. The monopoly wants them now; as prizes for good conduct, I suppose.

3: Small towns grouped together

The State of New York is divided into the city, which is within the East but not typical of the East, and the upstate area, which has much in common with New England in parts and much in common with Ohio and Michigan in others.

New York City is the only American community of more than a hundred thousand population that reminded me of Newnan and, therefore, of some thousands of other small American towns that are like Newnan. There is not just one Court House square, it is true, but scores of squares. It is many small towns grouped together. The people ride to work underground, instead of in autos and busses. Coney Island blares all year round, but it has the atmosphere of a country fair. There is a carousel in Central Park, on which children have ridden since the days of the Tweed Ring; the park also possesses a tiglon, a creature half-lion and half-tiger. The people of the community are singularly kindhearted and good humored, with none of the veneer of sophistication that is to be encountered in Chicago or Detroit.

Manhattan is a fascinating nightmare of architecture, from the magnificent Public Library with its delightful small park, populated after dark by youthful courting couples, to the towering hulk of the Empire State Building or Rockefeller Center, crowded with sight-seeing visitors.

Other Americans know New York as the city where the banks have the biggest resources, the buildings the highest altitudes, and the sucker the least break. Its inhabitants know it as the largest manufacturing center in the nation, as its largest college town, as a collection of small communities that ultimately total some eight million people, something more than twice the population of Georgia.

New York has excellent municipal government, partly as a heritage from the late Fiorello LaGuardia and partly because the government has to be competent to operate at all. It requires a high degree of efficiency to provide the water and move the garbage in a town that size.

New York has a liberal tradition in politics that goes back to 1796, when the rapidly growing urban center voted for Jefferson. It was the enfranchisement of the great mass of New York's mechanics and tradesmen through legal trickery that won the State for Jefferson in 1800 and cinched the election that ended the Federalist reign of terror. The city has been Democratic ever since, whether the Tammany Society has ruled from its wigwam or not; for sometimes Tammany fell into the hands of incontinent boodlers, who were nearly as thievish as the Hamiltonian crew that stole so recklessly in the earliest days of the nation.

The liberalism of New York City has been marred in recent years by a device, fastened upon the State by adroit politicians, by which ordinary jury trials can be denied persons charged with crime. It is painful to mention this about a community that houses the American Civil Liberties Union and so many other institutions and associations dedicated to civil rights; but the "Blue Ribbon Jury Law" is so offen-

sive to American principles and so obnoxious a weapon against freedom that even a campaign manager for Representative Rankin
would denounce it if it were attempted in Mississippi.

On the credit side of the ledger, New York City has done more to
try to give its citizens decent homes than any other large community
in America. There are still many slums, but there is not the smug
resistance to change that is found in Philadelphia nor the selfish
disregard for human rights that is found in Chicago. And New
York City has provided good parks for its children, and fairly good
schools, although too many citizens send their children to private
schools that are exceedingly dubious in quality.

This somewhat erratic conduct of New York's middle class is part
of the small town paradox, that displays itself in irrationality about
the operation of the splendid municipally controlled transit system,
which must be subsidized by the levy of a notoriously regressive
sales tax. It has somehow become fashionable to send middle-class
children to private schools. My conservative acquaintances, whether
rich or poor, send them to institutions that inculcate the rudiments
of learning according to the principles of 1896. My liberal friends,
some of whom are reasonably prosperous, send them to experimental
schools operated by the successors to the young ladies from Indiana,
Georgia, and Iowa, who used to seek life, spelled with capitals, in
Greenwich Village a quarter-century ago.

Any excuse will serve, and every excuse has been given me by
one New Yorker or another, varying from the I.Q. of the child, its
presumptive nervousness, and its exceptional talents for the arts, to
some mild form of racial or religious prejudice. It required a good
many conversations over several years with many New Yorkers for
me to ascertain that the private school habit was nothing more than
a fashion in the city, and really without significance. In its want of
significance, it is different from the general practice in the East,
where it is an aspect of the vicious caste system that permeates much
of the region. In New York, however, I am convinced that it does
not represent any retreat from a basic egalitarianism, except upon

the part of a few snobs who amount to nothing much in the reckoning of things American. The truth is that the public school plant of New York is obsolete and inadequate. An improved public school system would do much toward remedying the private school habit; private school development weakens public pressure for good public educational facilities.

Besides its tall buildings and its remarkable transit system, America's biggest city is notable for possession of one thing much needed in other major metropolitan areas: a responsible conservative newspaper. The irresponsibility of conservative leadership in the nation is a serious matter that traces back so many generations that it is difficult of explanation. Although they have a marriage of convenience with the upstate machines of their party, the conservatives in New York are the most intelligent to be found anywhere, collectively, and the *Herald-Tribune* is their mouthpiece.

It is a great newspaper, and an honest reporter of news as well as an honest critic with whom it is possible to disagree without heat. That the Reid family has been able to weld the creations of James Gordon Bennett and Horace Greeley into a publication that is delightful typographically, comprehensive in news coverage, readable in style, and consistent in policy is nothing less than remarkable. It is enormously influential because of those qualities, but its influence does not seem sufficient to provide the country's conservatives with responsible leadership.

4: The best of them will string along

The need for intelligent and responsible conservative party leadership in this country is intense. New York City itself provides a text for that discussion, because, while its conservatives today are the best in the nation, they are not fully trusted at home because of the record that lies behind them. Tammany, from time to time, has suffered an infiltration of demagogues, crooks, and cheats; it has never been really seriously set back on its heels, however, except during the period of LaGuardia's tenure of office. And the reason has been a distrust for the irresponsible conservatives.

The layers of consciousness and remembering of a community possibly can be laid bare, one by one, in the same manner and by the same devices that those of an individual can be revealed. Just as the man will act upon impulses acquired as a child, so a community will act, when fully grown into a city, upon impulses that derive from its village life. New York has forgotten that its citizens were disfranchised by the nation's earliest conservative party, that they were deprived of banking facilities except on terms of a monopoly, that their waterfront was enfeoffed, and that even their water system was the tool of exploitation. From that vassalage the city was rescued by Tammany, chiefly through two adroit tricks of that remarkable political prestidigitator, Aaron Burr.

Burr broke the financial power of Hamilton's associates by breaking their control over banking. This was accomplished by the expedient of a harmless-sounding bill in the legislature chartering the Manhattan Company, seemingly so clumsily drawn that the corporation would have difficulty in engaging in any really profitable competition with America's earliest monopolists; but out of the clumsy wording he constructed the Bank of the Manhattan Company.

He broke the political power of Hamilton's clique even more cleverly. The reactionary forces had established their usual property qualifications for voting, in order to disfranchise the mechanics and workers of the city. Burr acquired a few vacant lots, and his followers found themselves presently owning one one-hundredth or less interest in one of them, as tenants-in-common; they also found themselves qualified to vote, just on the eve of the important election of 1800. Neither Hamilton nor the lords of the Upper Hudson, who were too proud to engage in trade openly but who were not above turning a dishonest penny when they could, ever forgave Burr. Their successors never forgave Tammany, for that matter, but the voters somehow remembered.

Just what inward compulsion forces conservatives to string along with the lunatic fringe of reaction is a political mystery in America. Of the conservative presidents chosen by the nation, only three, John Adams, Rutherford B. Hayes, and Benjamin Harrison, widely spaced in American history, can be described as first-rate political figures or as responsible statesmen. Instinctively, the American conservative seems to prefer his Grants, his Blaines, his McKinleys, his Coolidges, his Hoovers.

A serious effort to make the conservative party in this country responsible was undertaken by Thomas B. Reed, who left politics in disgust not long after the triumph of Hanna and McKinley. Wendell Willkie tried it, without success. Currently that frank and intransigent Senator Robert A. Taft is attempting the same thing, though with even less political aptness and with the same foreknowledge of failure.

The American conservative always has placed his faith in voting restrictions, in bought elections, and in utilizing third-rate political hacks as tools. They rejected the leadership of the honest country lawyer, John Adams, for the frivolous glamor-boy, Alexander Hamilton, at the beginning of the country's history. Through the middle period, they neglected Hugh White and Daniel Webster in favor of Henry Clay. In 1896, at the most crucial Republican convention in history, they cast aside Benjamin Harrison in favor of William McKinley. The history of America is replete with rejected conservative leaders of the first rank, from John Adams to Frank Lowden.

Their employment, within their Southern and Western colonies, of arrant demagogues and common knaves is even more difficult to comprehend. For the average conservative is responsible, intelligent, and public-spirited as an individual.

Nevertheless, before the onset of the depression that usually bears the name of Warren Harding's Secretary of Commerce but that should bear the name of his Secretary of Treasury for greater accuracy, the utilities of the nation were dominated by the stock-swindling, holding-company-milking, Napoleon-obsessed group headed by Samuel Insull.

Of course, American conservatives are not proud of their leaders. They were not proud of the deterioration of our foreign policy to a point where the United States Marines, with a tradition of valor and gallantry, were made the bill-collectors of dubious claimants of Nicaragua. They were not proud of the alliance between the Republican party and the Ku Klux Klan in 1928. They were not proud of the use of poison gas and fire against the hungry, bedraggled bonus marchers who huddled at Anacostia. But even the best of them will string along; even a Lowell will serve on Governor Fuller's committee to whitewash a judicial lynching; even a Newbold Morris remains silent about the Blue Ribbon Jury Law.

This can be attributed, in a degree, to the refusal of first-rate conservatives to enter the field of government in their youth, and to make public service a career. Jefferson, the younger Adams, Forsyth, Taney, Cleveland, Baker, Glass, Norris, Hill, and Franklin D. Roosevelt devoted their lives to public service on the political and policy-making levels, and all were liberals. Few comparable conservatives can be named.

In spite of the bitter factional quarrels within the Democratic party, such as New York witnessed in 1924 when a certain victory was turned into a sure defeat in a seventeen-day battle of Madison Square Garden between William G. McAdoo and Alfred E. Smith, the Democrats have abler career politicians. Indeed, the bitter internal discord that sometimes negates Democratic success may arise from the fact that the two wings of the party each attract first-rate men by different routes. For the Democratic party, geographically, is an alliance of the great cities with the rural South, and in recent years, the Pacific Coast and Mountain States.

In the urban areas, a political career attracts men of marked ability, because it offers to youths like the Al Smith in 1912 a chance to earn a decent living and get ahead in life. In the South and the West, despite the well-financed campaigns of demagogues with Eastern masters, politics is a respectable profession by tradition.

The Republican party does not welcome career men, unless they are willing to become complacent party hacks like President Coolidge. The chilliness toward Senator Taft does not originate in disagree- ment with his views, which are hardly radical; the hostility toward Governor Warren is not because there is a suspicion that he might suddenly advocate nationalization of utilities, which is entirely un- likely; the opposition to these men, representing the ablest that either branch of the Republican party can offer, arises from a fear that they know too much about government. Conservatives are willing to trust foreign affairs to self-designated experts, because the career foreign service is a respectable playground for the younger sons of the rich; they are willing to trust career men at immediate levels of government, provided they display little initiative; but somehow they are unwilling to accept as a leader any first-rate man who has made government his lifework. Only twice have they relented, in the instances of two candidates for Vice President; and they were not pleased with either Chester A. Arthur or Theodore Roosevelt.

Each of these came from New York, and each worked his way up the political ladder by loyalty to the organization. Arthur owed his nomination to the desire of the convention that nominated Gar- field to placate the powerful Conkling machine that had supported Grant's third-term attempt. Theodore Roosevelt found it possible to work actively for James G. Blaine. Each displayed courage and liberal sympathies when, unexpectedly, he was thrust into the White House; but the Colonel was a better showman, and the party bosses had to bear with him and nominate him in 1904 and wait until 1912 and Armageddon to smash him.

The absence in the United States of a responsible conservative party is serious. It entails risks more grave than a mere anticipation of another Teapot Dome theft. Unless American conservatives purge their party relentlessly of the dangerous neo-Fascist elements within it, and of business interests that, like Stinnes and Thyssen, show a disposition to finance Rightest extremists, it is unworthy to be trusted with power.

5: The Hudson ties the State together

There is much more to be seen in New York than the metropolis. The State and the city are enormously different; the city is typical of any part of America that you may wish to select, while the State is New England in its attitude. Despite lingering names and traditions, the Dutch influence is little felt. Buffalo has a Polish population much like that of Connecticut, and some communities are predominantly Italian as a result of the importation of workers on the rail lines and the canal; but agricultural New York is Yankee, in the Down East sense rather than that understood in the South.

It is a region of dairy farmers. Two out of three homes have electric power, about twice the percentage of Georgia, which leads the Southeast. But rural New York is not as tidy as rural Pennsylvania, nor is it prosperous in the manner of the grain States. The land, while not so eroded and despoiled as in the ruined sections of the Southeast, is wearing thin and only the presence of a large urban population to consume the hundreds of thousands of gallons of milk produced daily enables the New York farmer to prosper at all.

The enormous industrial development of the State, however, is quite another thing. Syracuse, Monticello, Rochester, Ogdensburg, Potsdam, Schenectady, and Utica, all these amazed me by the variety of their commerce and manufactures. Most of their products were finished consumers' goods: cameras, clothing, household ware, machinery; the value added by manufacture was enormous, and the industrial population had incomes that deserved better housing.

Cheaper electricity would do much for New York State, just as it would do much for the Missouri Valley. The St. Lawrence Waterway, though it might stimulate the growth of Chicago at the expense of New York City, would reduce the power bill of householder and industrialist by at least a hundred and thirty million dollars annually. But although it has had the approval of four Presidents, and of the 1944 Republican nominee for President, who is not describable as a radical, the efforts of the rail and utility lobbies have been effective in blocking the development.

Unlike MVA, none of the delay in linking the Great Lakes with the Atlantic can be blamed upon rival bureaucrats. There is simply too much at stake for monopoly to relinquish its hold. The substantially lower power rates in Canada, just across the border from some New York communities engaged in competitive manufactures, indicate the measure of the opposition to the project.

Upstate does not like the city, and Upstate dominates Albany. Even when the Governor is sympathetic with the problems of the metropolis the legislature is hostile. The current arrangement seems to be for the city, which pays most of the tax bill, to suffer from a grave budgetary crisis while the State government develops an equally badly unbalanced budget by hoarding a surplus of a half-billion dollars.

It is the Hudson that ties the State together, and the story of the Hudson is one of the great romances of the country. Not always are scenes up to the expectation of the visitor, but the Hudson, like the Alamo, is an exception. There was a haze above the stream on the morning that I passed West Point, and the stream and the fortress must have looked much as they did on the day when Major André bore his message to its treacherous commander. And at night, the hills have the mystery that Washington Irving hinted in his tales, and one waits expectantly for the sound of the bowling as the Little Men frolic.

It was snowing when we left the Massena airport on the way back to New York City for a speaking engagement. Sitting in the co-pilot's seat, watching the snow, listening to the purring of the motors, I became drowsy and slept. Sometime later, my pilot, Ray Moulton, touched me on the shoulder to arouse me—the snow had stopped— he pointed out Hyde Park below.

6: Personal relationships and chance encounters

Already there is gathering around the memory of Franklin Delano Roosevelt a monumental mass of memoirs, from which presently there will emerge a myth. The myth will not do justice to the man. It will picture him as inexpressibly serious, and as preoccupied with the waging of the nation's greatest war. It will rob him of his human attributes, and transmute him into some kind of symbol.

The facts about Mr. Roosevelt, I think, are rather simple, and rather more important and significant than the myth. He was a country gentleman, apparently developed in the culture of an earlier era, as his involuted prose suggests. He was a sympathetic, sensitive, energetic individual, with a remarkable gift for improvisation in public affairs. He had an unusual sense of personal responsibility that became identified with an acute social consciousness. He possessed remarkable charm and singular dexterity in personal relationships and chance encounters. As a statesman, he based his policies upon a recognition that all citizens of our common country must be accorded their political and economic rights, and that institutions and techniques must be adapted to changing technological conditions without any surrender of basic freedoms.

Most of those aspects of Mr. Roosevelt's personality will find themselves a place in the myth, although they may be altered in emphasis to fit into the legend. Presently, no doubt, the myth-makers will delete from his collected speeches those that are not adaptable to their image. That will be America's loss.

For they will thereby distort the picture of the man. They will leave out the one essential: Franklin D. Roosevelt was a great pragmatic politician and it is necessary to be a great politician to be a great statesman. The First Inaugural was one of America's finest state papers, and it ended a period of economic collapse and individual fear. His final, undelivered address, scheduled for the 1945 Jefferson Day Dinner, remains and will remain an inspiration to his country. But the speech to the Teamsters Union was art. It was the kind of speech that Caesar probably delivered just before he sent his legions crashing into Pompey's men.

One of my friends, somewhat of a boxing fan in earlier years, gave me his reaction to that speech.

"It was just like Benny Leonard's last fights," he said. "I remember one of them. Benny was tired to death. His speed had been gone three or four years. He was slow moving around the ring. The boy against him was clever and fast and looked good until about the eighth round, and then Benny feinted and uncorked a short right that didn't travel six inches. The poor fellow never knew what hit him until they had carried him out. Well, the speech was just like that punch. Tom Dewey had been piling up points and his seconds probably were feeling pretty good, but when that sentence about 'my little dog Fala' got its laugh, I knew the election was over. Tom was down for the count."

There have been other great politicians in American history. Jefferson had endless patience and a gift of phrase and an insight into the real motives of men, their gallantry, their meanness, their fear. Henry Clay had prodigious charm. Amos Kendall had the technique of organizing. Lincoln had the power to evoke either laughter or tears. Franklin D. Roosevelt had everything; he was the most completely equipped politician in the nation's history.

The adroitness of his two losing fights, the Supreme Court "packing" and the 1938 "purge," illustrate his insight into political realities. There might have been an outside chance, had Senator Robinson lived, to make the changes in the court, although it is doubtful that Mr. Roosevelt ever expected such a victory. It is certain that he did not expect to win in his 1938 efforts to unseat certain leaders of his own party who had opposed his program. But the two battles were well worth while; they attained their ultimate ends. Mr. Roosevelt got a better treatment for his legislation at the hands of the court, which suddenly discovered, even before the resignation of some Justices, that the legal views of the Holmes school were correct. Mr. Roosevelt also obtained a measure of support after 1938 that had been absent since the more desperate aspects of the emergency period ended.

Of his four Presidential campaigns, I am certain that only that of 1940 gave him serious concern. He was sure of his ability to deal with the high command of the Regulars, who repeated the same old Liberty League propaganda ineffectively; but he had a hearty respect for Wendell Willkie, and he not only recognized the exceptional appeal of the Indiana man's sincerity but constantly expected him to utilize some new tactics. The 1940 race would have been much harder to win but for Mr. Willkie's concession to the organization in the matter of a party chairman; the young men who swept the convention before them and nominated him would have done a better job in control at headquarters.

Personal liking played a remarkable part in the Roosevelt career, it must be admitted. His taste was catholic enough to include both Carter Glass and Josephus Daniels, among elder statesmen of the South; and no men ever stood wider apart in viewpoint. Although he was a sound judge of ability, he could never refrain from finding places within his Administration for those whose loyalty and personal affection far exceeded talent.

His taste for political history and his knowledge of its American phase was almost unbounded, although there is a probability that Louis Howe was responsible for his acquiring it. The Jackson period especially stimulated him; his admiration for the political skill of Old Hickory's advisers equalled that for the General himself in his long and victorious fight against the Bank of the United States. I think his interest in Jackson colored many of his economic and political views, especially after the campaign of 1936.

Hyde Park contains the Roosevelt of history, in the Library that is filled with his souvenirs and personal papers. It was his boyhood home, and his simple grave is there, as is fitting. But Hyde Park seems to me to be less characteristic of Roosevelt than Warm Springs.

At Warm Springs, he learned how to use the courage that he possessed. There he taught himself the patience that is the essence of politics. There the tall young athlete of Groton discovered that no man is useless to society who has the will to contribute to it, and that no man is through who has the heart to get up again.

Of the many books about him and about the New Deal and the war, that of his son, Elliott Roosevelt, seems to me to give the most accurate picture of the man. Factually sound as are the treatments of FDR in the Morgenthau and Perkins memoirs, these seem to me to describe acts rather than delineate character. Of course, a man's actions speak for him; but they speak baldly and without eloquence and, very often, most inaccurately.

That which spoke best for Franklin D. Roosevelt was his littered desk in the White House. It spoke of a mind that was harmonious rather than orderly, of a mind that had no use for pigeonholes to classify men and causes, of a mind that was at its best in improvisation in emergency, of a mind that was so inquiring that every subject held interest. He recognized, as have few of the nation's Chief Executives, the value of the technical expert; but he recognized that the eventual decision must be made by someone whose interests were not channelled narrowly, and who could discern the interrelations of events. He was a strategist, not a tactician.

The desk spoke also of a man with a sense of humor that was spiced with wit. The humor was that typical American blend of fantasy and exaggeration; the wit was dryer than that attributed to President Coolidge. He was cautious in its use, because it could sting. Occasionally, dressed as satire, it appeared in his more political speeches, such as those he delivered on the trip through Connecticut in the closing period of the 1940 campaign.

The desk spoke of his love of variety, his enjoyment of new things to do. Perhaps, as a statesman, that was his one weakness; sometimes he did not follow closely the progress of an idea after it was once on its way. A few of the New Deal reforms halted prematurely, though in most of those instances it was probably his desire to feel his way safely, rather than loss of interest, that held them just short of their necessary ultimate goal. After all, FDR was an experimentalist and not a doctrinaire; he preferred to see plans tested empirically than to rely upon dogmatic conclusions.

He permitted me to make the first announcement of his willingness to run for a fourth term. From the conversations that I had with him in 1941, when I was a candidate for Governor of Georgia and sought his advice, and again in 1944, when I urged him to stay in office, I got the impression that only a sense of obligation induced him to make his last two campaigns. Had his opinion of Willkie in 1940 been the opinion that he held four years later, I do not believe he would have accepted the nomination; he honestly felt that any 1940 Republican nominee would be the creature of the irresponsible Old Guard, especially the inadequate House leadership, and that a possible Democratic defeat might entail the world-wide destruction of democracy as well as grave consequences to this country. In 1944, obviously, he had no choice but to continue his wartime task.

He enjoyed the campaigns of 1932 and 1936. He felt confident that the policies he was preparing could end the depression, which contributed to the force he put behind the Hoover contest. But 1936 was his favorite. He had licked the depression; he was moving into a period of experiment and reform; he had made some choice enemies in his first term, among men who were terrified in 1931 at the possible prospect of a revolution by the hungry but who forgot quickly their obligation to the Roosevelt policies for averting economic and political disaster.

I think he enjoyed 1936 best, because of his four races that was the one in which the opposition had most false confidence, resulting from the *Literary Digest* poll. With suitable irony, the opposition won two States: Maine and Vermont, respectively the most conservative and the most liberal Commonwealth in New England.

7: They like their homes and hills

Of all the nation, the one State that I have not visited is Vermont. I have seen it under a blanket of snow as I flew from Boston to upper New York State. Vermonters do not import lecturers, having debated everything for themselves many times; and I have not been able to take the time for a proper visit. What I know about Vermont is derived in part from having met a few native sons elsewhere; but they were few, for the Green Mountain boys do not travel extensively for pleasure, since they like their own homes and their own hills. The rest that I know is derived from the public careers and voting records of the men they send to Washington.

Nominally, all Vermont public officials are Republicans. There are Democrats in the State, I am aware; but they are never elected to office, and very likely remain Democrats because of a stubborn streak that has characterized the people of those hills for ten generations. The last Democratic governor retired in 1826. But Warren R. Austin, who went from the Senate to represent the United States at the United Nations council table, and Senators George Aiken and Ralph Flanders, are not representative of their party. Perhaps they are representative of nothing except Vermont.

Austin was a remarkable figure in the Senate. His domestic views were old-fashioned in their conservatism; that is to say, his was the conservatism of caution, which I am told, Vermont citizens have in plenty as one side to their natures. He was an intelligent and responsible conservative, who sought out what he believed essential weakness in measures he opposed and did not engage in the showman's trick of merely scoring points. His views on foreign affairs were intelligent, and colored with moral fervor. He understood the issues and realized the stakes at a time when many of the members of his party were playing politics with the country's safety.

Warren Austin did not like Hitler. He did not and does not like any brand of authoritarianism. He likes to be free and to see other men free.

His attitude is characteristic of the history of his State, which began its revolution in 1771 and sporadically fought New York and New Hampshire as well as the British Crown. The people of the hills not only did not intend to be swindled out of the land they had paid for, but they intended to be free while they were about it. When they got around to writing their State constitution, they abolished slavery; they meant for other men to be free, too.

When Senator Austin left the Senate to assume his duties on the United Nations Council, Vermont chose Ralph Flanders, a Willkie Republican, to succeed him. Senator Flanders is as close to the Center as will permit him to be described as a conservative; certainly he is no reactionary. Like his predecessor, he is the type of responsible conservative that his party needs so badly in a position of leadership.

His colleague, George D. Aiken, senior Senator from Vermont, is one of America's great men. If I were selecting the three outstanding figures on the Republican side of the Senate, I would place him in company with Taft of Ohio and Morse of Oregon in intellectual attainments and complete sincerity.

Aiken is a Vermont farmer, and the spiritual successor of George W. Norris of Nebraska.

Aiken's vision of the good America, I suppose, is a fruit farm in the hills of Vermont; and with that vision I disagree, for to me the good America is a white-shuttered house just outside a Georgia town. Aiken's concept of a good American policy, foreign and domestic, is a policy based on ethical concepts. Because of that, and because of his reliance upon logic in a sometimes illogical world, a comparison with the scholarly Charles Sumner seems to me justified. It is an impractical ideal, fatal in politics; Senator Aiken's campaign expenditures in his most recent successful campaign for reëlection were thirty cents.

Much of New England opposes the St. Lawrence Waterway. It has Aiken's support.

Most of New England objects to revision of the railroad's rate-

making machinery. Aiken believes in decentralization and in opportunity for every section of America.

Most Republican officeholders in New England opposed the New
Deal measures for relief, for agricultural benefits, controls over monopoly, and regulation of stock exchanges. Aiken supports them.

His is a passion for the lost causes and the underdogs: for the
migratory workers in the fruit orchards and cranberry bogs and
vegetable fields; for more public power; for educational opportunity
on a nation-wide basis.

His views on foreign affairs have been described as isolationist.
Although many of his votes have been in the company of isolationists, I do not think that isolationism is expressive of his actual position. He wants an American foreign policy that is coherent, that
is based upon good will and good morals. He does not want to see
America playing world power politics. I suspect Senator Aiken of
possessing a prejudice against both Russia and Britain, at times; it is
not an unreasoning prejudice, but one based on a belief that Communist expansion and Tory imperialism are essentially immoral.

Nowhere in New England, except Vermont, could George D.
Aiken be elected to the Senate. But his State, most fervently aboli-
tionist in the days before the War Between the States, must have
extraordinary citizens; citizens something like their hills, which,
they tell me, are green and gentle and rolling, but are made out of
granite.

8: CURIOUS CONDUCT OF THIS SECTION

Two States in New England present problems for any critic. It
is impossible for me to deny that I approach Massachusetts and
Connecticut with a degree of prejudice. I know that is unfair. The
people of Boston are not unlike the people of Charleston or San
Francisco or Mobile. They have the same emotions; as individuals,
they wake up in the morning and go to work, and return home in
the evening and play with their children.

Nevertheless, Massachusetts and Connecticut are unlike the rest of New England and unlike the rest of America, and about them I have an emotional bias. This bias remains unaltered by the knowledge that Massachusetts' bench has been occupied by an Oliver Wendell Holmes as well as by a Webster Thayer, that Massachusetts has been represented in the Senate by Charles Sumner as well as by the elder Lodge, that Sam Adams preceded James Curley as Mayor of Boston, that Harvard numbers Charles W. Eliot as well as A. Lawrence Lowell among its presidents, and that Bronson Alcott as well as Ira Calvin White wrote in Boston.

Yet there are unpleasant facts that must be recorded about the two States. In no section of America have there occurred so consistently violations of civil rights.

It is not necessary to go back to colonial days, with the rise of Boston's hegemony, the suppression of the liberties that the men of the *Mayflower* brought over with them to Plymouth, the witch trials that provided in Chief Judge William Stoughton a judicial predecessor for Judge Thayer, and the flight of Roger Williams through the snow.

It is not necessary to trace the spirit of totalitarianism through the Jeffersonian epoch, marked by the ruthless enforcement of the Alien and Sedition Laws by the courts and the destruction by hired mobs of the presses set up to advocate freedom, and to recall that religious liberty did not come to this area until forty years after the Bill of Rights had become a part of the Federal constitution.

It is not necessary to cite the existence of the New England Watch and Ward Society, which interferes with freedom of the press in Boston; nor the crowding of sixty thousand American citizens of Jewish faith into a ghetto where they have endured the assaults of thugs and seen their sacred edifices desecrated; nor the buffoonery of the police department censorship of plays on the Boston stage. Those are facts so commonly recognized throughout the nation that they are accepted as part of the Boston tradition.

But in Connecticut, far the more civilized of the two States and

one that in the past fifteen years has shown a trend toward remedying the evils of the past, enough violations of civil rights can be
counted in the single year of 1924 in connection with the Coolidge-
Davis-LaFollette campaign to shock sensibilities for many years to
come. At Darien and Meriden, and a dozen more small cities,
assaults on speakers were made with the coöperation of the local
authorities or workers were openly intimidated into support of the
Republican ticket.

History offers one clue, and economics another, to the curious
conduct of this section of New England.

The successful efforts of Massachusetts Bay Colony to obtain complete dominance throughout New England in the earlier colonial
period left its mark on the history of the State. With the rise of
Boston as the principal city and major financial center of the area,
the influence of one group of colonists became preponderant.

These were perhaps the most objectionable of all the groups that
settled America. The Pilgrims were simple men of piety. The indentured servants who built inland Virginia and Pennsylvania were
seekers after freedom. The Tidewater Virginians were gentlemen-
adventurers. The debtors of Georgia and the Scotch-Irish of the
Southeast were seeking better economic conditions. The Dutch and
Swedish settlers of New York and Delaware were traders and their
military escorts.

But the settlers of Massachusetts Bay were men belonging to a
unique group in society: the ambitious for power, who are unable
to attain their ends in the social order in which they found themselves. Essentially they were déclassé English landowners, unable
to fit themselves into the political structure of that country on the
side of either rival group.

The history of intrigue, of land speculation, of political double-
dealing associated with the rise of Boston as a commercial center
and of the dominant group in that colony into overlords of New
England is shameful in the extreme. Their attitude throughout the
Revolution was mysterious, yet they reappeared in power soon after-

ward, since there was no purge of "loyalists" such as followed the American victory in the other States. Not only did they reappear in power, but through the trickery attached to the assumption of the public debt by the Federal government, they obtained a dominant position in American commerce.

Only through the establishment of a near-totalitarianism were they able to check the normal aspirations of their fellow-citizens for political, social and economic democracy. Their reign of terror in New England ended approximately in 1830, with the disestablishment of their ecclesiastical structure; their power over the economy of New England and of the rest of the country has never lapsed.

Boston is the principal citadel of monopoly. The Union Pacific, one of the most princely thefts in American history, was financed there. The headquarters of the shoe monopoly is there. Until fifteen years ago, the textile trade of the nation was tightly in Boston's hands, and the woollen mills of America are still in their control. Incidentally, Boston is pretty nearly the boss of Hollywood.

Exposures of Boston's business underworld are a commonplace of America. Retaliation by the powerful monopolies that cluster there has been speedy and usually effective. True, they failed in their effort to crush Louis D. Brandeis, while he lived there, and failed to prevent his confirmation as a member of the United States Supreme Court; but they have been effective in preventing the Anti-Trust Division of the Department of Justice from getting sufficient funds for operations, so that such brilliant fighters against monopoly as Thurman Arnold and Wendell Berge left government careers.

Boston is controlled by Irish politicians, nominally; South Boston dominates the voting of the community. Although Governor Tobin and other men of ability and integrity have emerged from the welter of Boston politics, the leadership is not sound, and one must suspect an alliance with the trustees, the bankers, the investors' counsels, and the shrewd manipulators who dominate the State.

Boston thrives on hate. Many of the dirty books, seeking to array race against race and religious group against religious group, are published in Boston or its suburbs. Apparently these never face any danger of suppression by the Watch and Ward Society; it is more concerned with the doings of serious artists than with the publishers of such masterpieces of pornography and hate as are locally produced. *Only Blondes Are Angels* is an accurate example of Boston's current literature; this volume, by Ira Calvin White, is more or less a sequel to his opus, *The Lost White Race*. Goebbels was his superior, both as writer and propagandist.

I spoke twice in Boston on one of my trips to the East. I was just a little apprehensive about my reception, since I had been a trifle critical of some Bostonian practices; nevertheless, I had overflow houses. My arrival was coincidental with newspaper stories of the conviction of Boston's Mayor for mail fraud and with headlines charging other municipal scandals involving graft and bribery.

On my invasion of Boston, I had induced Jack Leban, a friend then living in New York, to accompany me. When we entered the auditorium, he deposited his hat with a personable young woman who promised its safekeeping. When the talk was over, and we had caught a cab, I noted that he was hatless. I asked if he had decided to leave his head bare in the future.

"When I went back for my hat," he said, "the young lady said that she remembered me quite well, and that she had noticed that I was not wearing a hat when I came in. So what could I do?"

"I guess there isn't much anybody can do in Boston," I told him.

Connecticut has been saved from some of the horrors of Massachusetts because its industries, primarily, are craft manufactures, and the skilled workers are less subject to intimidation and less influenced by hate propaganda than those engaged in other processing.

The conclusion that hate is a deliberate product of the master race in Boston is inevitable. The pattern is the same as that utilized in the South, when outside exploiting interests engage the services of some local Quisling. There is the same appeal to racial or religious hatred; neither the Jews nor the Irish in the Boston area have ever become a part of the population; each lives in its own ghetto of Warsaw.

Liberal forces exist in Massachusetts. The State can call the roll of many, from Sam Adams, who deserves the title of Father of the Revolution, through Garrison and Sumner and Thoreau and the two Holmeses, father and son. But it remains the home of exploitation; its own workers are exploited; its utility rates are above the level suggested by any yardstick; it not only stands at the bottom of the list of States in the preservation of civil liberties, but has an appellate system that is an affront to any American concept of justice.

It was in Boston that Paul Revere started his ride on behalf of freedom. He was the son of a French emigrant, not a Brahmin.

9: THE BOSS IS A SENSITIVE PERSON

New Jersey is the doorway to New York's port. The major rail lines of the East must pass through the State. It has many cities that are object lessons in the gradual decay of urban life, with extensive slums and the problems that go with slums. It has the nation's largest convention center, Atlantic City, once the worst boss-ridden community in the country, but now apparently well administered.

Politically, the State is a study in the rise and fall of urban political machines. One after another, machine bosses have assumed dominance over the entire State. Normally the Republican party is in a minority, but sometimes, when there is a Democratic dispute over leadership, the State elects a Republican Administration.

This usually occurs after the Democratic organization is compelled to select a candidate for Governor who will have a wider appeal than usual, because he is not identified with the local machine then dominant, and ultimately a break between him and the machine results. Most recently this was the case of Charles Edison, who not only headed great business enterprises but was identified with the

Roosevelt Administration as Secretary of Navy, where he performed brilliantly. But the battle between Governor Edison and Mayor Frank Hague of Jersey City merely followed a pattern traditional in New Jersey.

The classic combat was that when James Smith, Jr., one of the most charming of American bosses and suzerain of Newark, selected a college president with a progressive philosophy as the ideal candidate to regain Democratic prestige in the State. His candidate won, the students at Princeton celebrated the victory, and the head of the organization learned that he could not control the Governor of New Jersey, who went from that point toward a campaign that swept him into the White House.

As an incident in the battle within the State, New Jersey emerged with what in 1911 was the East's fairest workmen's compensation law, a reasonable system of regulation for utilities, a liberalized measure for municipalities, and one of the most drastic corrupt political practices laws in the nation. From his experience in State government in New Jersey, his first practical experience in public affairs, Woodrow Wilson evolved those ideas on national questions that he expressed as the New Freedom.

It is unfortunate that Wilson is associated in the public mind today principally with his idealistic efforts on behalf of world peace and with his frequent ineptitude in political matters. His domestic policies deserve far more attention than is customarily given them, and the thesis upon which he developed those policies is even more important.

Wilson essentially was a conservative progressive, for all his devotion to democratic processes. He believed that the country faced grave danger from the slaughter of the middle class, especially the small business man, that followed the defeat of Thomas Reed's wing of the Republican party in 1896 by the irresponsibles that clustered around Hanna and his magnificently chiselled replica of a statesman, William McKinley.

The objective of the principal Wilson measures, the Federal Reserve Act, the farm bank measures, and the Clayton Act, was the restoration of a middle class in American society. With a profound sense of justice, he desired to eliminate aspects of regional exploitation; but, primarily, his desire was to maintain the kind of society that he regarded as stable, as capable of retaining political independence for its members, and as offering an opportunity for economic and social advancement to every citizen.

In his New Jersey campaign of 1910, as well as in the Presidential campaigns of 1912 and 1916, he received considerable support from elements that styled themselves progressive. Upon the State level, this was natural enough; for the New Jersey progressive movement which, ironically, originated in Jersey City, was designed to eliminate specific abuses in local and State government. But that Wilson should have been the beneficiary of the movement, of which Albert Beveridge of Indiana was the authoritative spokesman, is wryly humorous.

It is doubtful that two men have shared as few views upon public affairs as the philosopher of 1912 progressivism and the Democratic candidate for President that year. Whether Beveridge and his crew kidnapped Colonel Roosevelt, or whether Theodore Roosevelt used them as window-dressing for his own ambitions, is a matter of debate. Personally, I doubt that the Colonel ever was taken in by another politician, and I doubt that he took seriously the totalitarianism of the doctrinaire progressives.

While there were associated with the progressives in 1912 many men who, within the ranks of the Republican party, had fought against corruption and complacency, and who were disgusted with their failure to get results, the leaders of the group were in favor of many things not compatible with American institutions. They did not oppose monopoly; there were good trusts and bad trusts, they said. They did not oppose imperialism; America had a manifest destiny to become an oppressor of weaker nations. They admitted frankly an inevitable division of the nation into classes, and they desired ameliorative measures that would keep the exploited quiet.

It is no more fair to compare the rank-and-file members of the Bull Moose group with the extremists who systematized its thinking than it is to hold the uninformed citizens of Boston responsible for the existence of the Watch and Ward Society, to which they do not belong and which does not permit them to read anything but the more lascivious scrawlings on the walls of synagogues, if it can help it. But anyone who has read the Beveridge defense of the American Philippine atrocities, or the letter in which Beveridge, the man, endeavors to explain why Beveridge, the politician and hate-monger, would not permit Beveridge, the scholar, to admit the ability and integrity of Roger Brooke Taney as a jurist, will recoil with disgust from the doctrines that found their natural support from the money bags of Frank Munsey and George Perkins.

Wilson's availability as a candidate for Governor grew out of his battle both to democratize and to modernize Princeton, where, as president of one of the nation's great colleges, he was opposed by reactionary groups. Since the fight for education, and especially the fight to make education a force for freedom, always is a popular fight, Wilson became a figure widely known and respected, not only in New Jersey but throughout the country.

When the Essex and Hudson County machines, dominated by James Smith, Jr., decided to accept Wilson as a candidate, they recognized his economic conservatism but did not realize that, entrusted with power, any responsible political leader who is at heart a libertarian must arrive, reluctantly or otherwise, at the conclusion that political freedom must be accompanied by economic freedom. It is almost equally inevitable that he will clash with the machine, before too long.

In Wilson's instance, the break with Smith came quickly, over the Newark leader's demand that he be elevated to the United States Senate by the legislature. Wilson was compelled to reject him, and Smith became, except for George Harvey, his bitterest personal and political enemy. Incidentally, his liberal policies caught the eye of America, and Wilson went on to the White House; but Democratic control in New Jersey was lost in the course of the fighting and was not restored until Frank Hague took over Jersey City and began to extend his power, early in the twenties.

The Wilson-Smith incident suggested several things to me, when I visited New Jersey. I was interested in the reason for some of the failures of the Wilson Administration. I was interested in the reason why New Jersey had been dominated by a series of bosses, and why "boss government" seemed inevitable in its municipalities. And I was in search of a clue to the reason why bosses always broke with the men to whom they were compelled by circumstances to give their support.

One explanation frequently given of Wilson's occasionally disastrous political ineptitudes has been his personality, of which there has been a distorted picture given the nation. Beyond a certain stubbornness, there is nothing in the Wilson portrait, as truly drawn, that indicates any inability to work harmoniously with anyone. He had charm, a flexible mind, remarkable verbal dexterity, and a sense of humor. He was a capable administrator and a sound interpreter of public trends in most cases.

Lack of political experience more nearly accounts for his inability to grasp certain realities. He entered public life when he was past fifty; and while I will not go so far as one of my friends, who holds that to be a competent politician, as to be a great chess master, a start must be made before the age of ten, it is certain that most of the ablest political leaders began their careers early.

Obviously, Wilson's greatest mistake was the inclusion of the Shantung deal with the Japanese in the peace treaty. This alienated many Americans, among them Senator George W. Norris of Nebraska, who applied the same ethical tests to foreign policy that must be applied to domestic policy. A certain inability to evaluate the motives of men in politics prevented Wilson from accepting constructive criticism in a crisis.

On the other hand, he had a more accurate concept of the duties of a President, both as Chief Executive and as party leader, than any occupant of the White House between Lincoln's death and his own assumption of office. This included the recognition of the fact that the President often can appeal to the people over the heads of a reluctant legislative group and compel adoption of popular measures.

The prevalence of bosses in New Jersey is exceptional. Bosses exist or have existed in every section of the nation, although the grain belt and the South have had fewer than their share. But in most instances, the titular boss of an urban machine is no more than the head of a political group, and is responsible to the group if not to the people. In New Jersey, bosses have been responsible to nobody. When a modern New Jersey boss explained his status, he said: "I am the law."

Although I inquired in Trenton, Elizabeth, Newark and Jersey City, nobody that I met could tell me why boss government characterized the State's municipalities. It seems to be a State tradition. Most of the bosses have served the same function as the Southern demagogue, keeping the home folks busy with some kind of show while acting as the agent for external exploiters. New Jersey has been pretty badly exploited by railroads and utilities in its history.

The Wilson-Smith feud, however, offers a rather complete explanation as to why machine bosses always break with other elements in the party. The boss is a most sensitive person. To describe him as a sinister creature is most unfair, and to suggest that he is always dishonest is inaccurate. Some boss-dominated communities have been efficiently and honestly operated. But the political boss always has an intense craving for public recognition. The Smiths and Hannas and Vares all want to go to Washington and, since Mr. Ed Crump, to give him the title to which he is accustomed, is about the only boss extant who can get elected to public office, they are unhappy.

Personal vanity is one of the main driving forces in public life, and the boss is the vainest creature to be found anywhere. Realizing this, the great politicians of our country—Jefferson, Lincoln and Franklin Roosevelt, notably—always stroked the local bosses gently into a purring innocuousness. Lincoln even included Cameron in his Cabinet; FDR usually got by with an invitation to lunch and a "long talk about things up your way."

Informal government is bad and dangerous, but a certain amount of pity ought to be expended upon bosses; they can be rather pathetic at times, between their conferences in smoke-filled rooms.

10: Insubordinate to human governments

The average map of the United States, even those expanded affairs in encyclopedias and geographies that unfold to a full four pages, is not big enough to contain the name of the smallest State, and usually abbreviates it to a simple R.I. Indeed, there are not so very many Americans, I suppose, who know that its name is the longest of any State: The State of Rhode Island and Providence Plantations.

Providence is a thrifty and prospering New England community, where you may find evidence that the American melting pot continues to function. For there are many Celtic and Slav elements mingled there with the descendants of the basic population, itself containing many divergent factors. For Providence Plantations attracted settlers from all over the world who believed that religious freedom was important; and for a time, religious freedom existed nowhere else in the whole world except in this smallest of American colonies. There were Fifth Monarchy men, and Baptists, and Independent Congregationalists, and Seekers, and Quakers, from the British Isles; there were Brethren from Bohemia; there were Roman Catholics from Ireland; there were individualistic thinkers fled from New England; there was the first Jewish Congregation in any of the thirteen colonies, with a synagogue erected upon land given by Roger Williams himself.

The constitution of the State, only sixteen times amended since its adoption in 1842, is unique among such American instruments by making its first reference to religious freedom. Incidentally, the Fourth Section of the First Article is the briefest that I have encountered in any similar State charter, saying tersely: "Slavery shall not be permitted in this State."

Rhode Island can serve as a reminder to all America that one man sometimes can change the destiny of a whole world. Roger Williams always was in flight from antagonists who wished to cut off his head or to hang him or to imprison him for the rest of his days. He was always insubordinate to human governments, when they sought to interfere with human thinking. He rebelled against Charles I; but the triumph of Cromwell did him no good, because one police state was as obnoxious to him as another, and the young author of *The Bloudy Tenent* had to flee to America and the safety of Plymouth. But the religious zealots of Boston would not leave him in peace, for he argued that men had an absolute right to complete religious freedom. He was compelled to flee in mid-winter to the wilderness, and from the Indians, with whom the citizens of his colony never had a disagreement, he bought the lands of Providence Plantations.

Roger Williams detested one thing: "tolerance." He rejected it for himself; he refused it to anyone else; he insulted no man's honesty of conscience by disdainfully offering it to him. He believed in complete freedom, neither more nor less; and in open dispute, about government or religion or anything else. Some of his disputes were notable, especially for length; one of his debates lasted for ten days.

If Jefferson had not known of the Rhode Island experiment and had never read *The Bloudy Tenent,* it is improbable that the guarantee of religious freedom would have been written into the Federal constitution and, eventually, although Connecticut held back for long, into every State constitution in our land.

Delaware, the East's other tiny Commonwealth, once belonged to the Swedish Crown and was conquered by the Dutch, then annexed to England. Its three major products are corporations, Du Ponts and cranberries. Wilmington is headquarters for thousands of companies that do not function in the State, but that obtained charters there because of the lax corporation laws. Wilmington and its suburbs hold half the population of the State, which includes the highest proportion of Negro citizens to be found in the East, a reminder that once the plantation system flourished that far toward the north.

The Du Ponts, descendants of a French radical who was a staunch friend of Jefferson, control an enormous chemicals, explosives and synthetics empire and are the most influential stockholders of General Motors. They take a paternalistic pride in Delaware, giving the people roads as casual gifts. One branch of the family split off to establish a rival Florida satrapy about 1920, but the pattern of household government was not shaken by that incident.

Rural Delaware, inhabited by descendants of Swedish, Finnish and Dutch early settlers, reputedly is one of the quaintest parts of the East, yet untouched by visitors and unaffected by the industrial influences about Wilmington.

New Hampshire has the smallest coastline of any State fronting on the Atlantic, but I found Portsmouth's harbor filled with ships when I visited there. New Hampshire supplies something more than a setting for Stephen Vincent Benét's folk classic, "The Devil and Daniel Webster"; it contains two notable monuments, the United States frigate *Constitution* and Senator Charles W. Tobey, something of a pre-Pearl Harbor isolationist, which was rare for the East, and one of the most intelligently responsible conservatives on domestic issues to be found in the Congress.

Georgia's share in "Old Ironsides" made me take a special interest in the little vessel. The *Constitution* is the pride of Portsmouth's great naval yard. The victories of the fleet and maneuverable American ship in the War of 1812 enheartened the nation. Its tough oaken sides were cut from giant trees on St. Simons Island, Georgia, on the border of the battleground where Oglethorpe defeated the Spanish at Bloody Marsh, the most decisive engagement yet fought on North American soil, determining that the language and customs of the thirteen colonies should be English instead of Spanish.

Maine began its history as a lumber State, continued it as a builder of privateers and clippers, and now has been converted into a great playground. Portland, burned by Indians, devastated by the British, victim of a fire that wiped out almost every house in 1866, occupies so strategic a site on its peninsula, with 365 islands clustering at its feet, that it always was rebuilt better than before. Its industries, however, seem to be declining, but its prosperity as the center of the vacation area is mounting.

I remember Bar Harbor as the society center of the East. Its streets were lined with shops transplanted from Fifth Avenue or Madison Avenue in New York for the convenience of the party-going vacationers.

Looking at Bar Harbor, it took a great many statistics to convince one that Maine has a very large French Canadian population, much of which has been there since Wolfe's storming of the Plains of Abraham, and that Senator Brewster represents the State. Bar Harbor is rebuilding; the great fire of 1947 did not seal its doom.

11: THEY WANT FAIR SOLUTIONS

The East is conscious that it is losing its position of leadership in the nation. Economists of the modern schools, who seem to be somewhat pessimistic individuals, see symptoms in the region of a maturing socio-economic order; perhaps it would be better to describe the condition they say they see as one of calcification.

They discern in the falling birth rate, for example, a future in which the population of the East will be reduced. They see in the failure of Eastern incomes to rise as rapidly as those in other sections a tendency toward levelling off of its prosperity. They do not all agree that a "managed economy" is essential to the welfare of the East, but many of them think so.

That general pessimism was not shared by the people of the region. I detected few symptoms of a loss of courage and vitality among citizens of the East. Most of them concurred that decentralization was inevitable in this country. Most of them anticipated some resultant redistribution of population. But they did not seem to be distressed about these things.

I found them concerned about the same problems that concerned the citizens of other sections, although the emphasis varied somewhat.

There was a greater consciousness of the necessity of eliminating racial and religious prejudices. The East is not homogeneous, and it is essential that these tensions be reduced. Although I found no traces, outside Boston, of the tension that characterizes Detroit and Chicago, I found a greater consciousness of the problem. There was also a greater willingness to work toward a solution.

In New England, the issue of civil liberties is smouldering. Labor-baiting is a characteristic of reactionaries of that region, and in the industrial areas there is discoverable a greater class-consciousness than anywhere else in America.

The cost of living topped all other discussions. The effects of inflation are serious in some parts of the East. The tax structure bears much more heavily on the lower-income groups, intensifying the feeling of class exploitation.

Nowhere else in America did I find a caste system dividing ownership, management, professional groups, small farmers, and industrial workers so sharply. I construe that as one of the principal dangers to the nation at this time, and it is susceptible of only one solution.

To restore the American vision of a classless society, it is essential that opportunity be given to every individual and that every section of the nation be developed. The policy of retaining the Western and Southern States as colonial appendages, to be exploited for the benefit of an imperial East, has resulted in greater harm to the East than to the colonies. It has resulted in a decrepitude of Eastern agriculture, in a stratification of society, and in the development of many social tensions.

The solution of the East's problems is the restoration of a system of free enterprise in this country, the elimination of internal trade barriers, the reassertion of the doctrine of competition, and the decentralization of production. Economically the East suffers because the cost of transportation has advanced so greatly that its importance as a manufacturing and distributing center necessarily must decline. The artificial devices for profit-making, that temporarily stimulated its economy, have been as deleterious as an overdose of some powerful drug.

Centralization of industry and of financial power inevitably will be accompanied by a centralization of political control and regulation. Because of this, the East is America's danger spot.

On the other hand, there is detectable none of the effeteness and morbidity that some critics of the East assert they see; or the Chicago *Tribune* did not send its representatives to see the people with whom I talked.

For all the economic and social problems that exist, the people of the New England and North Atlantic States are seeking solutions. They want fair solutions. They want the same thing that all other Americans want: a decent home, a life of reasonable comfort, in a peaceful world.

☆ IV ☆

NERVE CENTER

Novus Ordo Seclorum.
—FRANKLIN'S MOTTO FOR THE
GREAT SEAL OF THE UNITED STATES

1: THE SERGEANT WAS CONSPICUOUS

Everywhere there are lobbyists and generals. The occupants of the lounges and coffee shop of the Mayflower Hotel hardly glance about at the generals, unless they wear more than two stars; but they watch the lobbyists, for lobbyists are important in this city that is named after George Washington and that was planted on a site selected by Thomas Jefferson and given a beautiful design by L'Enfant. Lobbyists have been important again in Washington since early in 1942. Prior to that time, they had been more or less underground for almost ten years. The war brought them back, to act as advisers to those who wanted war contracts, or who needed to know their way about Washington for one reason or another. The end of the war found them once more entrenched, their influence higher than since 1929 on Capitol Hill.

The generals came with the war, too. They also are reluctant to go. Many of them hold or hope to hold civilian appointments.

There are office buildings full of lobbyists, representing tin, copper,

154

rubber, the Peron government in Argentina, the Falangist dictator of Spain, Communist groups, fellow-travellers, public utilities, manufacturing groups, labor groups, farm groups, men who want their taxes reduced and your taxes ultimately increased, real estate speculators, world cartels in drugs, and, especially, oil and transportation.

The man who took me to lunch that day observed that the oil lobby was the most apprehensive in Washington, because of the critical association of oil with foreign policy, but that the transportation lobby was the most powerful and the most ubiquitous.

Three generals walked through the coffee shop. Their passage evoked no interest in my companion; they only wore two stars; in fact, one of them may have worn only one star, since he was hurrying and looked a little embarrassed. Then my friend broke off his line of conversation to indicate another visitor.

"He specializes in German corporations," he observed. "Those de-Nazification affairs and the like. It's going to be quite a business before things are through."

I expressed wonder.

"Some of the men behind the Nazi bunch were careful to take out insurance. They had a good many tricks, such as Swiss corporations that owned Swedish corporations that owned the stock of the German corporations. Some of them even had relatives who were conveniently anti-Nazi, and who 'escaped' from Germany just before the invasion of Poland, and who have strange claims to ownership of the assets. With a great many records destroyed during the war, some of the claims will stick," he went on. "The fellow you saw handles those kinds of things. I don't know the routine, and he may be a fake. Some of them are. But it's going to be quite a racket. Maybe you remember the days after 1921, and what happened in the Enemy Property office. This time the stakes are a hundred, maybe a thousand, times higher than they were then."

A free-lance lobbyist, or so he was identified, stuck his head in the room briefly, but vanished before my friend could tell me about his activities. A sergeant came in, with a pretty girl. I guessed, from the way he talked as he passed our table, that he came from Minnesota; my companion argued in favor of Michigan. We wanted to ask, but it would have been an intrusion; the sergeant was conspicuous enough without visitors to his table; he was the only man in uniform who wasn't an officer.

2: THESE ARE HARD-WORKING MEN

A certain tolerance should be accorded the lobbyist under any circumstance, and a definite respect is due him if he is openly identified. Not only is the presentation of the views of any group a basic right guaranteed by the Federal constitution, and not only does the aboveboard lobbyist perform certain useful functions, but the profession is as old as American government.

The glorious days of the lobbyist were during the Grant Administration, when land grants, bond guarantees for railroads, and tariff measures offered exceptional opportunities for the skillful. Indeed, the gossips of 1871 recorded that one lobbyist sold his influence with each member of Congress on each vote, contingently, and always to both sides; he prospered greatly until it was discovered that he knew not a single member of House or Senate by sight.

But the lobbyist has surrounded Congress from the beginning. Dignified men visited the members of the First Congress to argue effectively for a very adroitly framed measure assuming the various obligations of the Continental Congress and of the several States.

A marvelous lobby was assembled by the Bank of the United States, during the Jackson era. Like the lobby of the Era of Wonderful Nonsense, it moved on many fronts. There were friendly gentlemen with open purses, who paid in cash. There were genteel individuals, who could discount a note for a friendly Senator and assure him that there would be no hurry about settlement. There were local political bigwigs, who could argue that they controlled enough votes to make a difference. There were ladies, some of them part of the social lobby that glittered goldenly and some of them of quite a different kind of lobby that seems to have been gilded rather than golden.

Some of those lobbies were rather costly to the people. That of the First Congress obtained enactment of an assumption measure that wrenched sharply the economy of those of the thirteen States, including Georgia, that had paid their share of the cost of the Revolution in cash and supplies instead of in paper money. That of Jackson's day, except for incidentally almost embroiling the nation in war with treasonable intentions, had little success. That of Grant's era stole most of the public domain, or traded it for contracts giving the government preferential transportation rates, which the even more voracious railroad lobby of 1946 managed to get annulled. That of the 1920s helped speed the depression, but, on the whole, chiefly duped the gullible among business men, who contributed gladly to anything in an era when it was obvious to anyone, except those who could tell a plugged nickel from a twenty dollar gold piece, that prosperity was here to stay forever.

Most lobbyists, however, are hard-working men. Some of them have good political contacts, of course; but their principal duties are to analyze measures and present their client's side of the story as effectively as possible. There is no reason why this should not be done, if it is done openly. It may even be useful to the public. For there is no reason why a measure specially beneficial to one group or one interest must be hurtful to everyone else. Chiefly in a negative manner, by carefully checking legislation and examining proposals, some of the lobbyists perform a public service, even if unintentionally.

The trouble with the lobby business is that the people are not wholly represented. There is no consumers' lobby in any real sense, though every producer of importance has his lobbyist.

There are governmental lobbies functioning also. Again it is difficult to determine the precise limits within which they should be permitted to function. It is obviously legitimate for a Federal employee to present the case of his agency to Congress, in matters of legislation and appropriations. Yet some of the interdepartmental battles for power have been costly to the people of the United States; that between the Bureau of Reclamation and the Army Engineers over the development of the Missouri basin has been exceedingly expensive, for example.

To this lobbying by employees and officials may be charged the sometimes one-sided growth of departments. Due to the exceptional talents of America's early occupants of the post of Secretary of State, the State Department became a clutter of disrelated duties. Some years later, when it was decided that it would be desirable to utilize the services of West Point's well-trained men and give them practical experience in engineering, many duties of a wholly civilian nature were thrust upon the Army Engineers and much flood control work came to be associated with the Department of War. The maze of subsidiary bureaus under the Departments of Agriculture and of the Interior sometimes results in apparent duplications of services and authority. When Herbert Hoover was Secretary of Commerce, he set out upon a program of departmental expansion that resulted in a virtual duplication of the consular service and in the absorption of many functions into an agency not equipped to deal with them.

This struggle between departments and bureaus and independent offices has both comic and serious aspects. The lobbying efforts of officials sometimes are associated with the struggle for social eminence, a result of Washington's abandonment under McKinley of its tradition of republican democracy and its imitation of the protocol of European courts. Vice President Charles Curtis' battle for the precedence of his sister, Mrs. Dolly Gann, is only the most ridiculous of many such affairs.

But for all the vicious aspects of the lobbying techniques, I am heartily against any suppression of lobbying. The requirements for registration and identification should be more rigid, unquestionably; but the right to endeavor to persuade members of the Congress by argument is a basic right.

Interference with those rights represents a more serious challenge to democracy than their abuse. Freedom can be destroyed effectively by those who insist that it is best to give up some phase of freedom or another to protect the rest.

3: SOMETIMES THE GUIDE REMEMBERS

There are three sights in Washington that I try never to miss when I visit the city. They are in the guide books that sightseers buy, yet two of them often are missed.

One, of course, is the panorama of Washington from the Monument. You can see the government buildings, and especially the noble memorials erected to Jefferson and to Lincoln.

On my last visit, a small boy inquired of his father if someone had not caught a baseball thrown from the top window of the Monument. Somebody supplied the information that Gabby Street, who was with the Senators and the Cardinals, was the man that held onto the ball. Someone else observed that Walter Johnson once threw a silver dollar across the Rappahannock, in emulation of George Washington, and the inevitable wag observed that a dollar would go farther in those days.

In the old House Chamber of the Capitol is a small brass marker. Sometimes the guide who is conducting the visitors about the building pauses briefly to identify it; sometimes he passes it by. It carries no legend whatsoever, so that occasionally someone who is curious asks a Capitol attendant why it is there. It marks the spot where John Quincy Adams' desk stood, and where he was speaking on that day in 1848 when he crumpled to the floor in the midst of a final plea for the right of petition.

I have dealt harshly in my thoughts, sometimes, with Massachusetts. Yet as surely as a man deserves to be judged by his moments of selflessness and high courage, a State deserves to be judged by the best that it can produce; and Massachusetts produced John

Quincy Adams, and no public servant before or since in our history has possessed greater integrity.

You may charge him with every one of his faults: a certain pettiness in little things, a touch of self-righteousness, a temper not always agreeable, a tongue more used to dispensing vitriol than honey, a want of charity in interpreting the motives of other men, and even perhaps a certain pride of intellect. They were shy men, the Adams father and son, and they command respect long before they win affection. Sometimes they are slightly ridiculous; but they were good men in a brawl, and, with due deference to Jefferson's devotion to the father, I rather think the son was the better fighting man.

He started life with the intention of becoming a career man in government. His respect for the views of Madison led him to enter the political party that had defeated his father for President of the United States. He served ably as a diplomat, and entered Monroe's Cabinet as Secretary of State. In 1824, in the election of a President by the House, the Clay group swung to Adams and he defeated Andrew Jackson, the popular favorite, and Georgia's William H. Crawford. He faced an economic crisis, in the middle of which he was assailed for an alleged political trade with Clay. His accuser was John Randolph of Roanoke, whose command of expletive remains unequalled. He was defeated for reëlection by Jackson. His career appeared over, at the age of sixty-two. One might expect him to retire to his native countryside. He did; for two years.

But with his entry into the House of Representatives in 1831, he there spent seventeen years of his best services to his country.

In one sense, his greatest usefulness to America was in the dispute over the French claims. He supported President Jackson with an eloquence and effectiveness that was enhanced by the personal differences between the two men. He exposed ruthlessly the ignoble politics that verged on treason. He enabled the Jackson Administration to obtain preparedness measures that prevented war and preserved national dignity.

But his great victory was in the long fight over the right of petition. For ten years, almost every day, he fought for the enforcement of the First Amendment.

During the Van Buren Administration, following the leadership of John C. Calhoun, Congress made a practice of rejecting and refusing to read petitions dealing with any phase of the slavery question. At that time the issue of extension of slaveholding territory was a major issue. Kansas already was bleeding. Slaveowners wished new lands; abolitionists wanted slavery extirpated everywhere, with no compensation to the owners; yeoman-farmers in the Western areas were not too interested in the dispute, except that they were determined that neither slavery nor the plantation system should intrude themselves upon their way of life.

Adams insisted that the people had a complete right to petition the Congress for any action that lay within the power of that body. The correctness of his constitutional position can not be denied. No petition to the Congress could be acceptable that dealt with a matter upon which the body could not act; no petition upon a question within the scope of legislative authority could properly be denied consideration. Not only was Adams' position sound constitutionally, considering only the written words of the First Amendment; his position was sound logically under any rational concept of democratic processes under a representative form of government.

Not only the extremists among representatives of the slave states opposed Adams' views and denounced him; many conservative, compromising ostriches were even more bitter. The old man, they said, was stirring up unnecessary trouble; the right of petition was not that important.

The ingenuity of Adams' attack must delight all parliamentarians. His entry into the Chamber each day began a one-man filibuster. Almost each day he had a new petition with him, which he offered solemnly to the Chair. Sardonically deft in dealing with his opponents, he presented all kinds of petitions dealing with the forbidden subject: to extend the areas into which slavery might be permitted; to purchase and manumit slaves; to eliminate slavery within the District of Columbia. When some members talked of expelling him from the House, he solemnly provided a petition with many signatures urging that this be done.

The entire House of Representatives could not cope with his forensic adroitness and his tough-fibred tenacity. Ultimately the House acceded to his view, worn out with a struggle between an overwhelming majority in the wrong and an angry old man in the right.

Today the battle over the right of petition may seem a little thing. With the possible exception of the courageous fight in 1861 by Roger Brooke Taney for the preservation of civil processes, and the action of the Supreme Court in 1943 in reversing itself in the instances of certain school children accused of the grave crime of refusing to salute the American flag because of religious convictions, it was the most important triumph for constitutional liberties in American history. Once the people are denied the right to present their wishes and their complaints to their government, they have acknowledged a degree of sovereignty in their creation that leaves the gateway open for every possible abuse and every totalitarian practice.

The third of Washington's great sights is to be encountered at Tenth and D Streets and is passed daily by many hurrying hundreds. Few stop to look at the statue, which stands at sidewalk level and which is only a little bigger than life. It is one of not very many great portrayals of America's heroes; it is a very plain likeness of a plainly but prosperously dressed gentleman, a bit past middle age, who seems to be thinking as he walks, and thinking not unpleasant thoughts. Whether it is an accurate likeness of Benjamin Franklin, I do not know; it looks a little like George Babbitt become mellower and wiser, in fancy dress, and become somewhat taller in stature, too.

Here is the average man, grown great on food unlike that which the Caesars ate. There is nothing about Franklin as a man of his age that can be called remarkable except his versatility. Priestley was a better scientist. Sam Adams was a better revolutionist. Jefferson was a better diplomat. Tom Paine was a better pamphleteer. Morris was a more skillful financier. Washington enjoyed more prestige. Hancock made more money. But the only man who may be considered indispensable to the Revolution was Dr. Franklin.

Of all the men who made the Revolution, he had the most to lose. His prominence in American life was great. His acquaintanceship abroad was extensive. His position was assured. His wealth was considerable, and he had reached an age when ambition did not beckon. On July 4, 1776, when he joined Thomas Jefferson and John Adams in presenting Jefferson's text of the Declaration to the Continental Congress, he already had passed his seventieth birthday.

Suddenly this staid and successful elderly gentleman became the most radical figure of the Revolution. Risking a lifetime's accumulation of property and eminence, he threw himself into the fight for freedom. He found himself the companion of European libertarians, republicans, challengers of the old order. He became the foe of every form of intellectual complacency as well as one of the earliest of America's abolitionists. He discovered himself using his two most effective weapons, charm and satire, to build a new world. A Frenchman later was to say of him that Franklin "invented bifocals, republics, and hoaxes."

His sense of humor and his realism never deserted him. In 1776 he was to tell the members of the Congress that "we must all hang together or we shall hang separately"; the month before his death he was to quote mockingly fictitious passages from the Koran to urge, after the fashion of Swift's technique in *A Modest Proposal,* the reasonableness of Mohammedans keeping Christian slaves, in a reply to General James Jackson's defense of slavery in the United States. The gift of laughter with which he was born, his only heritage, never was lost or wasted or dissipated; he conserved it for emergencies with as much thrift as he conserved the pennies that he earned, or the youthful experience that he obtained in turning grindstones.

Whoever had the imagination to place Ben Franklin's statue on the street, where it might stand on the level of other men, watching them serenely and smilingly and compassionately and a little mockingly, understood the man. Whoever made him look like the epitome of all the average men in America read accurately the heart of the plain fellow who could draw down the lightning from the sky with only a schoolboy's kite for equipment and overthrow a king with the laughter of ordinary folk.

4: THE WATCHDOG IS CHAINED UP

Washington is many things. There is social Washington, which is important to old local families, climbers, diplomats, lobbyists, and those who enjoy watching all these in action. There is the half-world of the lobbyist, which somehow touches all other worlds. There is the political community, centering around the rival headquarters of the major parties and around the White House and the House and Senate Office Buildings. Finally there is governmental Washington, which looks after the collective affairs of some hundred and forty-five million Americans.

Official Washington is contained in a book. The Congressional Directory consists of nine hundred nineteen pages, of which nineteen are a table of contents and fifty-eight an index. The other eight hundred forty-two pages will tell you precisely who is who and where you can find the department, bureau, agency, division, authority, commission or board that you are seeking. Or the Congressman from your district; or any of the representatives of newspapers, magazines or radio, for that matter. There are forty-two pages of small type devoted to lists of those entitled to admittance to the various press galleries.

Besides the departments presided over by Cabinet members, and the welfare, social security and unemployment compensation units of the Federal Security Agency, and the great loan agencies, there are scores of independent units that have been created by the Congress or by Presidential order. These range from the skeletal remains of the great war production agencies to such permanent fixtures as the Caribbean Commission, the Washington National Monument Society, and the Joint Economy Board; the last appears to have no members of the board, but does possess a secretary.

If you enter the Justice Building, which occupies the space on Constitution Avenue between Ninth and Tenth Streets, you will find one agency that is entrusted with protecting the public against monopoly, and individual business men against conspiracies in restraint of trade.

Those who believe that employees of the Federal government live lives of leisure may examine the description of the duties assigned to the Assistant Attorney-General of the United States who heads this division. These are set out rather succinctly, and, perhaps, with more bluntness than literary grace, on page 575 of the Directory:

"This Assistant has special charge of all suits and other matters relating to and arising under the Sherman and Clayton Acts and acts with antitrust provisions.

"In addition he has, under current assignment, charge of matters relating to and arising under the Agricultural Adjustment Acts of 1933 and 1938, Agricultural Marketing Agreements Act of 1937, Anti-Racketeering Act (in conjunction with anti-trust violations), Ashurst-Sumners Act, Capper-Volstead Act, Civil Aeronautics Act of 1938, Commodity Exchange Act, Communications Act of 1934, Connally Act, Elkins Act, Federal Alcohol Administration Act of 1935, Federal Register Act of 1935, Federal Trade Commission Act of 1914, Interstate Commerce Act, Land Grant Act of 1866, Packers and Stockyards Act, Perishable Agricultural Commodities Act, Produce Agency Act, Public Utility Holding Company Act, Railway Labor Act, Robinson-Patman Act, Securities Act of 1933, Securities Exchange Act of 1934, Small Business Act of 1942, Sugar Act of 1937, Surplus Property Act of 1944, Tennessee Valley

Authority Act, Tobacco Inspection Act, Transportation Act of 1940, War Mobilization and Reconversion Act of 1944, and the Webb Export Trade Act. He has charge of briefs and arguments in the Supreme Court on assignment by the Solicitor General, and of special assignments by the Attorney General; also representation on the Interdepartmental Committee on Cartels."

To carry on all this work, there is appropriated by the Congress approximately two million dollars a year.

Each year, six hundred fifty complaints are made by business men to the Anti-Trust Division of the Department of Justice. About fifty actual cases are filed annually, because the division is kept without funds with which to conduct investigations and enforce the law.

Today, when two hundred fifty corporations control approximately two-thirds of all the manufacturing facilities of the nation, and considerably more facilities than even existed in the United States in 1940, the watchdog of the people is being effectively chained up. It is small wonder that such men as Thurman Arnold and Wendell Berge, who fought so effectively for the rights of small business, retired from the assignment eventually.

Berge described the predicament in rather blistering language,

"For more than forty years each political party rendered continuous homage to the principles of the Sherman Act, and yet in practical economic effect during that period the law was a dead letter. I think that today we are paying the price of our failure to make effective the principles of the Sherman Act. Someone has said that the only thing that history has proved is that we don't learn anything from history. I surely hope in this case, at least, that is wrong.

"The real source of the threat to free enterprise . . . lies in monopolistic control over our great industries. If we really believe what we constantly say about the necessity of preserving free enterprise, then the time to act on those affirmations of belief is now. The fight to maintain free, competitive enterprise should transcend purely partisan or political considerations. Now is the time when you must demand and require that your Government continue to act decisively and effectively to prevent the further spread of cóncentration of economic power. You must demand that the channels of free, competitive enterprise be kept open for small business. . . ."

He said:

"The future of enterprise is in many respects the major economic issue of our age. In most of the world today we are witnessing the disappearance of free enterprise in the aftermath of war and economic crisis. Because this country is the industrial leader of the world, because its institutions are still free, and because its natural and human resources are vigorous, we still have the luxury of choice between economic freedom and a system of control.

"It is sheer delusion to believe that we can tolerate regimentation by monopoly without in time necessitating regimentation by government. If we forsake the principles upon which economic freedom rests by failing to apply them, freedom will forsake us. There is no question as to which way freedom lies. The danger is that in the affairs of men it is always later than we think."

In Georgia's historic suit against the transportation monopoly, which was throttling industrial expansion in the Southern and Western States through freight rate structures that made shipments of Southern and Western manufactures to markets almost prohibitive, the Anti-Trust Division provided invaluable assistance. Indeed, Arnold, Berge, and Wiprud of this division tackled part of the same problem through action against the Western Conference, an organization of railroads that fixed rates and even prohibited imperative improvement in safety appliances.

Monopoly menaces every American. Among the products that are under the control of or menaced by monopolists are aluminum, magnesium, matches, optical lenses, shoe-making machinery, drugs and pharmaceuticals, nylon, explosives, synthetic rubber, special-alloy steels, and radios; certainly an impressive if by no means comprehensive list of necessities. There are also monopolies in communications and transportation.

In the field of communications, it is probably impossible to have competition, and the people must rely upon regulation for protection. Transportation, however, is not the natural monopoly that its long and highly profitable association with government suggests. The rail lines, like the roads we drive cars upon, were built largely by public rather than private enterprise. Strong elements of competition are possible between rails, highways, waterways and air transport.

Since 1876, when a group of Southern Bourbons made their ignominious deal with the Republican party and deserted the cause of Samuel J. Tilden by agreeing to the creation of the extra-legal Electoral Commission that defrauded him of the election, the Southern and Western States have been ruthlessly exploited with the "freight rate differential" as the device of the exploiters. Rail rates were so juggled that a subsidy was given Eastern manufacturers on raw products moving from the colonial South and West. Rail rates on manufactures in these regions were placed at a level thirty-nine per cent or more higher, to prevent competition with Eastern manufacturers.

Gradually, as ownership became less associated with operations of the railroads and the transportation companies fell into the clutches of bankers, on the one hand, and a vast, amorphous, expensive and wholly incompetent managerial bureaucracy, on the other, the condition grew worse.

If this criticism of the management of transportation companies seems a trifle harsh, there are two tests of its verity that the public may employ. One is a comparison of the average efficiency of operations, comfort of passengers, and safety of transport with that on those few lines where ownership, or at least limited ownership, exercises some control, such as those rail companies associated with the Vanderbilts. The other test is an examination of the record submitted by that annoying gadfly of the rail bureaucrats, Robert

R. Young, the brilliant adventurer who controls Chesapeake and Ohio and the remnants of the Van Sweringen empire, and who knows how railroads are financed and how they are run.

Young has been described as a social-minded individual by some people, and as an old-fashioned robber baron by others. In either event, he believes that competition is an essential element in American business and that efficiently operated railroads can make money. More annoying, to the slow-as-molasses bureaucrats of rival lines and the fast-as-a-botfly bankers who perennially place those lines in profitable receiverships, Young has demonstrated that his methods can make a railroad prosperous. The C&O makes money, and the dilapidated properties tied to it in the Van Sweringen scheme are getting back on their feet.

Young believes that comfortable trains would get passengers. He urges that the railroads replace their forty-four thousand antiquated coaches, sleeping cars, diners and baggage cars with new rolling stock. His investigations disclosed that there are 5,200 sleepers that average twenty-seven years old, and fifteen thousand coaches with an average age of twenty-eight years. To replace all this junk, the railroads are ordering cars at a rate of fifteen hundred a year.

Chesapeake and Ohio, however, ordered enough passenger cars to replace every piece of equipment on its main line. Passengers ride the C&O, in a day when general train travel is declining.

It appears to be Young's belief that financial manipulation is at the bottom of the collapse of the railroads, their inability to earn anything on their investments, and their loss of business. But he does not overlook the fact that they have been badly managed as well as badly controlled.

As a practical man, he would like to see the railroads prosper through a policy of cheap and efficient transportation, and contribute to the general prosperity thereby. He would like to see dividends for stockholders and an eventual elimination of long-term bonded debts. He thinks it can be done. Indeed, to the annoyance of his fellow-railroad monarchs, he is doing it.

I am inclined to think that perhaps Young's own experiences with banker-control over railroads, which were at least moderately unpleasant, may have caused him to put emphasis upon the lesser of the two evils. The refinancing of bonds under private bids, and some of the other financial hocus-pocus in the railroad picture have been very hurtful to the transportation system that the Federal government, the States and the towns of America presented to the promoters who built the railroads. But fundamentally, it is my contention in a dissent from Young's views, the greater injury has been the divorce of ownership from management and the erection of an irresponsible control over the lines.

Once the stockholder is turned into an investor, and we talk about private management instead of talking about private enterprise, we are heading for the kind of thing that happened in Middle Europe.

5: Words have a meaning

The railroads insisted, in answer to Georgia's suit, that they were engaged in no violation of the Sherman and Clayton anti-trust laws. They were innocuous, immaculate, innocent, law abiding, public spirited, and many other things that added up to being not guilty. Nevertheless, with the biggest and most expensive lobby that has been seen around Washington in twenty years, they descended upon Congressmen and asked for a law exempting them from the anti-trust statutes and permitting them to do the things they said they were not doing through their maze of bureaus, conferences, boards, commissions, leagues and associations. The measure they desired is known as the Bulwinkle Bill, after an obscure North Carolina Congressman who introduced it. The bill would permit transportation companies to engage in conspiracies in restraint of trade. If enacted, it would undo what Georgia has succeeded in doing by getting the Supreme Court to accept jurisdiction of the case.

There seemed, in 1946, to be some likelihood that the measure might get through the Senate, as it previously had the House, and prevent our presentation to the Supreme Court of the vast mass of evidence that had been collected. Because of this, I paid a call upon the President of the United States.

The room that I entered was the same in which I had talked with Franklin D. Roosevelt, but much of the atmosphere had changed. Gone were the scores of little ornaments that crowded the desk and that spoke of Roosevelt's magnificent versatility, sense of humor, occasional untidiness of mind that let loose ends gather, and his amazing capacity for improvisation. The desk of President Truman had on it a small pile of documents that he had been working with; otherwise it was bare; he likes a clean desk and quick decisions.

I outlined to him the position of Georgia's suit in the Supreme Court, telling him that we had won the right to a trial and that the evidence was being presented to the court's special master, Lloyd Garrison, and that the railroads hoped to get the Bulwinkle Bill enacted into law before the Supreme Court could hand down a decision. I urged that, if the bill were passed and came to his desk, he veto it.

"Governor Arnall, the people of the various districts elect the Congressmen," President Truman observed. "The people of the forty-eight States elect the Senators. The President and the Vice President are the only men elected by all of the people to look after their business. I am going to do that, to the best of my ability, and I'll look into this bill."

A few days later it was reported that the President would not approve the measure, on the recommendation of the Department of Justice. The bill did not reach his desk. Its advocates temporarily abandoned it, because they could not hope to obtain more than a bare majority at the best, and had no chance to get the two-thirds required to pass it over a Presidential veto. President Truman had done precisely what he said that he would do; he had looked into the bill and then had carried out his obligation as the only living

Federal officeholder chosen by all of the people of the United States to look after the business of all of the people.

That afternoon, as a taxi hurried me from my hotel toward the station where I was to catch a train for Atlanta, I drew out a dollar bill to pay the fare.

A dollar bill is something that you see every day. Its face is familiar, and you never stop to examine the different features. This time, however, I happened to really look at it and to note the reverse of the Great Seal, which is on the left of the back of the bill.

The motto for the seal was one proposed by Benjamin Franklin, who had a nice touch for providing phrases in Latin for superscriptions of that kind. It was: *"Novus ordo seclorum."*

I was an indifferent Latin scholar at Newnan High School, and when I went to Sewanee I studied Greek instead; but I remembered enough from the glossary in the back of my first-year Latin book to translate those words.

Perhaps not too exactly or too elegantly; but at least so that they have meaning for me and for most Americans:

"Novus ordo seclorum—a New Deal in the world."

SOUTH

1: SECURE IN THEIR HOMES AND PERSONS

The evening of March 18, 1947, had been unpleasant. The drizzle and the lowering skies continued as I caught a late plane from Pittsburgh to Baltimore. The next morning, when I went down to breakfast, the day had not cleared and a fine mist was falling over the city. But a little later the sun came out.

My engagement with Dr. Stanley A. Ginsburgh, Chairman of the Beth Tfiloh Forum for whom I was to lecture that evening, was for noon; so I set out to explore briefly the city that the Calverts had founded. Ultimately I came to a square, where there stood an obelisk honoring George Washington, believed to be the earliest monument to the First President. I turned from the monument and walked down one of the pathways, and came face to face with one of the most extraordinary statues that I have seen.

As if he were cold, an aged man sat slightly awry in a large chair, clutching about him his judicial robes. His face was calm and ascetic, with a high, intellectual forehead. Somehow in bronze had been caught the portrait of Roger Brooke Taney, Chief Justice of the United States of America, as he must have looked on that morning in May 1861, when he delivered one of the most important opinions ever handed down by a judicial officer in the history of our country.

Outside the very courtroom in which he sat, soldiers marched with flashing bayonets, jeering at the old man who had been the companion and fellow-warrior of Andrew Jackson. Every force in America was against him, except that of right.

Before him had come a petition for the writ of habeas corpus, sworn to by one George H. Williams of the City of Baltimore and the District of Maryland, who had made, in the quaint juridical language of that day, "oath on the Holy Evangels of Almighty God, the facts stated in the foregoing petition are true," and that one John Merryman of Baltimore had been aroused from his bed by an armed force, deprived of his liberty, and removed from his home to Fort McHenry, and was now in close custody, without any process or color of law whatsoever.

The facts in the case are plain. John Merryman sympathized with the South in the sectional quarrel brewing, and expressed his views with considerable vigor. Acting on the orders of Major-General William H. Keim, Colonel Samuel Hohe had invaded the Merryman home at two in the morning, awakened its master, dragged him away and turned him over to Major-General George Cadwalader, for safekeeping at Fort McHenry. John Merryman's counsel was denied access to him. He was charged with no crime, nor detained as a witness; neither was any warrant issued, nor was he carried before a committing magistrate.

Merryman's arrest occurred in the early hours of May 25, 1861.

On the following day, his attorney having been denied access to him, application was made to Mr. Chief Justice Taney in Washington for a writ of habeas corpus, which was granted promptly.

The Chief Justice did not order production of the prisoner nor answer by the officer holding him, in Washington, but travelled to Baltimore to hear the case, for the convenience of witnesses and because he did not desire to order a soldier away from his military assignment. At that time Taney was eighty-four.

General Cadwalader, in a courteously phrased letter, declined to produce the prisoner or to recognize the authority of the court. On Monday, May 27, Mr. Chief Justice Taney directed Washington Bonifant, United States Marshal for the District of Maryland, to apprehend the General and bring him before the court on a writ of attachment. At the gates of the fort, the laughing soldiers denied Bonifant admission.

Thus conditions stood at noon on May 28, 1861, when Roger Brooke Taney, Chief Justice of the United States, acting as circuit justice for the District of Maryland, sat down in the courtroom in Baltimore, in much the attitude that is represented by his statue in the pleasant little park.

He read the return of the Marshal of the District Court, and then proceeded immediately to summarize his position in terse language:

"A military officer has no right to arrest and detain a person not subject to the rules and articles of war, for an offense against the laws of the United States except in aid of the judicial authority, and subject to its control; and if the party be arrested by the military, it is the duty of the officer to deliver him over immediately to the civil authority, to be dealt with according to law."

That single long sentence was amplified later, in his written opinion, into the decision bearing the name: "Ex parte Merryman." The rather lengthy text, to be found in *17 Federal Cases, Years 1789–1880*, is worthy of very careful study. It is the leading case in the nation upon civil rights, as well as a thoughtful and mature scrutiny of the historical background from which those rights obtained. In the history of America, no more vigorous defense of human liberty has been penned, for all the judicial language employed. Merryman continued to languish in a military prison, but no case has done more to establish the rights of individuals to be secure in their homes and persons, to be afforded counsel when they are accused, to be safe from imprisonment except through due process of law.

Taney has been the victim of much cruel misrepresentation, and it is only fair to point out that the doctrine set forth in "Ex parte Merryman," while denied at the time by President Lincoln and by the military men who dominated the War Department while Cameron was Secretary, received the eventual approval both of the courts and of the Congress.

If I were to select the State that is most typical of the South, I am inclined to think that it would be Maryland. Yet Maryland has few of the economic problems of the Southern States; it lies beyond the boundaries of the freight rate tariff wall, and enjoys a much greater prosperity than the Southeast. Nor was Maryland, except in fiction, a part of the Confederacy. Nor is its population predominantly Gaelic, as is true of most of the rest of the South, Virginia excepted. Maryland is Southern because it thinks in those paradoxical terms that are peculiar to the Southern mind, and because its instincts, its emotions, its point of view are those of the South.

Repeatedly I have said that a section deserves to be judged by its best, and Roger Brooke Taney is most representative of the South among many that might be chosen: Andrew Jackson, George Mason, Robert Edward Lee, John Forsyth, James Monroe, Willie Jones; for, except perhaps in the case of Thomas Jefferson, I shall no more claim such Founders as Washington, Madison, Rutledge, and Bulloch to be Southern exclusively than I would admit a similar claim by Pennsylvania to Franklin or by Massachusetts to Sam Adams; these belong to the whole nation.

The myths that have been fabricated about Taney were an outgrowth of his courageous support of Andrew Jackson in the Bank crisis. Called into the Cabinet as Attorney-General, the Maryland lawyer, one of the most eminent in America, accepted the post of Secretary of the Treasury to withdraw the public funds from the vast, corrupt financial monopoly that Biddle had erected with the aid of the Whig politicians and at the expense of the workers and farmers of the nation. When a Whig-controlled Senate spitefully rejected his name for the Treasury post, Jackson named him Chief Justice during a recess of Congress.

An extreme Union man, as the leading Jacksonian Democrats all were, Taney had combatted the Nullification views of Calhoun and the political irresponsibility of Calhoun's followers with the same zeal that he had opposed the near-treason of the Whig leaders in the French crisis and their vicious economic policies. In 1861 as in 1831, he was unwaveringly opposed to the dismemberment of the Federal Union. But in 1861, as in 1831, he was also equally opposed to any invasion of the rights of the individual, to any usurpation of authority by self-designated leaders, to any abrogation of civil liberties. Government, according to his theory, existed for the security and convenience of the people and had no powers other than those willingly and expressly granted by the people; States' rights, as he defined them in "Ex parte Merryman," consisted of the rights to defend the property and liberty of the citizens, and was an equally limited sovereignty.

Taney was the product of the South, and the product of Maryland. Sometimes he had a violent, crusading zeal, as when he counselled unrelenting hostility to Calhoun's supporters. Sometimes he permitted himself to believe that law and logic could solve economic and social problems that require more direct political processes. But he never overlooked the fact that the individual is of more consequence than the state, because the individual possesses rights unalienable and innate, while the rights of the state are no more than transient loans by the individuals who make up society; nor did he forget that America is yet, and probably always will be, a coalescence of minorities, where individual rights in the field of civil liberties must be protected by the courts with vigor unless either totalitarianism or chaos is to result.

That last lesson was easy to learn in Maryland, where Cecil Calvert, second Lord Baltimore, established a colony for Catholics of England and Scotland in 1633, with religious liberties more firmly guaranteed than in any other spot in America at that time except Providence Plantations. And boldness was a thing one learned in Maryland, too; for one man dared brazenly to affix his place of residence to the Declaration of Independence, and Charles Carroll of Carrollton wrote his down in a fine, firm hand. The libertarian tradition is strong in the State and unchallenged.

Baltimore is one of the great ports of America, and will be greater as the South's industries grow. It is the seat of one of the great institutions of learning, The Johns Hopkins University. It has an almost incomparable charm, both of appearance and of manners, and the most courteous police officers to be encountered anywhere in the country. Personally, I think it has more good things to eat than almost any other community.

Maryland is a well-run State. Nominally the capital is at Annapolis, but most of the agencies are in Baltimore. New efficiency was effected in the State government during the long tenure of Governor Albert Ritchie, one of the ablest administrators of his day and a pioneer in governmental reorganization. Maryland has never been afraid of governmental experiments or of social changes, although it has generally engaged in cautious planning before taking action; but Maryland has always been notable for maintaining vigorously the independence of the individual and the obligation of the courts to defend the freedom of men against injustice or violence.

For twenty-eight years, Roger Brooke Taney spoke the language of Maryland's freedom from the highest judicial seat in America. No power ever convinced him that America could exist other than as a Republic governed by laws rather than by men.

I turned from the Taney statue and wandered about Baltimore's busy streets for a time before entering my hotel. It was noon when

I arrived, and reporters from the papers and the wire services were there to meet me. They wanted a comment from me upon the decision handed down that morning by the Supreme Court of the State of Georgia in the case arising from the seizure of the Governorship by the pretender.

2: The South of the Confederacy

It is difficult for a Southerner to write about the South. You cannot get into type the sound of the husky, lazy voices, nor the smell of pine forests and river fronts, nor the taste of fried chicken and red-breast perch and barbecue cooked long over hickory coals, nor the sight of peach orchards in bloom and cottonfields white for the pickers and little hills. You cannot find words for the feelings that are Southern, for the pride in battles fought whether lost or won, for the bewilderment over social and economic problems that have no ready solution, for the angry tenderness that wells up inside when the South is talked of, for the lifting of the heart and the tapping of the feet when somewhere outside its boundaries a band plays "Dixie."

The South that I know is the South of the Confederacy, without Texas, but including West Virginia and the three Border States of Missouri, Maryland and Kentucky. But that is a geographical South that you can outline upon a map, and it leaves out some of the South. For you have only to step out of the bustle of San Antonio and into the quiet of the Alamo to know that it belongs to the South. The men who died there with Travis and Fannin and Crockett and Bowie were Southern-born lads, from Tennessee and North Carolina and Georgia, for the most part. For the South is a way of thought that the Gaels brought with them from their hills. In the hills of Tennessee and North Carolina and Georgia, you may yet hear the plaintive story told in the "Ballad of Mary Hamilton," and Georgia's Byron Herbert Reece in his Ballad of the Bones and a score more of poems has caught the music and the inflections and the rhymes. The South aches with nostalgia, as if even here its people were not quite at home, as if they never will be at home anywhere on Earth for all their love of the soil on which they live. I express it badly; all who have attempted to express it at all have expressed it badly; perhaps we always shall, for the South is a mystery not to be put into words.

One April afternoon some years ago, when I was preparing to campaign for Governor of Georgia, I went to North Georgia to deliver a Confederate Memorial Day address. Almost eighty years had passed since the hillsmen who followed John B. Gordon to the war in their coonskin caps had come back after the surrender at Appomattox Court House, but the ritual of song and speech and decoration of the soldiers' graves continued.

I talked that day about Gettysburg. I do not know why, because Shiloh was the great battle of the War Between the States and Chancellorsville was the greatest of Southern victories. But the heroism of Pickett's men, their charge against the invulnerable Union lines, always evokes excitement in Southern minds. So I talked about Gettysburg and the charge and the Stars and Bars, and the pride of the South in those men who fought with such gay courage in a war that was a disaster to a great region, but that was as Homeric as the seige of Troy. Afterward I shook hands and drove away, visiting at this house and that along the road, perhaps talking a little politics.

I have a friend in those hills who has a beautiful small farm, with neatly terraced fields that he still tended himself in those days although he had passed seventy, and who served three or four small churches as minister; without much compensation, I am afraid, but certainly with rich rewards, for he possesses, I am sure, the Witness of the Spirit for which he prays and he speaks with authority and not as the scribes. When I came to his white gate, I stopped my car and walked into the yard past his friendly dogs, and found him sitting on his backsteps deep in thought.

We exchanged greetings, and he looked at me silently for a few minutes.

"That was a pretty speech you made today," he said.

With what I hoped was appropriate modesty, I told him that I was glad that he had liked it.

"I didn't like it," he answered. "I think I'm going to have to preach against it next Sunday. I was just rounding out my sermon in my mind."

"What did I say that was wrong?" I asked him.

"Son, you can't be inviting people to think back of them and to live on the past," he said. "I think I've about got me a text to talk from next Sunday."

He settled himself. His powerful hands had a grace of gesture that I have never seen elsewhere; I always think of them as good hands; it is the only adjective to describe them, for they were well worn with the work about the farm and yet retained an expressiveness and a sensitiveness that gave emphasis to his voice.

"Somewhere in the book of First Chronicles, you'll find an account of how David was penned between the Jebusites in Jerusalem and the whole Philistine army that was in front of him. It was going to be a big battle, a lot bigger than Gettysburg; and if the Philistines beat him, the heathen in Jerusalem would come out and cut what was left of his army to pieces.

"It was hot, and there wasn't any water for David or his fighting men either, and he started thinking about when he was a boy tending Jesse's herds back at home and drinking from the well that was beside the gate at Bethlehem," he continued.

"I suppose any of us might do what he did. I think I can quote you what he said: 'Oh that one would give me drink of the water of the well of Bethlehem, that is at the gate!' It was a natural thing for a man to say, and David was just a man and a pretty weak one. But Abishai and two other men heard him, and broke through the whole Philistine army and came back with a goatskin bottle full of the water from the well at Bethlehem and handed it to him."

He stopped and drummed a moment with a forefinger, and then looked at me squarely.

"Son, when they brought him that water, David showed some sense, more than he showed any other time in his life. He wouldn't drink it. He poured it out on the ground, and he said: 'Shall I drink the blood of these men that have put their lives in jeopardy? For with the jeopardy of their lives they brought it.' He knew you couldn't nourish yourself on memories. He did not dare drink the water that was yesterday. You can't use up the courage and the laughter and the tears that somebody else had in the past. It doesn't belong to you to spend that way. It is too precious to do anything with except to pour out on the ground as a sacrifice to God. It is good to have memories, but they mustn't be used up to feed your heart with today. You must go out and find other food to eat and other water to drink."

"But don't you think that people have a right to be proud of what their fathers did? Isn't it good sometimes for us to hear about them? It seems to me that it gives us confidence and strength," I interposed.

"Of course it is good to hear the old tales, just as it is good for children to hear about Red Ridinghood and Jack the Giant Killer. But you can't get strength out of those things, but only from inside yourself. You were inviting those folks to be proud of themselves because their fathers were brave men, when you ought to be telling them to try to be brave men like their fathers," he went on. "You ought to be saying this to them: 'Your grandfathers failed and the British took Savannah, and your fathers failed and the Yankees burned Atlanta, and you too will probably fail. But your grandfathers and your fathers had courage, and laughed and shook off the weight of their failures as a dog shakes water off his back; and if you have courage you can do the same.' That's what you ought to be telling them, so that they would know that they can do whatever is necessary today and live in the present."

"Men who have no memories of their past and of their fathers' deeds have no roots," I objected. "You wouldn't have me tell the people of the South to forget about the past, which is a part of themselves."

"Of course not; but they must use the past for what it is intended, just as they must use the future. No man can eat bread today from today's plantings, either. It is just as wrong to tell them to be hopeful about their future, and to live for that future and in that future. Now is the time that they must work and laugh and cry, and now is the time that they must eat and drink. And that's especially true of our people, because they have such grand memories that you can be tempted to lose yourself in them, and not do what has to be done right now."

3: BECAUSE I AM AN AMERICAN

Those who have seen Natchez or Williamsburg sense that which is unwholesome in the Southern atmosphere, a tendency of some to live in the grandeur of a bygone day that perhaps never was and certainly never will come again.

But those who have seen Charlottesville, and the dreams of harmony come true in the buildings that Jefferson imagined in his old age and then watched grow, see the other side of the argument. For here the South has builded upon its past, because the past builded well and enduringly. Here the sense of the past is different, because that past was romantic and realistic, not imaginary and sentimental.

Alabama has three cities that are illustrative to some extent. There is Montgomery, rich with traditions, where the Southern Confederacy was born, but none the less fronting to a new day. There is Mobile, which has its memories, but which is a significant example of the South's prodigious and successful efforts to raise itself by its own bootstraps; for the great port there, with its excellent facilities, is very largely the work of the people of Alabama and their intelligent Port Authority. Then there is Birmingham, which has no memories, and is the capital of exploitation in the South; a city dominated by the managers sent down to the South by absentee Eastern owners, where you can witness for yourself the exploitation of Southern resources and Southern workers and feel shame in the scalawags, the precursors of the Quislings, who aided in the exploitation.

Alabama is now heavily industrialized, with a considerable production of steel and steel products. Yet its per capita income is below that of several other States of the Southeast with less abundant resources, which gives some index of the penalty paid for permitting outside domination. At Birmingham, during the campaign for Alabama's Governorship in 1946, Lieutenant-Governor Handy Ellis, who was "Big Jim" Folsom's principal opponent, made a speech typical of one type of Southern politician; it lashed out not only at Folsom's somewhat original platform clowning, but at youth-voting, abolition of the poll tax, and at the Negro, and was devised to appeal to the managerial staff of the absentee-bossed enterprises in the State and their sympathizers.

Folsom won, sweeping the rural areas to the dismay of those who profess the belief that the Southern farmer votes ultra-conservative in every election, and giving the parlor-liberals a taste of embarrassment, because they thought his campaign methods quite uncouth and undignified. Since it is impossible to be a statesman without being entrusted with direction of public affairs, and since this requires considerable political skill to attain, it is still my suggestion to those interested in libertarian and progressive programs for the South that they bother to learn the rudiments of politics first.

But campaigning is one thing and governing is another. Folsom's well-wishers hope that he will not throw aside his opportunity. Already physically big, he could add to his political stature. His Administration will be measured by its accomplishments.

Montgomery gave me my introduction to politics, when I was a boy of eight. My grandfather, Joseph Matthew Ellis, long represented Bullock County in the Alabama legislature, and at two or three sessions I served as a page in the House, when he came up from Union Springs to take his seat. From my observation, while issues and problems have changed, the techniques of politics are not different from those days.

Alabama has a large number of educational institutions. Some are private or denominational, such as Spring Hill at Mobile, and Huntingdon at Montgomery, and Southern at Birmingham. Its two great State schools are Alabama Polytechnic at Auburn, and the State University at Tuscaloosa. Both are notable for large enrollments, excellent faculties, and powerful football teams. The University has developed a valuable service to the whole State in its Bureau of Public Administration, headed by Dr. Roscoe Martin, which is engaged in a continuous study of public problems, economic questions, and administrative methods, and which has contributed much to the growing efficiency of Alabama's government at both State and local levels.

North Carolina is generally looked upon outside the South as the most progressive of the States of the Southeast. Its excellent road system, its adequate public services, its fine educational establishment that includes the State University, Duke at Durham, and many other colleges, and its rapid industrial development have been well publicized. The succession of excellent administrators who have held the office of Governor: Aycock, Gardner, Hoey and Broughton among others, has assured efficient and economical government. Racial tension long ago was minimized in North Carolina by acceding to the legitimate requests of the Negro for political rights. During the depression years, when the earliest attempts at unionization of the textile industry was undertaken, there was a degree of industrial strife, but this subsided. The liberals of North Carolina can boast of President Frank Graham of the University of North Carolina, at Chapel Hill, as one outstanding leader, and they can look back to Josephus Daniels as a man whose statesmanship made a great impression upon the entire nation, both in its national defense establishment and in the formulation of an intelligent foreign policy.

By contrast, outsiders usually regard South Carolina as the most intransigent Commonwealth in Dixie. Although few members of the Constitutional Convention had as great a hand in the framing of the basic law of the Union as did John Rutledge, South Carolina has had since the era of Andrew Jackson a history of opposition to change and a tradition of political solitude unequalled in America. The shadow of John C. Calhoun still lies across the State's future, as it lay across its history from the day when he formulated his doctrine of Nullification.

Charles Town was a beautiful, prospering, urbane center of trade and culture when New York was a village, Boston a center for smugglers, Washington a swamp, and Savannah a disembarkation point for Oglethorpe's colonists. Charleston is still rich in beauty, in great family names, in tradition; but it no longer is one of America's three great ports and no longer the financial center of the South. Nor does it longer dominate South Carolina; the newer inland communities, like Greenville and Spartanburg, where textiles flourish and where hydroelectric power is plentiful, are coming into leadership.

South Carolina, with a greater proportion of Negroes among its population than any other State except Mississippi and with acute depression distress in its agricultural areas, has been afflicted with poverty since the Reconstruction era, when it suffered bitterly. Its economy is less stable than that of North Carolina, Georgia, Tennessee or Florida. A considerable part of its coastal plantation section has been turned into playground estates of non-residents. Its demagogues have been notorious, from Preston Brooks to "Cotton Ed" Smith.

But South Carolina has a justifiable pride in one aspect of its rigidity of mind. In the days of the War Between the States, South Carolina taught the people of America what free speech meant, and the sublime epitaph on the gravestone of James Louis Petigru attests the respect that an outspoken Union man could obtain in the city whose harbor saw the first shot of the war. You can still obtain freedom of speech in South Carolina, and you can get a hearing for what you have to say. Those who would write off a State, with such exceptional colleges as Clemson, The Citadel, the University of South Carolina, Wofford and Furman, and with an electorate that can be aroused enough to retire its "Cotton Eds" from office, are exhibiting blind prejudice. As industrialization increases, so that the citizens can afford more adequate public services, South Carolina will demonstrate that the toughness of its spirit and the vigor of its resourcefulness are not over.

Similarly a great many outsiders like to look down their noses at Arkansas. Here is one of the most liberal of Southern States, in many ways, with a reputation for reaction not at all deserved. Reactionaries do not elect such Senators as Joe Robinson, the Caraways, husband and wife, and J. William Fulbright.

Arkansas is underdeveloped, in contrast to the rest of the South. Although it suffered from the dust storms, from mortgage foreclosure, from the exodus of a part of its farm population, and from recent inroads into its economy by absentee ownership, it is obtaining a gradual and satisfactory readjustment.

The finest auditorium in which I spoke in my tour of America was that in Little Rock, named after Senator Joe Robinson. Acoustics in public buildings often are faulty; indeed, I have been told that perfect acoustics in a building occur only by accident. If so, the accident happened in Little Rock.

I also remember Arkansas as the State where I wore one shirt for five days. The airline mislaid my bag, and it stayed a day behind me for that length of time, and I never arrived in any community while the stores were open. The life of a lecturer is not all tea-and-cakes; and to create a phrase, into every life some rain must fall.

Mississippi is the State that delights cocktail-lounge liberals in New York, who can remain unconcerned about Blue Ribbon juries in their own State or anti-Semitic orgies in near-by Boston. It gives them a conveniently distant target. That Mississippi is the Commonwealth of L. Q. C. Lamar, John Sharp Williams, William Alexander Percy, Pat Harrison, Tom Bailey and Hodding Carter as well as of Bilbo and Rankin, these seem unaware.

That attitude has made some people in Mississippi angry, and Hodding Carter is among their number. As the State's most distinguished journalist, he has fought all the illiberal forces in the South with every available weapon, including a pungent humor and a gifted invective. He thinks the South would profit and that libertarianism would profit if the outsiders left the Southern problems to the South.

When I reached Mississippi in May 1946 to make a speech to the convention of the Veterans of Foreign Wars at Jackson, I was the guest of the late Governor Tom Bailey in Mississippi's charming Executive Mansion, one of the most beautiful in the country. Governor Bailey, a good administrator and a believer in middle-of-the-road policies, already was in bad health, and it was then apparent that he would probably have to abandon any thought of seeking the Senate seat held by Theodore Bilbo, whom he would easily have defeated. But Bilbo saluted my arrival nonetheless, with the typical Bilbo rhetoric, and we exchanged verbal shots through newspaper interviews.

Even then Mississippians were concerned that outside comment might tilt the scales in Bilbo's favor, and were showing signs of irritation. After the rest of 1946, when the outside critics were vocative, and of 1947, when they were silent and John Rankin ran fifth among five Democrats for the Bilbo vacancy, I can see what they mean, and understand how a man like Hodding Carter, who fights demagogues and quacks every day, can suggest that outsiders keep out. But I dissent.

America belongs to all of us. It is important to me that books are suppressed in Boston, because I am an American. It is important to me that New York has curtailed fair jury trials, because I am an American. It is important that Illinois has a ridiculously complex

judicial system, because I am an American. It is important that
Michigan has imprisonment for debt, because I am an American.
This book may never be suppressed in Boston, and I may never face
a jury in New York nor have a case in court in Illinois nor go to
debtors' jail in Michigan; but other Americans will write books
that will be suppressed and other Americans will be denied honest
juries and be denied justice through a maze of outmoded technicalities and go to jail because they are poor.

The fact that many of the criticisms of Mississippi were half-truths,
that Theodore Bilbo and John Rankin are represented as representative of a people whom they misrepresent, does not terminate
America's interest in Mississippi. Every section of America can
learn from every other section, and should welcome criticism from
every source. Every good cause needs as many followers as it can
find, from every part of America. While I think that the South,
from long familiarity with somewhat perfervid critics, perhaps ac-
cepts criticism with less complaint than any other section, I think
that most Americans are willing to have other Americans point to
things that need correction. I think that Hodding Carter will agree
with me, when he recovers from his immediate irritation about the
misunderstanding visited upon his state. He will realize that Mississippi fathered both the proprietor of the Dream House, "The Man"
Bilbo, and the master of fabulous Trail Lake, William Alexander
Percy, just as Wisconsin offered the nation quite different kinds of
Senators in John C. Spooner and Robert M. LaFollette.

Mississippi is aggressively striving for a readjustment of its economy, and seeking industries, possibly a little too desperately so that
exploitation may also be invited. Much of its richest farming section
has passed into absentee ownership, and its once immeasurable forest resources are diminishing rapidly. The wealth of the Delta soil,
however, is incalculable, and the potential wealth in oil and natural
gas within the boundaries of Mississippi is also great. Meridian,
Hattiesburg, Vicksburg and Jackson, the capital, are growing stead-
ily. With increasing industry, and a more diversified agriculture in

those sections of the State where cotton farming is less profitable than in the Delta, Mississippi will move forward rapidly.

4: CIVIL WAR WITHIN THEIR BORDERS

The Border States are sometimes classified as a separate entity. Some other observers, selecting other criteria, group them with Virginia and West Virginia into a special classification, because the five escape some of the exploitation of the rest of the South, including some aspects of the freight rate trade barriers.

That overlooks the essential of Southernness, which is a way of thought and an emotional quality. It overlooks also the similarity of population, which, despite large German elements in Missouri, and an English base to the Virginia and West Virginia citizenship, comes predominantly from the same Scotch and Scotch-Irish stock as the rest of the Southeast.

I think that Kentucky, Missouri and Maryland are Southern; primarily because they think of themselves as Southern, and are thought of as Southern by the rest of the South. It is true that the War Between the States was civil war within their borders, and that Kentucky vainly sought neutrality in the fratricidal struggle; and that Missouri, strangely enough, supplied full quotas of men to both the Northern and Southern armies; but the traditions and the talk of the people of all these states are those of the South.

Kentucky was the home of the Kentucky Resolutions. They owe much of their authorship to Thomas Jefferson, but they were the expression of a bold people who had plunged into the Western wilderness and built a home while fighting a war. They were more than protests against the Federalist "white terror"; they were the definite expression of the responsibility of State government to protect its citizens from interference with individual freedom and civil liberties.

When I was a college student at Sewanee, I learned the charm of Kentucky; or at least the charm of Bowling Green and of the girls who attended Western Kentucky Teachers College on the hilltop. To me the charm of Kentucky is still unmarred, after speaking at many of its colleges and before many audiences: at Lexington, at Ashland, at Murray, at Paducah, at Louisville. Lexington was the home of Henry Clay, upon whose political genius, personal charm, and violent ambition I looked with less favor than do most people in Kentucky; Lexington also is the home of the University of Kentucky, which has a distinctive Southern flavor, a devoted faculty much hampered by the State's curious salary-limitation law, and a terrific basketball team that habitually wins championships.

Louisville is where Reynolds Metal, the only rival of Aluminum Corporation of America, started off, and is a city of diversified industry. It possesses also a great liberal newspaper, the *Courier-Journal,* headed by a former Georgian, Mark Etheridge. Louisville also possessed a great Mayor, in Wilson Wyatt, until he quit to become Federal Housing Expediter in an effort to bring order into the field of American housing and discovered that some Congressmen will play politics with human misery just as some Caesars will fiddle while Rome burns.

Kentucky has rich mineral resources, and a history of warfare in the coal areas during the era of unionization. It has a mountain population even more removed from the modern era than those of the North Georgia, Carolina and Tennessee hill country, to which the Kentucky hills bear so close a resemblance. Kentucky also has a beautiful bluegrass country, famous for horses and colonels and mint-juleps; it has other rich farming areas as well, somewhat similar in appearance to the lands to be found in Virginia and Pennsylvania.

Kentucky always had bitter politics. The prestige and political genius of Crittenden could not prevent dramatic dissolution of Kentucky's peace nor that of his own household in 1860. As the aftermath of a bitter election, the assassination of a Governor, and many charges of balloting irregularities, Kentucky counts its votes at the county seat on the day after the voting. Generally there is a small Democratic margin, but sometimes the Republicans slip in a Governor or a Senator.

Kentucky does not go in for colonels, really, much more than any other Southern State, except facetiously; but Governor Ruby Laffoon had something over a thousand colonels on his staff in his day. Although Kentucky is the home of Bourbon, on my visits there I was surprised to find occasional Scotch drinkers.

Kentucky has an ordered economy and enough money for good public services; but it has one problem unique in America: a constitutional provision forbidding payment of any State salary of more than five thousand dollars. Competent administrators, highly trained technical and professional workers, and college deans and presidents are hard to get at that figure. The college folks have found expedients, including various private donations, that meet the financial problem in some way, though not satisfactorily. The courts may determine, however, that teachers are not State employees at all. Other State agencies suffer.

Americans who have not seen the industries of Louisville or the wealth and variety of Kentucky's farmlands believe that the Commonwealth exists as a place to run the Derby.

Missouri possesses two of America's greatest newspapers: the St. Louis *Post-Dispatch* and the Kansas City *Star*. The *Post-Dispatch* is all that is left of the Pulitzer press empire; newspapermen regard it with the same affection that they regarded the New York *World,* which was fabulous enough to have been a Southern institution. The *Star* is as conservative in tone as in typography, but, like the New York *Herald-Tribune,* it is an example of intelligent and responsible conservatism.

St. Louis is not the largest railroad center in America, but strategically it is the most important. Industrially it is amazing, producing everything from delicate aeronautical instruments to shoes. The Edison boys, from Atlanta, went there and made a fortune in shoe manufacture and sale. In skilled craftsmen, St. Louis rivals New England, as a result of the number of trained journeymen who arrived there from Germany when the liberal movement was crushed in the 1840s. St. Louis was haven for Carl Schurz, among others; his fight for decent treatment for the South, for preservation of what remained of our public domain and our natural resources, and for human liberty wherever menaced is one of the stories of America's debt to those who came here as refugees from a Europe that denied them freedom and opportunity.

Kansas City is a great wholesale, distribution and manufacturing center, associated in my mind with one of the nation's great men, Thomas Hart Benton. He was another of those tough, tenacious, individualistic Americans who loved Andrew Jackson, and who hated Whigs and disunion. He worsted Clay and Webster in debate, and the great moment of his life came when he triumphed over them in the "expurgation of the record" of the Senate's unconstitutional vote of censure against Jackson for his actions in the fight for the people against the Bank of the United States. Benton remained a Union man to the last. He fought his own much-loved son-in-law, Frémont, in 1856, because he believed that the Free Soil party might bring about dissolution of the Union.

Benton's oratory, like the bluntly factual *Thirty Years' View* that is one of the most neglected source-books of American history, was rough-and-ready rather than polished; but he attained true eloquence when he sent Andrew Jackson a message on the eve of his victory in 1832: "Have faith in the people and the people will have faith in you."

Missouri's smaller cities, like Warrensburg, Maryville, Kirksville, and Independence, are pleasant, prosperous and possessed of a charm that is a combination of the neatness of New England and the hospitable laziness of parts of the South. Despite a substantially prosperous agriculture, I was surprised to learn that Missouri lagged far behind Georgia and the rest of the Southeast in rural electrification, although perhaps the stimulus of the Tennessee Valley Authority in those States accounts for their more rapid progress.

Maryland, third of the Border States, did not listen to its exiled son's appeal nor to the call of Potomac to Chesapeake and enter the Southern Confederacy; but it is more Southern in atmosphere and thought than many parts of Virginia, North Carolina, Tennessee or Georgia. It is a rival for Kentucky in the matter of horse races and the manufacture of alcoholic potables.

It is possible that it was a sound sense of strategy that led Abraham Lincoln to use force in Maryland and diplomacy in Missouri and Kentucky: the loss of the Chesapeake, and the encirclement of Washington, might have loomed as sufficiently dangerous for him to rely upon the military. Likewise, the danger of secession was more acute in Maryland, for Kentucky was bent on neutrality and an effort to bring about a compromise and a rapprochement, while Missouri was strongly Union in those sections that were militarily important. However, I believe the Lincoln success in Kentucky and Missouri was due to a better understanding of the men and women of the Western Border than of those of the Bay. He had lived among them; they were his own; he understood their language and their desires, and he utilized his much underrated political skill to prevent them from joining the Deep South. While the result was that Kentucky sent large numbers of men to both armies, and Missouri suffered from cruel guerrilla warfare that ultimately descended into banditry, from the Union side the result was satisfactory strategically.

The Border States resist classification, and so does West Virginia. The men of the mountains had objected to the domination of the State of Virginia by the Tideland long before the War Between the States broke out. They were strongly Union in sympathy, and they took advantage of the conflict to establish their own government and secede from Virginia. Although violative of the Federal constitution, the Congress permitted them to do so, and after the war Virginia reluctantly accepted the *fait accompli*.

West Virginia was settled by Virginians, in the main. Its sympathies, its institutions, and much of its way of thought come from the Old Dominion. Article III, Section 15, of its constitution is couched in the identical language of Jefferson's Statute for Religious Freedom, and Section 11 contains an even more drastic safeguard for the enjoyment of political rights, and is worth quoting in these days of witch-hunts:

"Political tests, requiring persons, as a pre-requisite to the enjoyment of their civil and political rights to purge themselves by their own oaths, of past alleged offenses are repugnant to the principles of free government, and are cruel and oppressive. No religious or political test oath shall be required as a pre-requisite or qualification to vote, serve as a juror, sue, plead, appeal, or pursue any profession or employment. Nor shall any person be deprived by law, of any right, or privilege, because of any act done prior to the passage of such law."

West Virginia is emerging into prosperity at last, after an era of exploitation of its mineral and forest resources; but prosperity only underwrites further what West Virginians already had attained: the right to the prideful words on the State Seal, *"Montani Semper Liberi* —The Mountaineers Are Always Free."

There are those who will assert that Tennessee must also be unclassified. It was disputed territory during the War Between the States. Its Ordinance of Secession was unique; disdaining the legalistic language of all the other Southern States, Tennessee took high and unanswerable grounds for quitting the Union, asserting that the right of revolution was the unalienable privilege of all free men. That suited the temper of a State that had existed independently before its recognition. For Tennessee contains the territory that once was the State of Franklin, which parted from North Carolina soon after the Revolution and wrote one of the most liberal constitutions in American history, containing such innovations as suffrage for youths of eighteen.

Tennessee has given America some unusual public figures, including Andrew Jackson, James K. Polk and Andrew Johnson among its Presidents and Hugh White among the stalwart independents who examined everything and rejected all that they did not like. It is a curious footnote upon Tennessee's history that, although Jackson is the State's greatest hero, White won Tennessee from him in the campaign of 1832. It is also a comment upon the character of White that, when the Senate Chamber was deserted by every other Whig or dissident Democrat who voted against Benton's resolution to expunge from the Senate Journal the criticism of Jackson in the hour of Jackson's and Benton's victory, Hugh White sat in his chair and watched the proceedings through.

The four large cities—Memphis, Nashville, Knoxville and Chattanooga—do not dominate Tennessee's industrial, agricultural or business life. Memphis, of course, is the market town of the Delta, more closely affiliated with the cotton States that lie to the west and south of Tennessee's borders. Knoxville is the center of the activities of the Tennessee Valley Authority, which has transformed the ravaged basin of the Tennessee and its tributaries into a new area of prosperity and opportunity. Nashville, besides being the greatest mule market in the world, is a college town with Vanderbilt, George Peabody, and Fisk located there, and publication center for many religious denominations. Chattanooga is a railroad and distribution center, as well as a flourishing industrial community.

The rapid advance of Tennessee has prevented the statistics from keeping abreast with its progress. It is rich in resources. Some of them have been so ruthlessly exploited that the very soil has been destroyed and the countryside turned into a wasteland; a visit to Ducktown and Copper Hill will frighten any American into a belief in decent conservation methods. But the bluegrass of Tennessee produces fine herds; the diversified farming throughout the State is bringing profit to farmers; and new industries have poured into the State with the availability of a plenitude of cheap electric power. Many of the industries, such as Aluminum Corporation and subsidiaries of United States Steel, are absentee owned and controlled, but they do not dominate the life of the State.

Politically Tennessee is in ferment. Inherently one of the most liberal Commonwealths of the Union and a land of independent industrial workers and prospering yeoman farmers, it is looking toward libertarian leadership today. The test is in the making. Wherever the issues have been clear, the people have won victories upon every level. That political control has rested in the hands of "Boss Ed" Crump and his Memphis organization for many years, ever since the collapse of the Caldwell financial empire and the Lea political aspirations simultaneously, is undeniable. Partly this has been due to a strange affection felt for Crump himself, who has a peculiar popularity with many citizens. The popularity does not extend to his satellites. Younger men outside the Crump organization, like Estes Kefauver, are coming up. The machine's alliances elsewhere in Tennessee are breaking. Nevertheless, in Memphis itself, where all the Delta goes for holiday and shopping, the rhyme is still true:

> "Oh, the river's up and cotton's down;
> Mistuh Ed Crump, he runs this town."

5: THE ONE THAT'S A COMIN' UP

There is something else in Tennessee. There is the University of the South, at Sewanee, where I went to college.

The Mountain is the largest campus in America, but Sewanee is not the largest college. It is a small school, but I shall not quote Webster's speech on Dartmouth; I love it, and so do many more; and of the honorary degrees that have been given me, I appreciated that from Sewanee in 1947 most of all.

In the chapel there is a picture that caught my imagination when I was a freshman. It represented a desert scene, so imaginatively done that you could feel the parching heat of the sun upon the barren sands. A group of travellers were struggling over the barrenness. Some of them were prostrate; some were urging their weary camels onward. In the foreground was a great rock, that cast its shadow over a shining stream that seemed to flow from it, and beside the stream some travellers were resting. The inscription said: "For faith is like the shadow of a great rock in a desert place."

It seems to me that the small colleges, usually church supported, have made a great contribution to the growth of America. Fundamentally, especially in the South, the libertarian movement is less secular than ethical, and stems from roots that are religious rather than economic.

Essentially the doctrine of equalitarianism is a religious tenet, and the fear and instinctive distrust of social programs and ideologies, such as communism or fascism, that are founded upon the concept of a wholly material Universe arises in America from a deep-rooted belief in God. In the reforms that the South has achieved in the past three decades, notably in those advances that Georgia registered during my own term of office as Governor, the support came from the people of deep religious conviction.

The small college performs another useful function, in an America that is menaced somewhat by the spectre of specialization. Usually the smaller institutions place emphasis upon the humanities. They provide, therefore, a considerable number of the individuals who think in terms of life as a harmonious entity, rather than a hodge-podge of unrelated specializations. The strength of the eighteenth century was that men, like Franklin and Jefferson in America and the Encyclopaedists in France, believed that statesmen should think in terms of well-rounded knowledge. Franklin invented bifocals and investigated the flow of the Gulf Stream and dabbled with Greek and Latin; Jefferson not only founded the science of comparative language and made very great contributions to zoology and botany, but found time to invent weather vanes that registered indoors, and that boon to Manhattan's cliff dwellers, the dumb-waiter. Greater versatility and a broader point of view is essential to counteract the mass-production psychosis.

Sewanee is famous for its great Negro trainer, Willie Six. Although it is one of the South's smallest schools, there was a day when Sewanee played football against the best of them on equal terms and won the Southern championship more than once. Those teams were trained by Willie Six, who rubbed muscles and dabbed iodine on scratches for more than thirty years.

Sewanee's elevens no longer can stop the behemoths of the great State Universities but Willie Six still pounds and massages and anoints the members of the squad. They decided to honor him, to award him a letter at the year's last big game, to declare the day to be Willie Six day. Athletes of two generations came back to the Mountain to pay tribute to him, and they led the old man to the middle of the field with the band playing and made their awards. They had a radio hookup that day, and the climax of the program was to be Willie Six saying a few words for all Sewanee men everywhere.

The announcer tried to lead him, when the old man's voice froze up.

"You've seen a lot of Sewanee teams in the years you've been around here," he said. "Tell us which one would you say is your favorite."

For a minute he was silent, was Willie Six, there in the middle of the field with thousands of people looking at him, and then he spoke: "I guess my favorite team is always the one that's a comin' up!"

The sundial records neither the hours of yesterday nor of to-morrow.

Once when he was a visitor at the Mountain, I saw one of the South's last great feudal barons, William Alexander Percy of Trail Lake. He had his own solutions for the problems of the South. This scion of Hotspur's house had a plantation that was a tradition in his father's day and that became a myth in his own. From all over Mississippi, tenants sought to get on his land. Neither the needy nor the shiftless were ever turned away. He was a medieval lord of lands, like his ancestor who met the Douglas in tragic battle at Chevy Chase; he protected his own. He was scornful of the demagogues, the nigger-haters, the dirty talkers, and they feared him. Feudalism is not a way of life for any part of America, except Trail Lake, but

Percy taught the South something of the assumption of responsibility by the individual that cannot be forgotten.

Because it seemed at the time to be a good thing to do, I studied Greek at Sewanee. This accounts for a lamentable fondness for compound adjectives, which comes from blind Homer's tendency to describe his protagonist as "much-travelled Odysseus." I can no more rid myself of the words I learned at Sewanee than I can rid myself of the way of thought I learned there.

6: Proud of their great men

Three States of the South have well-coördinated economies, according to the study of the McCarran Committee of the Senate, which investigated the concentration of industry. It is significant that one of them, Virginia, lies largely outside the transportation tariff barriers, with more than half the State in what is known as "Official Territory." The others, Florida and Louisiana, have unusual economic aspects and access to cheap water transportation to an extent unknown elsewhere in the South.

Average incomes in the three States were well above the general Southern level in 1940, and remained in that position through 1944. It is unlikely that the relative position will be retained throughout reconversion and decentralization, although there is no indication that there will be a reduction in their prosperity.

In some ways the statistical approach to the three States presents pictures not wholly accurate. Virginia's prosperity is better distributed than that of the other two states, with an older and better established industrialization. Florida's agriculture has undergone a tremendous transformation within the past twenty years. Once a territory divided rather sharply between cotton and forest products in the north and citrus in the south, it has become one of the great livestock producers of the country and its production of table vegetables is prodigious. The same evils affecting the system that depends upon large numbers of migratory workers beset Florida, though perhaps to a lesser extent than California. Louisiana has some rural areas that have low incomes and that were underdeveloped to a grave degree until a few years ago.

Virginia is libertarian in many ways, but intensely conservative in others. It is the only one of the Southern Commonwealths that can be said to be under the complete political control of a State organization. Public services maintain a high standard, but the political bureaucracy is exceptionally large and exceptionally political.

Florida may be regarded as liberal, in spite of the adoption of somewhat repressive labor legislation and the existence of a somewhat regressive tax system. Its delegation in Washington demonstrates that. Actually, the critics of Florida's system of taxes overlook the competition between States in the matter of taxation on the one hand, and Florida's status as a playground for the rich and even more for the prosperous middle class. Floridians are satisfied with their tax system, and the public services of all kinds are well supported.

Louisiana was the most Bourbon of Southern States, despite its possession of some strong progressive elements such as those once led by John Parker. Then Huey Long burst upon Louisiana politics like a bombshell.

At least three full-length novels, including John Dos Passos' bitter *Number One* and Robert Penn Warren's idealization, have appeared about the Long era in Louisiana. Hundreds of magazine articles have appeared. He is still a figure of controversy in his State, and his grave on the Capitol grounds at Baton Rouge is always decked with flowers. I have seen impoverished farmers and their wives from the Louisiana upcountry, which had not a passable road until Long built scores, with tears in their eyes spell out the sentimental epitaph on his tombstone:

> "Green be the turf above thee,
> Friend of my better days;
> None knew thee but to love thee,
> Or named thee but to praise."

Whether Huey Long was entirely demagogue and posturer, whether he was partly sincere and partly knave, whether he was a modern Gracchus and a friend of the people, whether he was an ambitious neo-Fascist opportunistically seeking power and wealth, he did two things: he woke Louisiana up and he left behind him the most rapacious political machine in the recent history of the South. Waking Louisiana up was good. It is true that the reform groups that eventually ousted the Long satellites from power and sent some of them to jail were conservatives, but they were intelligent and responsible conservatives, very different from the antique Bourbons who preceded Long. They have not turned Louisiana back to its absentee owners, although the State still is afflicted with exploitation. They are providing good honest government and a much higher level of public services than Louisiana knew before Huey Long came upon the scene. The Long influence remains strong in the State; it is currently spearheaded by Earl Long, Huey's brother, who won the 1948 primary.

Louisiana is a State of contrasts. Shreveport, the home of Governor Jimmy Davis, looks and smells and talks like a Texas community; it is a fine, clean, modern city. Ruston, home of Louisiana Polytechnic Institute, is a typical college community. Monroe, which I knew before my visit there only as the original home of Delta Airlines, is an oil and natural gas town, and I discovered that gas for home cooking and industrial furnaces in Atlanta and Newnan was piped from that city. Baton Rouge, a delightful river city, home of Louisiana State University, is dominated by the skyscraper Capitol that Long built when Governor, ripping down the decrepit if historic edifice that preceded it.

In New Orleans when I spoke at Tulane University, I was introduced by Mayor DeLesseps Morrison, probably the most controversial figure in the new Louisiana. He is something of a symbol of the new middle-of-the-road libertarianism that is becoming increasingly the Louisiana school of thought. He is giving New Orleans less excitement than it enjoyed in the days when Huey Long was sending in soldiers, but he is giving the town excitement enough by a somewhat thorough housecleaning politically and administratively. New Orleans likes him, because he is one of its own, but I suspect that secretly the city shrugs just a little.

For New Orleans is as incredible as people believe. The food is good, of course, but it is the atmosphere that gets the visitor. The city has seen much of history. The French came, and then the Spanish, and then the French again. The Americans came, and Edward Livingston wrote a code for the new State. The pirates came in and out of the harbor, not raiding but only visiting and trading. The British came, and Andrew Jackson borrowed help from Jean Lafitte and his buccaneers and beat them back with incredible slaughter. The victory was unimportant, it turned out, because a treaty of peace already had been signed; that is, it was important only to the people of New Orleans, who escaped a promised looting, and to the Democratic party, which henceforth observed the anniversary of the victory at Jackson Day Dinners that gave party stalwarts an opportunity for much excellent rhetoric rebuking the reprehensible rapacity of Republican rascals.

Politically, Louisiana has been divided along geographical lines, with the poor and submerged upstate fighting New Orleans and the plantation owners. Prosperity is reaching all sections of the State now, so new alignments are in sight, though the geographic cleavage is still the same.

Florida, too, is divided. The usual division is North Florida, the West Coast and the East Coast.

Florida contains many things, including, until the development of the atomic bomb, the most important strategic base in the United States. For Pensacola is the key to New Orleans, and enemy control of New Orleans would threaten every point on the Great River, including vital St. Louis and the railroad system of the country. Jefferson pointed this out, at the time of the Louisiana Purchase, and diligently sought acquisition of the two Floridas.

Florida long remained underdeveloped. The people of North

Florida were almost indistinguishable from those of South Georgia, and planted cotton. Tampa was the port that communicated with Cuba, and had intense excitement during the Spanish-American War, and then went back to sleep. Jacksonville shipped the lumber and rosin and turpentine and cotton of North Florida, and was something of a winter resort. St. Augustine, with its ancient Spanish fort, was visited by tourists, once in a while, who wanted to drink from the Fountain of Youth that Ponce de Leon found there; at any rate, there was a spring-well identified with the Spanish adventurer who quested for youth in the Land of Flowers.

Then came the first citrus and tourist boom and its collapse, and the second. The hurricane disaster and the realty collapse and the depression would seem to be enough to bother any State; but the cattle tick slipped in from Georgia and the fruit fly had to be eradicated from the orange groves. Florida was hit by almost every mishap, and therefore, or in spite of, prospered amazingly.

On the West Coast, there is a string of beautiful citrus and tourist towns, with Clearwater, St. Petersburg, Sarasota, Venice, Naples and Fort Myers drawing thousands upon thousands of visitors from the North, especially Ohio, Wisconsin and Michigan. Indeed, Michigan looks on Florida's West Coast in a certain proprietary manner. On the East Coast, Daytona and Palm Beach and Miami draw tourists from the East, and are crowded to capacity. Jacksonville, Tampa and Miami are great ports, and Miami is one of the major centers for air transit.

Orlando, the county seat of Orange County—and incidentally Mrs. Arnall's home town—is Florida's finest inland resort city. It holds many memories for me.

I made a good many talks in Florida, before college groups and business groups and women's clubs, and talked about the same things that I talked about in Connecticut and California and Texas. I also talked at Miami Beach, where Governor James M. Cox, the Democratic nominee for president in 1920 and a staunch, fighting liberal and a great publisher, introduced me to the Committee of One Hundred. The collective wealth in the room was something over a billion dollars, perhaps something over five billion dollars; after you quit the millions figures become a little meaningless. I said the same thing to them, and they reacted in the same way. After the meeting I talked with a millionaire whose investments included stocks in many corporations that occupy semi-monopolistic positions; he had never heard of the freight rate differential; he was shocked that it existed, although his economic and social views belonged to the pre-McKinley era; he really meant it when he said he believed in a free competitive economy, but he thought it existed everywhere in our country.

I told the same story to Virginians in Roanoke, Bristol, Danville, Norfolk, Lynchburg and Richmond, and the response was the same. Everywhere in America people want simple justice for all Americans; but not everywhere are they aware of the unfair operation of parts of our economic system, where competition has been eliminated and where exploitation is practiced.

Virginians have written adequately of the beauty of Virginia, of the charm of Tidewater and Valley. They are proud of their great men; all of them, although Robert Edward Lee probably stands first in their affections. They are proud of the historic spots in their State, and mark them clearly; perhaps cannily, for the tourist trade is a great element in the prosperity of parts of Virginia.

Virginia at its best is to be encountered in one spot. Charlottesville is approached by scenes of great beauty, and the buildings of the University of Virginia deserve the praise bestowed upon them by architects and the admiration of lay visitors. They have a dignity and a grace unequalled anywhere. They make you conscious of their builder's consummate genius in so many fields.

Somehow, I did not hear so much talk of the author of the Declaration in Virginia as I did of others of the Old Dominion's great sons. Except, of course, at Charlottesville, where the squire of Albemarle County has his shrine.

You go to Monticello up a steep incline. The grounds are hidden in early summer by the green of the trees. Then the sight of the house excites your imagination. It is the expression of democracy in terms of beauty, utility and comfort; for it has all three, as any object must have them to attain perfection.

It is not the house, however, that is important. It is not the house that is the best thing in Virginia. It is the epitaph on a weathered obelisk above the grave of a man who dreamed dreams in his youth and saw visions in his age.

Here was buried
Thomas Jefferson,
Author of the Declaration of Independence,
of the Statute of Virginia for Religious Freedom,
and Father of the University of Virginia.

I will swap you ten Williamsburgs and its hundred Olde Gifte Shoppes for one sight of Monticello.

7: THEY DID IT AGAINST ODDS

There is left of the South one State about which I have written nothing.

How shall a man write about his native countryside? There is not a town or village in Georgia that I have not visited. I know the bustle of Atlanta, the busiest distribution point in all Dixie; I know the quiet drowsiness of St. Mary's, with great oaks draped with moss that were old when Oglethorpe's settlers landed; I know the beauty of Georgia's hills, that are prettier than a young girl at Easter when they are dressed in green and more lovely than a much-loved woman when they wear the brown of November. I know the taste of every Georgia dish: the ubiquitous fried chicken with hot biscuits, crisp-fried lake bream with hush puppies, shrimp low-mull that they cook on the coast, collard-greens cooked with salt pork with which butter-milk is greatly to be desired, barbecue, hot both from the hickory coals and from the sauces, watermelon rind preserves that have spent three years in a crock, well seasoned with ginger.

I know the people of Georgia: those of the mountains with a culture that goes back to Elizabethan times, and those of the sections that were not settled until long after the War Between the States when the pine forests were felled, and those who work on farms or in textile mills.

I know that Georgia has sustained more wounds from war than any other part of America. It was the youngest of the thirteen colonies when the Revolution broke out; not only were half its homes razed in the struggle, but, unlike many of the States, it paid its share of the cost of the war with money and supplies instead of scrip, and faced an economic crisis when peace came. It struggled back, until only Virginia among the States that made up the Confederacy had more industries when secession came, and its farming was so diversified that Georgia bore the burden of feeding the armies in gray. Then Sherman came, and his men ravaged a path across the State from Atlanta's cinders to the sea at Savannah, and the thing had to be done over.

My grandfather helped do it, tending store and farm and rebuilding an abandoned cord mill near Newnan. My father helped too. And the grandfathers and fathers of all other Georgians.

They did it against odds. The economic scales were weighted against them. They had to sell their products on a buyer's market, and buy what they needed on a seller's market. They were effectively restricted in establishing industries. They were driven to cutting down their forests, mining their soil, wearing out their muscles and hearts and hands; it is not cotton that they sell on the New York Cotton Exchange, it is the very soil of Georgia and the blood from the hearts of Georgia men and women; it is the youth of boys and girls, and the happiness and the dreams of men and women.

They were beset by absentee taskmasters, who learned their trade from that Pharaoh who had Israel to make bricks without straw. They were harassed by scalawag demagogues, who shrilled racial hate and sectional disunity at the bidding of those who hired them with the interest on the thirty pieces of silver that Judas would not keep.

They have won again. There is prosperity in Georgia. There is a modern outlook. There is a new standard of living. Every third Georgia farmhouse has electric lights. The schools are open for a full term. New industries are arising, more closely identified with Georgia's products of forest and farm and mine than before.

I can no more write of those things in objective terms than I can describe Newnan to you, with its tidy little square and the Confederate soldier who stands guard upon the little monument before the Court House door; he has stood there since 1885, and he is not weary of his watch nor are we of Newnan weary of him, nor do we forget in April to place flowers there in memory of the men who fell with Johnston at Shiloh, and with Gordon at Seven Oaks, and with Hood before the gates of doomed Atlanta.

I sit there, in a small white-shuttered house, and think about America; and America means Newnan and Georgia multiplied by the number of every State and every town in our common country. Other towns and other States have their memories, too; and their statues on Court House squares; and there are other white-shuttered houses, very like my own. About them I am writing, as objectively as I can; and as understandingly as I can; objectively because I have seen much of America in a journey of some seventy-five thousand miles and I would like for you to see it as I have seen it; understandingly, I hope, because I am trying to see the home towns of other Americans through the same eyes that see Newnan and that love it.

VI

WEST

*Besides fate or determinism, there is creative intelligence
in the world, and there is also opportunity to exercise our
powers, intellectual and moral. America is well endowed
with such powers.*
—THE REPUBLIC, CHARLES A. BEARD

1: THE FOUR POINTS OF THE COMPASS

The West has neither geographical nor ethnic unity. It is an artificial classification, as I am employing it, and embraces all that enormous region that lies on the far side of the Mississippi River that is neither definitely Southern nor Northern. Thus it includes Texas, a vast empire within itself which considers itself Southern; and the Pacific Northwest, where the citizens of Washington, Oregon and Idaho have a feeling that they are a separate region; and California, which, like Texas, is huge and contains so many different elements that it is entitled to individual consideration.

The best that I can say for the division that I have undertaken is that the four points of the compass provide convenient name-tags for divisions of this book, and that the corresponding regions have identifying economic characteristics. Thereby East becomes that area which is dependent upon exploitation for its prosperity. North is the section where opportunity and natural resources have permitted a development that is well integrated and well rounded. South is an area of exploitation, as well as a tradition and a way of thought. West is the vastness beyond, that is underdeveloped but not completely exploited, that is absentee controlled at present to a very large extent but that is struggling for economic and social independence.

Such an economic division of America is necessarily inaccurate, though no more inaccurate than a division by other characteristics. If it results in the people of Wyoming and Utah being grouped with those of Texas and California, I can only offer apologies; when it is necessary to file things in pigeonholes, you are almost certain to select the wrong one on occasion. Certainly the people of the West have no more reason for complaint than those of the three Border States, whom I choose to regard as Southern on the imperfect grounds that much of their area shares the exploitation of the South and that many of their memories are Southern memories; and yet, as I have said, the Border fought a war in 1860-65 that was a civil war, whatever name North or South might choose to call it by.

So Texas and California and Wyoming will have to be grouped together, differ though they may, if only on the grounds that all three need development, suffer from absentee control, and are looking toward a tomorrow that they must find if America is to prosper and endure.

The people of the West, despite the presence of such racial groups as Indians, Mexicans, Spanish, Chinese, Filipino, and Japanese, are American in a sense somewhat different from that meant when one says that New Englanders or Carolinians or Ohioans are Americans. The South was settled principally by Scotch and Scotch-Irish; New England was English and now is Irish and Polish, as well; Scandinavia, Germany, Middle Europe, the Balkans, Poland, Finland and the Ukraine contributed identifiably to the growth of the grain belt and industrial States of the North. But the West was settled by other Americans, from the other three regions.

Some critics, notably the very angry Philip Wylie, have complained that the West is divided into dissenting groups by State-of-origin. Except upon the moderately prosperous emigrés of Southern California, I have not noted myself any such tendency and the trend to be observed there seems to me to be chiefly a lingering nostalgia that is not very hurtful; I do not think that the members of the Iowa Club or the Michigan Club or the Texas Club in the vicinity of Los Angeles are engaged in any dark plots against each other or any plans against all of us to establish an Iowan suzerainty, for example, in the United States. There are no bloody battles between the Arkies and the Okies, both of whom tour the nation yet in battered vehicles seeking employment and a home. In Oregon you can find people from the South, from New England, from the grain belt, and from California and Florida. Indeed, everywhere in the West this is true; for the American still likes to adventure, and the setting sun still attracts those who seek for fortune somewhere over the hill.

There are some things in common in all this enormous area that justify the classification that has been imposed.

The entire area is subject to exploitation, through vicious freight rate differentials that average somewhat higher even than those that have paralyzed industry in the South.

Excluding the Northwest and Utah, but not Texas, there is more external interference with the political life of the people of the West than of any other Americans, including even those of the South.

Because American occupancy of the region is new and American supremacy was superimposed upon the customs of small groups of other racial origin, and because direct foreign emigration to the West has been from the Orient chiefly, the racial tensions sometimes flare into greater violence than in the other three regions, and the repression of minority elements has been more drastic.

The entire area is underdeveloped, despite the immense new installations on the Coast and the almost unlimited wealth of the region.

There are some customs that the entire vast region may be said to share, too. It is an area where food is good and plentiful, although the prices are not so low as in the North. Except for the viands of Mexican derivation, there is nothing that can be said to be a Western culinary school; or if there is, it is eclectic, for you can find all the goods of all the other sections of America. But what passes for barbecue usually is an atrocity.

The people travel great distances casually. A hundred-mile drive, each way, to attend a sport event or a lecture or a show is commonplace with the average family in Texas, it seems.

The people love outdoor movies and outdoor spectacles of every kind. These range from drive-in-theatres, which you can find sprinkling almost all of the States I have cataloged as West, to great amphitheatres for the presentation of opera. Some of the drive-in-movies in Texas can accommodate astronomical numbers of cars, and every space seems filled every night.

The entire West seems to have a remarkable feeling that history is in the making. Although it is a long time since Drake put into the Golden Gate with his swashbucklers from the *Golden Hind,* the West is new. It was not many years ago that Austin and his settlers reached Texas, or that Frémont stormed through California, or that Brigham Young led his followers to Deseret. The youth of the West emphasizes the youth of America, its newness, its resources, its freshness of viewpoint. It serves as a rebuke to those who believe that "America has reached economic and social maturity" and that what small future we have as a nation is one of sitting in slippers by the fire, waiting for dissolution; half of America remains unsettled, and yet there are those who assert that there are no frontiers left to be conquered.

The very vastness of the West is exciting. A lecturer bent on filling engagements on schedule must take to the air, and that gives him a chance to see the panorama of America beneath, magnificent in its proportions and rich in resources that have not yet been developed.

2: "A Graphic Guide to Decentralization"

The *why* of that underdevelopment of the West has been examined in the almost invaluable report of the Special Committee to Investigate the Centralization of Heavy Industry in the United States, authorized by the United States Senate. The report is entitled "A Graphic Guide to Decentralization." The Committee is usually called the McCarran Committee, after its chairman.

Its membership was predominantly conservative. Besides the Senator from Nevada, the members were Bankhead of Alabama, Gillette of Iowa, Murdock of Utah, Thomas of Idaho, Nye of North Dakota, and Robertson of Wyoming.

The report was prepared in 1944, as a guide for the Congress in dealing with the problems of reconversion, disposition of government-owned war plants, and legislation in the field of transportation.

The achievements in production of the Western States during the war period were summarized in the report, which concluded that ten million more residents were needed immediately in those States and that industrial production should be increased and diversified. The West was described as "underdeveloped and underpopulated." Said the summary of the report:

> "The development of industries in the West, sufficient to take care of the new army of industrial workers, would undoubtedly under present circumstances provide work, according to known ratios, for another 3,000,000 men. Eastern industry would profit enormously. There would be a large demand for refrigerators, radios, washing machines, electric appliances of every sort, furnaces, plumbing fixtures; also hardware, paint, and so forth."

The report had pointed to the three million new citizens of the West, who had gone there patriotically to work in the war industries and the need for finding them permanent employment in that area. To provide homes and essential services, it was estimated that these additional three million workers could be absorbed with their families.

> "All this depends upon our allowing the West to establish industries to provide permanent employment for 1,500,000 workers now engaged in war industries," this prophetic summary reported. "The West has the mineral, the timber and sea resources."

The report examined one of the principal causes of the underdevelopment of the West, and found the freight differential system guilty, recommending its elimination. However, although the Congress directed its elimination, the Interstate Commerce Commission has not seen fit to carry out instructions, and relief must depend, I am afraid, on the aftermath of Georgia's suit under the anti-trust laws.

But the report did not examine one other factor in detail, although employing language that is exceptionally strong for such political conservatives in pointing to the eventual calamity:

> "Let us face the facts. Europe is in ruins. Capitalism in Europe has been dealt a grave blow. It may never recover fully. The elimination of the important European countries as free-enterprise countries tends to place us more and more in the position of the nation with the isolated economy. If our system is to survive, we must avoid such a position. Who has ruined Europe? Obviously the apostles of centralization who, through the instrumentality of Hitler and the Nazis, had hoped to seize all economic power and hold it for the large corporations and a few international cartels."

Thus did the concerned, honest and forthright conservatives of the McCarran Committee deal with the real problem of the West: the problem of absentee domination.

As I travelled about the West, there was adequate evidence of this condition and of the state of mind that it engendered. There were citizens who were indignant about its existence, and there were citizens who were indignant that it should be observed. This latter type of indignation was encountered most frequently in Texas, Wyoming, California and Colorado, the four States in which the interference perhaps has been most effective, most openly insulting to the sensibilities of the people, and most damaging to the political and social institutions.

The South, more used to such outside interference in its affairs, hardly feels the same sensitiveness about discussions of the question of absentee owners and bosses as does Texas, represented in the Senate by O'Daniel, or California that had a Merriam inflicted upon it as Governor. But then the transportation and finance barons who looted the South possessed more finesse than the oil and sulphur overlords of Texas or the cannery crowd, the mass-production farm owners, and the movie-finance and transportation moguls of California.

The fact remains that, until the advent of the New Deal, there was little industry worthy of the name in the West, and no opportunity for Western investors to put their money into Western enterprises. Political independence, in any actual sense, had been narrowly won, but not fully retained in California, but did not exist in any of the Mountain States except Utah or anywhere else in the West except the three Northwestern States of Washington, Oregon and Idaho, which attained a political maturity of viewpoint soon after World War One.

The people of the West, however, are making a fight for independence and making an effective fight. Bronson Cutting's first victory in New Mexico was the actual beginning of the end for the absentee masters and their Quislings, such as the Fall machine that Cutting pulverized. Although much of Wyoming's land is owned by non-residents or by citizens whose residence is nominal and for tax reasons, that State is represented in the Senate by Joseph C. O'Mahoney, one of the most valuable leaders of liberalism in the nation. Gradually, by such victories, absentee domination is being eliminated; the reëlection of W. Lee O'Daniel was by no large margin, while such liberals as Sheridan Downey, Dennis Chavez, and James E. Murray have had relatively easy victories.

The problem of reconversion emphasized for the people of the West the interference by monopolists in their lives and livelihoods.

The policy of the transportation bosses in attempting to help to throttle the Kaiser steel projects drew attention to the entire industrial helplessness of the area. Since water is the big need of the West, the citizens could not help noticing that reclamation projects which might be associated with public power developments were eyed with hostility by Eastern reactionaries.

Personally, I consider the estimates of the McCarran Committee extremely low on the subject of Western population. Allowing for every possible handicap in solving the requirements for irrigation, assuming that the trend toward decentralization is not rapidly accelerated, and recognizing the magnitude of the transportation problems involved, I still believe that the West, as I have defined it, can absorb not less than thirty million additional Americans instead of the ten million suggested by the McCarran Report. An America of a quarter-billion population is very possible, if we develop our resources instead of wasting them.

What are the people of the West like?

They are like all the other Americans that I saw elsewhere, although their costumes are decidedly more varied than those you will find on Broadway in New York or Peachtree in Atlanta, or State Street in Chicago, or Main Street in Sauk Center, Minnesota. The people of the West certainly are not standardized as to clothing; they are bold, and dare to wear what they like, from seersuckers to chaps, from California's casual costumes to dinner jackets. Otherwise they might be people from Newnan or Des Moines or Binghamton.

The West is a synthesis of America. When you think that the Midwestern influences predominate, you notice the egalitarianism that is peculiarly Southern. When you decide that Missouri furnished the basis for the Western variety of drawl, you listen to the tongue of a Wyoming citizen with the sharpness of New Hampshire. You can find anything you like in the way of customs in the West, for the West has absorbed all the customs of all the rest of America, and improvised upon them.

What do the people of the West want?

They want an equal place in their common country and ours. They want a chance to develop their resources. Translated into practical terms, they desire help with their problems of power and water, assistance in their housing needs, and elimination of all trade barriers that keep them from developing needed industries. On foreign policy, they are somewhat against a "soft peace" that will return Japan to its financial overlords or Germany to the Junkers, and there is no trace of isolationism in the West except that which stems from a feeling that our foreign policy is not always coherent and democratic: the Pacific is wide, but distances in the West are so great that it is looked upon as little barrier for our defense. In domestic politics, the West is a little Left of Center; not much, but enough to make it an area in which a wholly American brand of radicalism might flourish if somebody is foolish enough to permit another depression.

The West wants more Americans for citizens, and more development of its amazing resources, and an end to the policy of exploitation that makes of South and West colonies to be drained of profit. That seems to me little enough to ask for, on the part of the inhabitants of something over half the area of the continental United States.

3: CALIFORNIA IS COLOSSAL

All I know about California is what I saw from the air and what I read in the papers. They would not let me see the State.

On February 9, 1947, I arrived in Los Angeles, in the late afternoon and the cab whirled me to the Biltmore. They take pictures of everybody in Los Angeles, and the row over the Georgia Governorship was going full blast and I had just resigned and turned the office over to the Lieutenant-Governor chosen by the people in 1946; so I was not surprised to find a delegation of cameramen, both still and movie, awaiting me. They took their shots, and I went down to dinner with some friends.

During the meal, I was paged twice, but I did not answer. I was much too hungry and the conversation was much too good for me to interrupt either food or talk to go to the phone. But when the meal ended, and my friends left, I went by the desk to get the calls, intending to go outside and await other friends who were going to pick me up to go to the Auditorium to talk.

At the desk, however, a group of six men closed in upon me.

One of them asked if I were Ellis Arnall, and I confessed that I was.

"I'm a lieutenant in the homicide squad," he said, flashing his badge and a folder full of credentials. "I have instructions to keep you under surveillance."

"I haven't anything to do with the Black Dahlia case," I replied, mentioning the current Los Angeles page one murder. "I just want to go ahead and do my lecture, and my friends are waiting outside."

"We'll tell your friends where they can meet you," he said. "You are coming with us, mister. Don't you listen to the radio? Walter Winchell just broadcast that you are going to be assassinated tonight while you are speaking. We're going to see that nothing happens."

They whisked me away to the Auditorium. They seated the audience from the rear, so that some twenty rows were bare in front of me, a great inspiration to any speaker. Uniformed policemen lined the walls. The lieutenant advised me that, if I heard a shot, whether it hit me or not, to drop to the floor and lie still.

"We'll get him if he shoots you," the lieutenant said amiably. "The exits are covered. He can't get away."

Walter Wanger, the motion picture producer, was scheduled to introduce me. I noticed that our chairs on the platform were very far apart, and I suggested that we move them together. He said that he could hear me perfectly well at that distance.

I lectured. I talked for an hour and fifteen minutes, glancing at Wanger occasionally. As the only other target in sight, he did not appear to be enjoying my speech any more than I was. I am certain

I was not the least afraid, but it must have been quite warm in the Auditorium, for my hands kept perspiring.

I did not see much of Los Angeles from my hotel room. It is the center of the motion picture industry, and of the transplanted Americans of comfortable means who enjoy the climate of California to its utmost. It is the largest city in the world in area, and if it builds up completely will have a population as great as that of Canton, Bombay, London, Buenos Aires and Chicago combined.

I next went to Fresno. While I protested, the Los Angeles homicide squad provided me with an escort to the plane. The Fresno police provided me with an escort to the hotel. Fresno is in the valley, about midway between Los Angeles and San Francisco, and is the center of the fruit industry in California. Those portions of it that I saw while being transported from plane to hotel to auditorium to hotel to plane were pleasant and there was a look of substantial prosperity about its streets.

They relaxed their guard somewhat in San Francisco, where the St. Francis is one of the best hotels in America into which no assassin would dare enter. The city has a charm something like that of Savannah or Baltimore or New Orleans, but with a flavor of its own and beauty quite unusual. The bridge is all that a visitor might ask, and the view of the Golden Gate makes one wonder why Drake did not settle there with his men instead of returning to England to destroy the Armada.

It was not until I reached Salt Lake City that there was any explanation of the Winchell broadcast. I had wired Walter Winchell from Los Angeles, but his reply did not overtake me until the plane deposited me in Utah.

He wired me back: "I was merely trying to protect you from those crackpots and I did."

Winchell has many interesting sources of information, and I wish he would give me the lowdown on this some day. Especially since I wanted to see California.

Not that California can be observed closely in a short time. It is colossal, with many industries and a varied agriculture. Almost every crop known to America, from apricots to wheat alphabetically, is produced by its rich soil. Its mineral wealth is almost incalculable. People went to California to seek gold, but the oil of the State is infinitely more valuable.

California is an impressive instance of the waste on one hand and efficiency on the other that may be attained by large-scale agricultural projects. Yet one wonders what might become of California's prosperity if the supply of migrant workers were reduced sharply by their absorption into industry or their acquisition of small yeoman holdings. To cultivate large farms, or what might more properly be termed agricultural factories, under a system of mechanization is comparatively simple, but harvesting requires workers in large numbers. Although the Mexican population is engaged in such work, the majority of migratory fruit pickers in recent years have been drawn from the dispossessed farmers of the Dust Bowl.

Whether agriculture lends itself with genuine efficiency to mass production techniques has not yet been satisfactorily determined. Endeavors to find an historical parallel in Roman Italy, where yeoman-held tracts were absorbed into large estates and the land literally worked out by slave gangs, in the days when Caesar and his successors provided Gauls, Britons, Saxons, Greeks and Germans in inexhaustible numbers for such servitude, fail because mechanization had not been introduced and scientific knowledge of soil use was not even sought after.

It would seem reasonable to assume, however, that non-exploitative efficiency in agricultural mass production can be attained only where the same degree of mechanization is applicable to harvesting that is applicable to cultivation. That would tend to withdraw fruit and table-vegetable growing from mass production ultimately, since these present no true counterpart to the mechanized production of grains, or of cotton when the mechanical cotton picker shall be perfected and effects its inevitable revolution in the South.

Industrially, California is growing rapidly and its industries are certain to expand. For all our immediate preoccupation with Europe, the Pacific offers invitation to America for trade, and the fact that California is the base for trade with the Orient makes it a great potential industrial producer. A tremendous labor force was assembled there during the war, engaged in shipbuilding and airplane construction primarily. But there are other industries, and the day will come when California will rival the South as a manufacturer of textiles.

The political history of California since the turn of the century has been fascinating. In few other States, Texas again excepted, is there such a bitter struggle between reaction and libertarianism, and in California the cleavage perhaps is sharper than anywhere else. The State long was dominated by the transcontinental railroads, which interfered with every unit of government down to the smallest village. This control was broken, at least in part, about 1908, the building of the Panama Canal contributing rather more than political historians, usually bent on finding words of adulation for the opportunistic Hiram Johnson, seem willing to discover. The utilities retain great influence in public affairs, sufficient to hamper the development of power and irrigation projects. The great landowners dominate the agricultural picture.

But the California climate has attracted many people to the State, including a large number of retired residents of the grain belt, who agitate lustily for old-age pension systems of great liberality. The labor movement is influential, although unhappily divided between Rightist and Leftist wings.

As a result, California's Democrats once nominated Upton Sinclair as their candidate for Governor, although the novelist and pamphleteer was a Socialist nominally and somewhat of a visionary in the field of economics. It is difficult to make an evaluation of Sinclair. His fierce integrity blazes from the pages of *The Jungle* and *Boston,* which the dignified *The Atlantic Monthly* published as a serial, and from such pamphleteering ventures as *Little Steel* and *The Brass Check.* He always has been energetically democratic, and never compromised with any of the Communist ideologies, wanting no dictatorship of anybody, master race or proletariat either. As a critic of social and economic evils, he has been valuable to America and to the cause of freedom; but I rather doubt that he would have made California a satisfactory Governor in the trying period when the country was recovering from the collapse that was associated with the name of another Californian, a now happily forgotten resident of Palo Alto named Hoover, who served as Secretary of Commerce in the boom period and made ready the depression of his own Presidency.

The Democrats were beaten with Sinclair as their nominee, and the victor was Frank Finley Merriam, a feeble reactionary, who paved the way for Republican collapse in the State. The Democrats of California have now forced the Republicans to something close to a middle-of-the-road party in local affairs, with Governor Warren, a sound administrator and a sensible and effective politician, becoming one of the most available candidates for his party's nomination for President. The party battle remains intense, in spite of Governor Warren's dual nomination in 1946, and the California delegation in Washington is rather evenly divided between the major parties.

California is divided into two parts, and the political lines coincide somewhat with the geographic division; Southern California is Democratic, while the upper part of the State is Republican. Sacramento is the nominal capital, but in truth about half of California revolves about Los Angeles and the other half about San Francisco.

California's unique cross-filing system in the direct primaries adds to the confusion of its politics. Governor Warren was the nominee of both Democrats and Republicans. Some of the Congressmen won in both primaries. Cross-filing and cross-voting provides excitement, but the State would profit by somewhat more rational an election system in the view of many political experts; I do not know; perhaps anything that gets as many people to the polls as have voted in California since 1930 is a good system pragmatically; and it is desirable that experiments be conducted on the State level to ascertain what is sound practice. While it is true that there have been instances in which organized groups have invaded both primaries in an effort to force a decision between the two major parties upon a definitely unfair basis, the damage has not been too serious to date.

The people of California, like the people of Georgia and Maine, undoubtedly have both their own problems and their own local ways. Perhaps the climate has attracted a certain number of crackpots, too, both Leftist and Rightist, who mouth and parade and break up meetings. And once a silly police chief arrested some bobbysoxers because they wanted to hear their favorite crooner make a sincere plea for racial understanding. The treatment of American citizens of Japanese extraction has been exceedingly unjust, and Mexicans, Arkies and Okies have been denied civil rights and have sustained exploitation. The racial tension may be a little higher than in most American States, but I have memories of the forlorn community of Mexicans in Manhattan, Kansas, and of the wave of hatred that banned the German language in many states in 1917, and of South Carolina's repeal of its statutes against frauds in primaries in a futile effort to deprive Negroes of the right to vote: though Southerners are used to the practice of indicting a whole people, I concur with Edmund Burke that the practice is indefensible.

Part of the racial tension in California, I suspect, is fanned by the same elements who encourage it in the South. It helps to create a false issue and to divert attention away from exploitation. It is successful for a time. Exploitation always has its successes, but long after the Stanfords and Huntingtons have gone, the people and the earth and the sky will still be here.

4: FORTY DECIDED TO STAY

Through the heart of the city winds the river, which though occasionally turbulent usually is placid and lovely. About San Antonio are scattered many pleasant squares, breaking into the bustle of the community, and underneath the trees on the park benches, you will find men playing dominoes and smoking pipes solemnly. There are many uniforms on the street, even in years of peace, for Fort Sam Houston and Kelly Field and Randolph Field are busy military centers.

The town is a cluster of tall buildings and fine homes and hovels. The St. Anthony is one of the finest hotels in America, visitors always agree, with most comfortable rooms and most agreeable food and the prettiest hatcheck girls in the country.

San Antonio is gay. In spring the squares are dressed in green that conceals the mediocrity of the monuments, and young people stroll through the parks hand in hand, or along the banks of the river; and the bluebonnets are as sweet as a girl in love for the first time. On April 21 comes the Battle of Flowers, which Texans will tell you commemorates Sam Houston's victory at San Jacinto in 1836, but which everyone knows in his heart commemorates an older victory, the mystery of Spring's recurrent and so brief triumph over Winter.

San Antonio has been an important military and trading center since Spanish days. It has changed hands in many wars: in Mexico's Revolution twice, and three times in the days when Texans fought for independence. It has been capital of a Spanish and a Mexican province. It is one of the major transportation centers of Texas, and one of the gateways to the West. Rich as is its history, however, it seems most of all to be a place where people live.

There is poverty in San Antonio, especially among the Mexican population, which is large. But, except in the bitter depression years from which Maury Maverick rescued the town, the poverty has not deteriorated into squalor, because there is a lightheartedness about San Antonio that rejects immaterial things.

It is a city of contrasts. There is not quite the hurry of Dallas or Fort Worth about its streets, but San Antonio is a busy town. Yet you can step from the noise of the thoroughfares into the quiet of the Alamo.

For eleven days Santa Anna's artillery hurled cannonballs against the walls. Gradually the defenders retreated to the chapel. Then came the final assault, and every man died with Travis and Fannin and Bowie and Crockett. One hundred eighty-seven men can not withstand six thousand forever, even if they are cast in heroic mould. Among them were forty men from Gonzales.

All of us have our favorite heroes, and they are mine. Not the aging Beowulf girding on his armor for the final duel, nor Alfred at Ethandune, nor even Douglas following The Bruce's heart to his last battle, were braver than they. For they broke through the enemy's lines and into the doomed citadel and refused to leave it. They were farm boys from the Southern hills, for the most part. They had come hundreds of miles over hard trails and rushing rivers to a new land and a new life; but they could travel yet another seventy-one miles to die.

In Texas you are never far away from memories of the Alamo, or of the single-starred flag of the Republic that Austin and Houston and Lamar established, and that is unique among American states because it was admitted by treaty into the Union. Texans do not forget, nor do they fail to impress upon the visitor, that Texas fought its own war for independence.

To that war, as to the building of the infant Republic and early State, the South made the greatest contribution. Tennessee, Georgia and the Carolinas supplied the families that founded Texas. Houston, the hero of Independence and the victor over Santa Anna at San Jacinto, had a distinguished public record in Tennessee before he cast his lot with the rebellious settlers. Mirabeau B. Lamar, second President of Texas, was a member of a famous Georgia family, and founded a notable Georgia newspaper, the Columbus *Enquirer,* which still carries on its masthead, this quotation from his address to the Texas Congress:

"An enlightened mind is the guardian genius of democracy. It is the only dictator that free men admit. It is the only security that free men desire."

The early Texas was founded by men who wished to see a civilization of yeoman-farmers develop. Its leaders were Jackson Democrats and strong Union men; to the last Sam Houston fought secession, but San Jacinto was twenty-five years away and he was an old and bitter man; moreover, "The Bonnie Blue Flag" was a catchy song, and Texans marched away to it behind Albert Sidney Johnston, and many of them fell with him at Shiloh.

There are many ethnic elements in Texas that differentiate it from the Southeast, including the influx of German settlers into the San Antonio area. The Mexican population is considerable, and maintains in many instances a kind of dual culture alongside the rest of the citizens. The Negro population is much smaller proportionately than in the Southeastern States. Many Negroes removed from Texas after the War Between the States, and few have moved there from other sections since that time.

The variety of Texas' agricultural products is hardly imaginable. Everything grows somewhere within the tremendous empire-within-a-State. Cattle and sheep and the feeding of them is a big enterprise, but so is cotton and citrus fruits and table vegetables. Oil is big business. Sulphur is big business. Corpus Christi is a newly built city, in large part, because chemicals are produced there and it was necessary to move a great portion of the community to make room for the giant facilities.

They also have weather in Texas, about which they talk and tell big tales; and many of the tales are justified. All weather anywhere in Texas is compared with that in Amarillo. I spoke in Amarillo one evening in February. The next morning, expecting to catch an eight-thirty plane, I got up at six, and looked out at the cold bright dawn, and went down to breakfast. When I got up from breakfast, the skies were overcast and a heavy snow was falling. Within thirty minutes, four inches came down.

I was glad that I saw Amarillo the day before. It is the most colorful town in the country, capital of the Panhandle, center where the westbound railroads converge, and a city where almost everyone you see is wearing broad-brimmed hats and high-heeled boots. It lived up to my boyhood images of the cowboy West.

Austin provided my introduction to Texas, and I have visited the State's capital city several times and its magnificent University of Texas, one of the great liberal institutions of the nation, with a fine faculty and an equally fine campus. But my memories of Austin are associated with the strain of two weeks there in 1939, when I was Attorney-General of Georgia, and found myself with one of the most difficult cases of my career on my hands.

With another youthful companion, Dick Gallogly, a teen-age college student, had staged a holdup of an Atlanta drug store in 1928. In the course of the holdup, the druggist was slain. The two boys were apprehended, and brought to trial. The other youth was convicted and sentenced to death, but a mistrial occurred in Gallogly's case. On his second trial, he entered a plea of guilty, and both boys were sent to prison for life.

Gallogly had served ten years in prison, when he made an escape, assisted by his pretty young wife. They went to Texas, and she made a dramatic and effective plea to the chivalry of Texans; one photograph showed her wrapped in the Lone Star flag.

Before my term as Attorney-General of Georgia, I had represented Gallogly in a clemency appeal, which was unsuccessful. Because of the prominence of his family, he had become something of a political prisoner and his case was a *cause célèbre* in Georgia.

I could not afford to ask any member of my staff to represent the State of Georgia in the case; if there were to be a failure, it would have to be mine. For two weeks the case stayed before the Governor of Texas; finally he decided to grant extradition.

When I returned to Georgia, where I could hardly have come back had the decision gone against me, my wife, who had followed the case in the newspapers and who felt a strong sympathy with the young bride of the boy, greeted me by saying that she had hoped that they would have been allowed to stay in Texas.

5: THEY ALL FEEL THE SAME WAY

I have a special affection for Texas because my career as a lecturer began there, somewhat by inadvertence, and because so many pleasant things have happened to me on my trips across its vastness.

Early in 1946, my friend S. Russell Bridges of the Alkahest Celebrity Bureau at Atlanta, who once piloted William Jennings Bryan's lecture tours, urged me to accept some lecture dates. Ivan Allen, Jr., secretary of the Executive Department, helped talk me into it, with the argument that I had talked a great deal about America and seen very little of it, while here was an opportunity to see it. My first fully booked, really-paid-for engagement as a lecturer was at San Antonio on February 11, 1946. I was scheduled to speak at an open forum, presided over by Henry B. Dielman, and soon after noon I checked in at the St. Anthony, and then walked out to view the town. In the late afternoon, panic struck me. What should I talk about, two hours from then. I sat down, and on the back of an envelope, I sketchily outlined a few points. With that as a guide, I stumbled through the performance.

I have used the same, now somewhat worn, envelope and the same notes to deliver essentially the same talk in almost every State of the Union, and especially all over Texas.

At Beaumont, the Junior League's Welfare Club sponsored my talk before a sedate middle-class audience in an oil production center where organized labor has become a great political and economic factor. In Wichita Falls, a new city and one of the most important sheep towns in Texas, I had the same things to say, and discovered that people there felt much as they did elsewhere; indeed, someone at Wichita Falls had saved me a copy of the Boston *Post* with an editorial saying that talk about Western and Southern woollen mills was nothing but "the ranting of Ellis Arnall"; I also found that Western textile folk share my slight prejudice against Boston as a symbol of exploitation.

At Southwestern University at Georgetown, at North Texas State

College at Denton, at West Texas Teachers College at Canyon, I said the same things that I said before the Chamber of Commerce at Childress, and before the Knife and Fork Club of San Angelo up in the sheep-raising hills, and before the forums at Colorado City and Monahans and Plainview and Bryan. It was the same talk for the Junior Chamber of Commerce at Waco, where Pat Neff, then head of Texas' great Baptist university, introduced me; and for the Athletic Club at Dallas and for the Women's Club of Fort Worth.

And every time, the people nodded at the same places, and applauded at the same places, and seemed to feel the same way. Americans differ much in their incomes, in the kind of homes they live in, in the kind of work they do to earn a living; but they agree that fair play is due every citizen, that every section is entitled to opportunity, that every child should have an education regardless of race or color, that every American should be able to speak his mind anywhere freely and without fear.

They are interested in all of America. In many respects, the interests of the citrus growers of Texas are as removed from those of its sheepmen or cattle ranch owners as from those of the copper miners of Montana or the lumbermen of the Northwest. But in every town in Texas that I visited, I found the citizens interested in the rest of their State and in the rest of their country. They were better informed and more alert to domestic and foreign issues than many of their leaders believe, and they understood that we can not disassociate our national economy from the affairs of the world.

That was emphasized for me one day in El Paso, when I picked up the newspaper and discovered that a considerable number of veterinarians, bacteriologists and technicians were being sent by our government to help the Republic of Mexico eliminate an outbreak of hoof-and-mouth disease that threatened the herds of that nation and that might cross the border.

If we can fight the contagious diseases of cattle, that might affect our prosperity and well-being, why can we not fight the contagious diseases of mankind? Not only those that can be combatted by doctors and nurses with vaccines, serums, and drugs, but those that are disorders of society, brought on by poverty and by pernicious propaganda.

At Houston, which is one of the fastest growing of Texas' large cities, I shared the platform with Upton Close, the radio commentator, under circumstances that were a little trying for us both. He had been invited to address the Texas Education Association, but the invitation had been withdrawn. My Western agent, M. C. Turner, of the Dixie Bureau at Dallas, had accepted the date for me. James V. Allred, one of the most distinguished of liberal Texans, presented me, and I talked. Then someone seized the microphone and said that Mr. Close had been invited; that he was there; that he had a speech prepared; and that he ought to be given an opportunity to deliver it. Mr. Close apparently refused to accept the cancellation of his invitation, insisting on his right of free speech. That day the members of the Texas Education Association had an opportunity to weigh divergent economic and political views, at any rate.

Throughout every visit that I have paid to Texas, I have never been bored even for an hour: something always happens and the local customs are pleasant. As when they have a coffee hour on the trains of the Texas and Pacific Railway each morning at ten-thirty, because everyone in Texas must have coffee at mid-morning. Indeed, when I last left Texas on a December morning, the people of Monahans had forgotten all about oil wells; they were heading for coffee and half an hour of gossip and tall tales.

Much of Texas' vast resources are absentee controlled, and much of the new industry brought in during the war emergency through the zeal of Jesse Jones is dominated by Eastern management. The same fight between the local middle class and the absentee lords that Sam Houston forecast a hundred years ago is going on. On the whole, it looks as if the Texans will win their second War of Independence.

The philosophy of the average Texan, I am assured, is summed up in a clipping that I found from the Bryan *Daily Eagle*. Mrs. Lee J. Rountree is a first-class editor, and what her shears select must appeal to her readers. It says:

> "I don't want any money I can't spend;
> I don't want any whiskey I can't drink;
> I don't want any secret I can't tell."

6: JESSE JAMES SLEPT HERE

They have land and scenery in Wyoming, and they stage rodeos in Laramie. Much of the land is absentee owned and a good deal is owned by the Federal government. Much is still controlled, directly or otherwise, by the railroads that received such lavish grants from the Congress back in the days of Crédit Mobilier.

Laramie was named for a legendary figure, the French-Canadian trapper Jacques LaRamie, who competes with Paul Bunyan for vigor; if Bunyan could fell a forest in a day, LaRamie could trap a pack of wolves in a night or skin a herd of buffalo before breakfast. The town has other legends. On August 30, 1876, Jack McCall was arrested for shooting Wild Bill Hickok, and Jesse James once occupied a cell in the same stouthouse. Bill Nye founded his fabulous paper, *Boomerang,* there in 1890. It was a wild town in those days, was Laramie, just after the Union Pacific tracks had reached the site.

There are plenty of cowboys in Laramie now, and the Union Pacific is still one of the mainstays of its economy, but the University of Wyoming, only college in the State, dominates the community. The streets are bordered with cottonwoods and poplars, which are conspicuous against the barren prairie. The Laramie Mountains glow in the morning sun. The few industries are hidden on the outskirts of the city, and do not infringe upon the residences and stores of downtown Laramie.

Wyoming has space, and only 2.1 persons to the square mile. It has beauty and a great possibility, and despite the influence of absentee owners, it has a tradition of progress and libertarianism, from its introduction of woman's suffrage in 1869 to its election of Senator O'Mahoney, one of the most stalwart independents in the Congress. It supplied America with its first woman Governor, when Mrs. Nellie Tayloe Ross was elected in 1925.

They joked about women voting and women serving on juries when Wyoming tried that innovation in 1870. In Laramie, they showed me in the library of the University a score of the mocking cartoons of that period. One was captioned:

> "Baby, baby, don't get in a fury;
> Your mama's gone to sit on the jury."

7: THE SLOPES OF THE ROCKIES

I read about Denver before I visited it for the first time, to talk to the Western Governors Conference and argue to them that the South and West must end their tutelage as colonies and assume their responsibilities as parts of our common country. The accounts of Denver told that an English army officer, accompanying the American forces as an observer of the Mexican War campaigns, described the site as the most beautiful he had ever seen. I expected to see mountains, but it was a cloudy day and not a mountain could be seen through the obscurity.

But they are there. Lieutenant Ruxton, of Her Britannic Majesty's forces, was not too exaggerative about the site in the Platte Valley, with grassy stretches and a wealth of cottonwoods, and with wild cherry and plum trees outlining the curve of Cherry Creek, and with the mountains in the distance brooding.

For all that Denver is the country's "Little Capital," with a horde of Federal employees, with more main offices of Federal agencies than any other city except Washington, and with the immense personnel of the Reclamation organization's engineering force, and for all its immense tourist business, Denver reminds me much of Newnan grown big.

It has a fair diversification of manufactures, from auto tires and candy to trunks and fancy crackers, but it is a wholesale town, a white-collar town, a market town. They handle more sheep there than anywhere else in the world, and it is the center of range cattle shipments. But it began as a stopping-off place for the Forty-Niners on their way to pan for California's gold; it sold them supplies. It sold supplies to those who came for Colorado's gold rush a decade later. Wholesaling is still its first and biggest business today. Someday, of course, they will have tremendous textile mills in Denver, to convert the wool from the sheep that grow in the Western States. That will come when the grip of the railroad monopoly relaxes and the West ceases to be underdeveloped and gains the population that it needs.

The tourists love Denver, for its dry air and its sunshine. It is the convention center for the West, and on every visit that I have paid it, its hotels were filled to overflow.

Colorado's principal scenic wonder is the Garden of the Gods, which I saw on my way to Colorado Springs. Although the Governor of Colorado, five of his predecessors in that office, and Senator Ed Johnson attended the meeting where I spoke, my real memory is of awakening in the Antlers Hotel and looking out toward the Rockies, which you felt that you could almost touch, and of staring at the height of Pikes Peak.

On a bus the next morning, that was taking me to Denver to catch a plane for Grand Junction and another talk, I was the unintentional beneficiary of a conversation between the occupants of the seat in front of me. One was a very professional-looking gentleman, who might have been either educator or medical specialist—probably the latter, because his clothes were expensive.

"I stayed over at the Springs to hear Ellis Arnall last night," he told his feminine companion. "He had a big crowd, but I was a little disappointed in him. He's not a profound man, just straightforward and sincere."

I wished afterward that I could have found some way to introduce myself and thank him for such a nice compliment.

On the Western slope, over the mountain ranges, almost exactly opposite from Colorado Springs is Grand Junction where lives one of the finest men in America, former U.S. Senator Walter Walker. He is publisher of the Grand Junction *Daily Sentinel* and one of the State's leading Democrats.

Colorado's problem is water. Colorado's politics are middle-of-the-road, with Democratic inclinations in the party divisions. Until a few years ago, the principal issue was local self-government, but a home rule measure eventually was passed that seems to satisfy most of the communities. It is difficult to understand why State leaders, who weep such abundant tears at the inroads of the Federal government upon their authority, should be so reluctant to give a demonstration of decentralization by allowing counties and cities to run their own business; it took Colorado more than a score of years to win independence for Denver and its other towns; it took Georgia a fight of thirty-two years before home rule was written into the new State constitution of 1945.

8: THE TRAIL OF TEARS

You would think that lecture tours would be arranged logically, and that once in the heart of the Mountain States, one would proceed by convenient stages of a few hundred miles a day toward the West. It is never so. The lecturer fills a date before that newest of dinner organizations, the Knife and Fork Club, at Denver, where the members eat and listen to visitors and have no programs, no objectives, and no discussions, and then he hurries away to catch a plane for Oklahoma.

I rather think that this is because American geography is not emphasized. It seems to be a common belief that, because Tulsa is west of New York and Seattle is west of New York, they must be no more than an overnight train-ride apart. America is so big, that we have no conception of its size or its power or its resources.

Oklahoma is new as a State, but it has some old problems, such as soil use and exploitation of natural resources. It is cotton and oil, and the homeland of the Okies, who were displaced from their small holdings after the collapse of the nation's economy, and replaced by machines. It is a State with a heavy Indian population, about ten per cent of the whole, and with the original Americans an influential factor in business, social life and politics.

One of my earliest appearances as a lecturer was in Oklahoma City. I knew the town, which is the cleanest that I have seen in America except Wichita, Kansas, because I made speeches for the Roosevelt-Truman ticket in Oklahoma in 1944.

Indeed it was an acquaintanceship made during that campaign that led to my invitation to talk to the Oklahoma Education Association. Roy Turner introduced me in 1944, and when I got back to Atlanta I sent him a commission as a Lieutenant-Colonel and Aide-de-Camp on the Governor's Staff. Then I met him again at a cattle show in West Virginia and discovered that he was a song writer and a former oil man who was now gentleman-farming at Hereford Heaven near Oklahoma City and serving on the local school board. My friends at the West Virginia show and sale said that he had a fine eye for Herefords, and I could see that he had a tremendous interest in public affairs and knew more about State government than most public officials. I suggested that he run for Governor of Oklahoma. He laughed, because he had never sought office of any kind or dabbled much in politics. But he changed his mind; he was elected in 1946 and demonstrated that he had as great a feel for politics as he had insight into government.

Governor Turner has an oil well in the backyard of the Executive Mansion. There is oil on the Capitol grounds. There is oil everywhere in Oklahoma, except in the cotton-growing regions, and Tulsa and Oklahoma City battle vigorously for leadership in the State.

Politically Oklahoma oscillates between liberalism and reaction, depending on the economic situation. It voted for Hoover in 1928, but it gave Roosevelt thumping majorities every term. Oklahomans with whom I have talked suggest that there is more outside exploitation of its agriculture than of its other resources, and this was an accident of the depression and the incident mortgage foreclosures. Since the restoration of some degree of economic stability in 1934, Oklahoma has been increasingly prosperous, and it enjoyed something of a boom during the war years, and has not suffered any recession since.

Georgia contributed more to the building of Oklahoma than any other Southern State, but I can not think of Georgia's contribution without shame. For the leadership among the Indians of Oklahoma belongs to the members of the Cherokee Nation, and it was Georgia's ruthless expulsion of the Cherokees that sent them down the Trail of Tears to the Indian Territory. Today in Georgia, except for a slight admixture of Cherokee blood in the people of some of the mountain communities, all that remains of the greatest and most civilized of the Southern tribes is a recollection of injustice and some names of great beauty, such as Rising Fawn, Coweta, Tallulah, Nacoochee, Amicalola, and Trahlyta. In neighboring North Carolina, having bought back some remnants of their tribal lands, the Cherokee Nation East continues to exist, almost as it did before Scott's soldiers rounded up the tribesmen and marched them away to lands far across the Father of Waters. But in Georgia, none remains to remember the tragic words of Tsali as he faced his executioners:

"If the Cherokee people now beyond the Mississippi carried my heart in their bosoms, they would never have left this beautiful land, these our mountains. Let my youngest son, whom you have spared, not pass beyond the Great River, but die where he was birthed. It is sweet to die in one's own country, and good to be buried by one's native stream."

The Cherokee Nation West gave to California an able Congressman in Will Rogers, Jr. and gave all America a great master of laughter in his father, who had the eloquence of The Ridge, bravest and most tragic of the Cherokee chieftains, who chose death rather than flight.

It was inevitable that, in the twilight of responsibility that existed in the first third of the nineteenth century, when no boundaries defined the obligations of State and Federal governments, the Indians remaining in the original States that had ceded their western lands to the United States should be victims. The Federal government had solemnly promised a legitimate and reasonable extinguishment of their claims and their peaceful removal to western lands, and had failed to keep its bargain in full. But the rapacity of land speculators, and the cruelty of the Georgia government in its dealing with the people of John Ross and Sequoya and Elias Boudinot, can not be defended.

The Cherokees, like many another Eastern tribe, yielded acre after acre in a slow retreat into their hills; but always the white settlers, and the land-grabbing speculators, pressed down upon them. Finally the troops came, and herded them along in a march almost half-way across the nation. When the end came, they were torn by internal bickerings, about which it is profitless to take sides, for The Ridge is dead where his assassins left him and John Ross, his rival as leader of the Nation, is dead likewise, though long thereafter in Philadelphia.

The Cherokees, now citizens of Oklahoma for the most part, are Americans; and those that I have met are so very like all other Americans that it is hard to believe that they were here in the Southern hills long before a ship from Europe touched the coast.

9: They have everything

When I started for the Northwest, a friend of mine congratulated me on the chance to see that corner of our common country.

"Washington and Oregon and Idaho have everything," he said,

and he was right. It is magnificent country, with a stimulating sense of knowing what it wants and where it is going. Though conscious of the transportation rate discriminations as almost no other section of America, it is enjoying a genuine prosperity. Its woodlands, probably the most impressive remaining in America, are suffering from exploitation, but a conservation program is in the making. The reactionaries win some fights, but you can write reaction off when a Wayne Morse can win the Republican nomination for the Senate from Oregon.

Portland was settled by a lone visitor from Tennessee in 1844, and Bill Overton did not value what he had found enough to keep it, but traded it off to Lovejoy of Boston, Massachusetts, and Pettygrove of Portland, Maine. These gentlemen each desired to do honor to his hometown, but they came to no blows. They tossed a silver dollar for it, and Pettygrove won.

The first thing you notice about Portland is the bronze drinking fountains on the corners, made to accommodate four thirsty souls at once. They are there, I was told, because a lumberman named Simon Benson believed that his loggers drank whiskey because water was unavailable; they add that he may have been right, because saloon sales dropped nearly a third after the fountains were installed. They will also tell you that the water in Portland is so pure that it does not have to be distilled for use in electric batteries or druggists' prescriptions. The air is pure, too, since Portland is an all-electric community and no smoke or soot defiles the atmosphere.

Many of the pioneer families that settled in the Portland area came from the Southeast, turning toward the Northwest Territory when Texas became unattractive to yeoman-farmers with the introduction of slavery. I have wondered for years whether the families in their covered wagons actually sang "Oh, Suzannah" or not. The Southern element was large enough for Portland's first Mayor to have been a Georgian, Hugh D. O'Bryant, who was elected in 1851.

Oregon lost population, a little, when the California gold rush came, but regained it quickly. The salmon fishing began to bring prosperity in 1864, but the Northwest now is diversified as to agriculture and industry to an amazing extent and does not depend upon the mere exploitation of depletable natural resources.

There is one main reason: cheap electric power, such as I saw produced at Bonneville. Dr. Paul J. Raver let me see what had been done with this immense project for the Columbia River basin, from the giant generators to the fish-ladders that permitted the salmon to return to their native creeks to spawn. It was a fascinating exploration, although essentially the pattern of development resembles what I had seen at some of the Tennessee Valley projects, although Bonneville does not deal so extensively with regeneration of an area because there does not exist the same problem of land destruction as in the basin of the Tennessee.

I saw the Bonneville project, and Salem, where Oregon's State Capitol struck me as the finest and best arranged in the country, superior even to the skyscraper that Huey Long built for Baton Rouge, and travelled on to Eugene, a delightful college town that is the home of Wayne Morse and of the University of Oregon. Both of them are major institutions.

Wayne Morse is Senator from Oregon and one of two Republicans in the United States Senate that I wish would shed that party's label and become Democrats, so that both parties would feel happier. The other, of course, is Vermont's amazing George D. Aiken. Of the two, I think the change would benefit Morse more because his discomfort as a Republican is greater; I suspect that nothing makes too much an impression on Aiken's constitution, which is made out of granite from Vermont quarries.

Wayne Morse was born in Wisconsin, but the Northwest welcomes newcomers. He was born in 1900, and educated at the University of Wisconsin, where undoubtedly his thoughts were influenced by the LaFollette brand of genuine progressivism. He moved on to Minnesota to get his law degree, and then to Columbia in New

York. He did not reach Oregon until 1929, when he joined the faculty of its law school and soon became dean.

He was an able and liberal teacher of law, and he developed a great many friends about Oregon, but he still was not in politics. But in 1941, President Roosevelt drafted him for the Railway Emergency Board; then he did a three-year stint on the National War Labor Board. In 1944 he ran for the United States Senate. At first they did not think he would win, and then he won.

In the Senate, he has been a nuisance. Within the Republican party he can find few to agree with his philosophy that the country must be given a good dose of democracy to keep it in health. He is critical of regressive taxation, of regional inequality, of economic discriminations because of race or geographical location. As is to be expected, he is both a specialist in and an advocate of public power. Very few care to meet him in debate, because he acquired a respect for facts from his Wisconsin associates and developed a gift for argument; his wit, which can occasionally be savage, seems to be a birthright.

Morse insists that he intends to stay inside the Republican party and reform it, and whenever it is suggested that he become a good Democrat he points to the predominantly Democratic city machines and says something or other objectionable.

In Portland, I asked for an explanation, and was assured that it made very little difference in Oregon whether a man was a Democrat or a Republican anyway, although Oregon usually was Republican just as neighboring Washington usually was Democratic.

"Just so long as a man is for more electricity and against high freight rates, he's all right," I was told. In that event, Republican though he is, Wayne Morse is all right.

I noted one curious fact about Portland. Of all the groups that have migrated to the Northwest and settled there, and these are many and diverse, only the Chinese seem to retain their national customs and to form a self-contained community. They come out, again I was told, at the Rose Festival, which is more than forty years old; they come out with massive papier-mâché dragons that breathe fire, and with such an explosion of firecrackers as has not been heard since their fathers left Canton a hundred years ago.

Washington centers about Portland's great rival, Seattle. It is one of the most liberal States of the Union, politically and socially. The labor unions are influential, and some of their leaders have forgotten the stormy days after World War One when Washington was the center of persecution of the "wobblies," as they called the members of the International Workers of the World, a tough catch-all outfit with syndico-anarchist leanings, a belief in direct action, and a feeling of expendability.

Seattle is built on seven hills, and I am glad that I visited there in warm weather, for I do not see how the citizens negotiate the steep streets with their complicated twistings if there is ice and snow. You can look out to the waterfront and see all the ships bound for Alaska, or look inland and see the snow-covered ridges and the spire of Mount Rainier.

In Seattle there is a hodge-podge of nationalities: Irish, Italian, German, Balkan, and French, as well as Chinese, Japanese, Filipinos, and Hawaiians. Since 1917, there has been a considerable Negro population.

The city was built by trade, and still dominates the shipments of lumber and fish from the Northwest, but the advent of cheap electric power has brought industry and this is growing diversified. In both Washington and Oregon, however, they will tell you that the war industries centered too much about ship-building and plane-making and that ultimate reconversion may present difficulties.

Idaho makes up the rest of the Northwest. It is famous for Sun Valley, where movie stars go to get away from it all and to be publicized by Steve Hannagan and where I did not get to go. Boise is in a pleasant valley and is a delightful city.

Idaho possesses one group of settlers that are unique: the Basques. Whether these hardy folk from the Pyrenees, great lovers of freedom who defeated mighty Charlemagne's army at the pass and slew his favorite nephew and his best knights, came to Idaho because these mountains remind them of those they left, I do not know. They are there, raising their sheep in the hills; and they are stout lovers of liberty still. More important politically, they are now very thoroughly organized Democrats, and were heavy contributors to the victory of Senator Glen Taylor in both primary and election.

There is one joke about Idaho that is obligatory. It is told to every visitor by every resident, on sight, and repeated in every book that mentions the state: If Idaho were flattened out, it would be the biggest State in the Union.

Of all of America that I have seen, the Pacific Northwest seems to offer the most obvious opportunity for wise development, and the greatest temptation to exploitation. On the other hand, though the development may be retarded by high transportation rates and by various barriers to its expansion as an industrial area, the exploiters have less chance there than in either Texas or California. Public sentiment in Washington, Oregon and Idaho is informed and intelligent; more effective, it is well organized. The Northwest means to develop sanely; it asks nothing but an opportunity to do so.

10: THE STORY OF FAITH

The story probably is apocryphal, for I have never seen it in any of his biographies and I have read much about him, because he was a first-class politician-statesman whose career was so limited in play that it offers ready opportunity for study. Sometimes, however, the stories about a great man that are not true are more thoroughly in character than those that can be authenticated. For example, it is somehow improbable that Abraham Lincoln once retorted to a pouchy, punch-swilling diplomat who asked him if it were true that he shined his own boots: "Of course, I do; whose boots did you think I shine?" Nevertheless, incredible though it is, it is the Lincoln story I like best.

So of all the stories of Brigham Young, and they are innumerable in Salt Lake City, the one told me as I travelled away from Utah late in September 1947, pleased me the most.

An elderly member of the Church of Jesus Christ of Latter Day Saints came to the Mormon leader and complained that, in the crossing of the continent, he had somehow lost his left leg. He wished it restored.

"You could work a miracle and give me a new leg, couldn't you?" he asked.

"It might be possible; if we both have faith, I could," Brigham Young replied stroking his patriarchal beard. "But how old are you?"

"I'll be seventy-two at my next birthday, Brother Young," the supplicant replied.

"Well then, you'd only have a few years' use of that leg to pay for having to have three legs throughout Eternity," he was told. He went his way, somewhat hastily.

Brigham Young's vision and statesmanship brought the Mormons to Deseret, as they called the pleasant site by the Great Salt Lake. He built a sturdy community, and a tremendous prosperity. The members of the group, no longer quite a majority in Utah, are distinguished for sobriety and industry. The Church is great in influence, and looked after its own during the depression years. It dominates many business enterprises, and permeates the life of the community, as the Temple and the Tabernacle dominate the city.

On my visit to Salt Lake City, I went to see James Albert Smith, president of the Church of Jesus Christ of Latter Day Saints, and discovered in him a pleasing patriarch with a quick sense of humor and a great understanding of the problems of the West. He told me to visit Ogden, the second city of the State, and in the fall I did.

It is a great agricultural center, with sugar refineries and other enterprises. The trip from Salt Lake City carries one along the Great Salt Lake, surely the most dismal expanse of water in the world. Ogden is built in the mountains, and has unusual beauty surrounding it.

The long journey of the Mormons across America, seeking a refuge from persecution, is one of the great stories of faith. Across rivers and prairie, across deserts and mountains, the band fled. They never doubted that they would find what they sought: a home. They selected a spot by the brackish waters, and they built for themselves a city that is beautiful and an economy that has endured.

The cynical say that the institution of marriage developed two States: Utah and Nevada. They refer, of course, to the plural-marriages authorized in the early days of Mormonism, and to the principal industry of Reno and Carson City, which is the dissolution of marriages that did not prove successful. Nevada is underdeveloped, and sensitive about the jokes about dude-ranches, divorces and gambling establishments. Much of its land is still in the hands of the Federal government.

That also is true of New Mexico, where the national parks and the forest reserves under Federal control are enormous. New Mexico, the only bilingual State, with legislative debates conducted in English and Spanish, is a blend of Indian, Spanish and Texan. With a population of but four persons to the square mile, it also is a study in underdevelopment. There was a gold rush and later a cattle boom, but both died. Oil, natural gas, and the making of dry-ice from flows of carbon dioxide are new developments. Politically the State has not yet become predictable. It was long under the dominance of a machine based on an alliance of Tweed-like politicians of the Fall breed with padrones who controlled the water holes indispensable to the Spanish and Mexican and Indian population; but Bronson Cutting broke the machine after Fall's exposure, and dominated the Republican party until his untimely death. The Democrats have had some innings, including the present one, which has put a solidly Democratic delegation in the Eightieth Congress.

The Pueblo Indians, with their rain dances and other magic, fascinate the students of anthropology. The medieval rites of Holy Week in the Spanish-American villages in the mountains, carry visitors back to an earlier and simpler culture. The poverty of the Indians depresses the economy of the State, it is recognized, but the Federal government has devised no solution to the problem, which has been acute for thirty years.

The Indians fare somewhat better in Arizona, although I am told that the Qahatikas living in isolation away from any highways or other avenues of communication are among the most impoverished and wanting among the aborigines. The State of Arizona entered the Union after a history of Spanish, Mexican, American, Confederate and Union occupancy. Phoenix City became the capital because Tucson had been too friendly with the Confederate expeditionary force in 1862.

Until the Colorado is completely tamed, Arizona probably will continue to rely upon its two big crops: cattle and dude-ranch customers. In Arizona they still assert that the Colorado is "too thick to drink and not thick enough to plow."

Politically, Arizona is safely with the Democrats. Its delegation of Senators and two Congressmen all belong to that party. It has its first Arizona-born Senator in Carl Hayden, who has been active in Democratic politics since he attended his first national convention in 1904 and watched them nominate Alton B. Parker to run against Theodore Roosevelt.

Montana has fifty-six counties, and one of them is unique in the country in name; it is Lewis and Clark County, named after the expedition that Jefferson sent out to explore the great West. Montana has a population of about six hundred thousand, and a Congressional delegation evenly divided between Democrats and Republicans. In Senator James E. Murray, a somewhat fabulous character reminiscent in his great wealth and broad sympathies with Michigan's late Senator Couzens, it possesses a distinguished national figure and a great liberal. He succeeded another great liberal, Thomas J. Walsh, who exposed the Elks Hill and Teapot Dome steals by one of the Senate's most important investigations.

Copper dominates Montana; and sometimes Anaconda Copper, which is known throughout the State as "the company," bosses public affairs. Anaconda Copper has a city of its own, twenty-six miles from Butte, where it smelts its ore. This has relieved Butte of the pall of sulphurous smoke that once, so residents say, hung over the city and necessitated street lights in the daytime.

Butte itself sits squarely on top of the greatest deposit of mineral wealth yet uncovered in the world. There are 253 miles of street in the city, and more than two thousand underground, where three billion dollars' worth of copper and silver has been removed since 1864.

You might describe Butte as the nation's smallest melting pot. Welsh, Cornish and Irish miners settled the community, and were joined by immigrants from the Balkans. Other elements came later, and now there is a small Finnish district, an Italian colony, and a miniature Chinatown. For all the rough-and-ready atmosphere of Butte, they live together in harmony, as Americans always can if they try.

11: No PICTURESQUE VACATION COUNTRY

I spoke to a good many people in the West, to college students and forums and women's clubs and luncheon meetings. I talked with a good many folks and asked them what they thought of their section and of their country. The theme of their conversation always is the same.

They want to be part of America as equals, not as subordinates. They want to control their local destinies, not have them arranged somewhere in the East. They want to fill their underpopulated areas with free Americans, not with serfs. They mean to do this, and they are succeeding. You can not write the West off as picturesque vacation country, or as a producer of raw materials alone; you have to think of it as a part of a nation that must have equal justice for all its citizens.

☆ VII ☆

COMMON WORLD

Among all the strange things men have forgotten, the most universal and catastrophic lapse of memory is that by which they have forgotten that they are living on a star.
—GILBERT KEITH CHESTERTON

1: MEN WILL PRESS ON

Our world's heritage is not destruction and chaos and engulfing night; neither is dust the eventual destiny of men. Between them and the dreadful nothingness that they fear, men may interpose their own stoutness of spirit, their own integrity. There is too much of courage and devotion and pity in the human heart for men to fail to solve their problems, to survive their difficulties, to triumph over their frailties, and to make their Earth as pleasant as a garden.

After the last tyrant and the final dictator shall have strutted across the stage of mankind's history, mouthing their concluding rhodomontades, and disappeared forever into the wings, the curtain will not fall to end the play of men's tragedy of high hopes, of men's comedy of disappointments, of men's drama of fulfillments. I do not know the play's denouement, nor do you; but of this I am convinced: free men shall stand. I do not say that there is nothing for them to fear, for there is much of terror in the untamed Universe. I do not

247

say that many of their wishes will not be long deferred; they are promised as their heritage not happiness, but the right to a pursuit of happiness: and happiness may long elude them. But that men will win the ultimate victory, I do not doubt: they can be happy if they have the will to be.

What is it that the people want?

They want peace, and a home that is their own, and freedom. They want freedom from fear, and freedom from want, and freedom to live their lives as they desire. They want it, not as a gift from someone else, but as something that they have made for themselves. They do not want a scientifically planned existence; they know that living is an art and not a science.

The people want that everywhere. The vision of freedom is not our vision, alone. It is the vision of people in every nation. It is the vision of men of good will everywhere. They desire freedom for themselves and for others, because they know that every man's freedom is jeopardized if one man anywhere remains a slave.

It does not require any hermetic knowledge or esoteric logic to reason so. The people that throng the sidewalks of Newnan on a late Saturday afternoon in autumn after the crops are gathered are not unlike the people that I saw in Pennsylvania and Kansas and Utah and Idaho, thronging the streets of other towns that resemble Newnan as you resemble your cousin. They are not unlike the people that go to the county fair in Shropshire, or that celebrate Christmas in mid-summer at Melbourne, or that crowd the centuries-old Red Square in Leningrad on May Day, or that scurry laughing as a wedding procession files through the streets of Canton.

Men will not get their desire in a day. They must move forward toward their goal clumsily and experimentally, tasting of this or that forbidden fruit, and wandering from the highway down one or another bypath that leads nowhere. But they will press on.

Nothing that I have seen in the United States alters that conviction. Nor is the conviction altered that the best defense of democracy can be provided by an extension of democracy, and that the application of democratic methods to a solution of our domestic and foreign problems is essential if we are to have either national or personal security. There is nothing the matter with America or the world that a good dose of democracy will not cure.

2: FOR THE DREAM IS THE SAME

Freedom is what men live by, but each man defines freedom in different terms. In a democracy, which recognizes that, while freedom is indivisible, it has many different facets, the policies of the government must be determined in accord with the will of the citizens. Government is only one of their agents for carrying on their daily lives, but it is their biggest agent; government is only a convenience, but it is an almost indispensable convenience. What citizens desire should be the objective of government; indeed, it is government's only legitimate objective.

What do the people want?

I asked that question in Georgia and in every State that I have visited. Although there were differences in emphasis, because of different local conditions, the answers always were essentially the same.

Always, during the question periods that followed my talks, they asked the same questions. It is not so surprising as it may seem. The people of America read the same newspaper accounts of public events, furnished by the great wire services; they read the same columnists, the same magazines, the same books; they listen to the same radio programs, and laugh at the same jokes. The community of interest in America is much more in evidence to any traveller than the differences between the various sections.

The people want peace and national security, but they want these as elements in individual security and not at the sacrifice of any essential freedom. They are hostile to imperialism, and have a convincing faith in democracy as the best safeguard for peace in the world.

The people want homes in which to live with their children, and they want these to be available to all classes of citizens. The American tradition is a home for every family. The American dream is of a comfortable home; perhaps, a little overcrowded with gadgets, this home of their dreams may be, but it represents their belief that comfort is not a reprehensible ideal in a free country.

The people want a fair tax system, that neither robs the lower-income groups nor penalizes thrift; that neither retards venture nor restricts incentive; especially they want Congressmen to reëvaluate their concept of luxuries, for the American standard of living is a democratic standard and a modern standard, and not the standard of Bourbon France in the seventeenth century when only nobles or highwaymen were entitled to comfort.

The people want jobs. They believe in an economy of abundance, in full employment for every person able and willing to work. They believe that depressions can be averted, if government, labor and industry show good sense.

The people distrust monopoly. They distrust those American industrialists who enter into private trade-treaties with European cartels. In the South and West, they are especially concerned with the transportation monopoly. In the Missouri Valley and New England, it is the electric-power monopoly that they fear. While they recognize the expediency of monopoly in some fields, which they think should be regulated drastically, they believe that competition is the basis of the American free economy, and they want freedom of competition restored by vigorous law enforcement.

The people want labor organizations held accountable for their contracts; they oppose unreasonable and restrictive labor practices in the same way that they do monopolies which slow down full production. The song of scarcity, whether sung by monopoly on the one hand or labor on the other, is out of tune with American aspirations.

The people want a reasonably stabilized cost-of-living. Throughout the nation, the standard of living of the white-collar worker has declined since 1942, while that of the industrial worker has dropped sharply since 1945. Throughout the country, there was a suspicion that many shortages were deliberate, and that full production was not being attempted. Characteristic of the sound basic judgment of the average citizen, they recognized the difference between the shortages of agricultural products and those of manufactured consumers' goods, and they noted that the greatest shortages occurred in those industries that were cartelized.

The people want a program of education that will be both realistic and democratic. Among the younger Americans there was a demand for more instruction in history and government, as well as a greater variety of vocational training. The people wanted good schools and, in most sections, felt that Federal assistance through an equalization fund to economically depressed sections of the nation was essential.

The people want a health program. They are weary of a discussion of this-or-that alternative plan of providing health insurance, of the failure of the colleges to provide more physicians so that quacks and charlatans are thriving, and of the political disputes over their ability to pay for a comprehensive public system of hospital and medical care. They want more doctors and nurses and dentists and hospitals and clinics. Rural America is especially sensitive to this acute need.

The people want an end to the preaching of racial and religious hate. While they suspect some minorities of an unjustified sensitiveness, they are weary of the failures to adjust these problems upon the American ideal of freedom. They want no special privileges for minorities or majorities.

The people want their civil rights protected. Many were perturbed because of the un-American attitude of some Congressional committees. More were concerned with censorship sprees that are common at this time in many States and communities. Labor leaders were concerned about the reappearance of the labor spy, whose pernicious influence was exposed years ago by the LaFollette Committee.

The people want equal rights and justice for all citizens and all sections of our country. Sensibly, they recognize that no American can be deprived of his rights politically or economically without establishing a precedent that may rob all of us of some essential freedom. Except among those who profited directly by injustice, and not even among all of them, did I hear a voice raised against economic liberty for every section of the nation. And except among those who enjoy the irrationality of hatred, or who obtain satisfaction out of cruelty, did I hear objection to political liberty and responsibility for every citizen.

The people want one country. They are Americans. It is the tradition of this land that, if you do not like it where you are, you may load yourself, your family, and your furniture in a covered wagon or a trailer, and set off for some other part of the country that suits your fancy. It is the tradition of this land that, if you do not like the economic status you have, you can save your pennies and dimes and dollars and go into business for yourself and become a millionaire.

The subdivision of our nation into regions, each with a peculiar economic problem due to the distortion of our principle of domestic free trade or the exploitation of the people and their land by colonial methods, is distasteful to every citizen.

The division of our country into classes and castes is also distasteful. Essentially, the American dream is of a classless and equalitarian society. Equality is not a matter of the size of houses or the number of automobiles owned; equality is the recognition by each citizen of the dignity and worth of every other individual.

Americans see all those things as desirable, in themselves; but they see them as only means toward an end. The end is freedom for the individual. There have been many changes in our country since the first colonists appeared. The great forests have been cut, and the prairie has been broken by the plow, and cities have been founded, and rivers harnessed. But the changes in America have been superficial, for the dream in the same. It is the dream of a country in which men and women can do as they please, where they can live their lives as they choose, where they are the masters of their fate, and where they can pursue illusive happiness in the manner that best satisfies their hearts.

3: AMONG THE PEOPLE I FOUND AN UNDERSTANDING

The people want peace and national security.

They want a just peace. They want the kind of national security that is represented, in the life of a householder, by an honest police force, capable of protecting the public against thieves and killers.

They believe that the experiment in collective security that the United Nations is undertaking is a good one. Probably not more than half the Americans with whom I talked were too optimistic about its success, but three-fourths of them believed that the experiment was demanded by morality. About the same three-to-one majority believed that the structure of the United Nations was imperfect, especially in its failure to give adequate representation to the smaller nations. A great many felt that the United States might embark upon too many unilateral undertakings.

The people of America expected too much too quickly from the United Nations. Somehow, they were led to believe that it provided a magic formula for peace, when there is no magic formula for peace or for anything else. But they still believe in collective security. They believe that peace can be obtained through forbearance and patience, because they know that a nation is not a color on a map or a section of the globe, but a composite of the people who make up a nation, so that relations between nations are not essentially different from relations between individuals. They believe that the United Nations offers a pattern and a structure and a beginning and an opportunity. Gradually it can be entrusted with a degree of sovereignty sufficient to enforce acceptance of peaceful solutions to international problems.

I found, among the people themselves, a clearer understanding of the relationship with Russia than is to be found among many of their leaders. The suggestion that America was threatened seriously by communism was not widely held; godless materialism is not characteristic of American thinking; the techniques of the police state are not popular, so that even legitimate emergency measures in wartime grow unbearable when hostilities cease and even before the economic emergency is ended.

Personally, I have excellent reason to believe that individualism is not abating in this country. Throughout the years that I have known her, Mrs. Arnall has had an abiding fondness for French pastry. Whenever we dine in a restaurant where French pastry appears on the menu, she asks the waiter to bring the tray. She examines every possible item, sometimes until I fume a little with masculine embarrassment. Then, without fail, she selects the inevitable chocolate éclair. If I had ordered one for her to begin with, she would have refused to eat it with the usual obduracy of American women, or Americans of any sex, age or section for that matter.

There is too much democracy and too much individualism in America for communism to make much progress in any ideological war. The American Communists are a very ineffective potential Fifth Column, if they are intended as such, by the Kremlin. Most Americans regard communism as an ineffective domestic threat. They know that communism will never appeal to the rank and file of Americans.

That Russian imperialism represents a serious threat to world peace and to American security, they believed. It made no difference to them that the economic views of Russia differed from ours; it made a profound difference in their thinking that Russian political methods were different. Any dictatorship, whether Right or Left, lives only by aggression and is essentially imperialistic.

This view was especially prevalent, I found, in the grain states. It can not be denied that, in a measure, it was influenced in two ways by national background. Scandinavian elements are plentiful in the grain belt, and they are not unmindful there that the countries from which their fathers came are close to the Soviet orbit; the people of that part of Europe have feared Russian imperialism, with good reason, before. Likewise, socialism has been a commonplace in those countries, and has proceeded through a completely democratic pattern; and while socialism has little appeal to these Americans of Scandinavian origin, they recognize that it is an economic and not a political doctrine, shrug their shoulders and suggest that its success in Sweden does not argue its success in America, and get to the heart of the question of individual liberty.

There were Americans, neither Communists nor fellow-travellers and of unquestionable sincerity, who insisted to me that much of the Russian aggression was inspired by fear of the Western powers. While I do not doubt that the military clique and the ruling bureaucracy in Russia have made such a fear general, as a substitute for carrying out Lenin's promises of popular government, I do not believe that it lies at the heart of the present Kremlin policy.

Most Americans approve the Marshall Plan and prefer to call it, correctly, European Recovery Program. That the program perhaps aims in some degree at the containment of communism within the borders of the USSR and its satellites is less important than its endeavor to restore Europe to productiveness and to assist democratic governments in Western Europe. Except in those instances where there have been regrettable dealings with neo-Fascists, the policy meets with wholehearted approval and is justified by American tradition in every way. The recovery of Europe is essential to check the growth of totalitarianism, either Right or Left. It is essential to the economic well-being of America. It is a case of going to put out the fire in a neighbor's house before it spreads to your own barns and bedrooms.

But if I found a majority of Americans concerned about Russia, I found a majority puzzled and somewhat disappointed with our foreign policy. We have done much, they pointed out, toward providing a democratic regime for Japan, although we did not have faith enough in our own republican institutions to replace the Son of Heaven with a Chief Executive chosen by the people.

They disliked our intervention in Greece on the side of the monarchy. Again this may be attributed to the influence of Americans with roots in the country affected. Apparently a preponderance of the Americans of Greek ancestry are strongly in favor of a republican form of government, both here and in Greece. A good many of them, men in the late forties and early fifties, were enthusiastic followers of Venizelos and came to this country when the Republic fell. They have dispersed themselves individually all over America —for I have encountered sizeable Greek communities only in New York City and Tarpon Springs, Florida—and they have made friends, to whom they argue the righteousness of a Republic in the first home of democracy with genuine eloquence. And sometimes with terseness, as did the proprietor of a café in South Georgia, who summarized his views in four words: "King is no good."

This feeling about our policy in Greece was intensified by the attitude assumed in Italy, where, until the British people themselves rebelled against Tory imperialism, we tacitly supported the pretensions of that miserable scion of the House of Savoy whom Samuel Grafton, with blunt truthfulness and to the displeasure of a number of tea-toting diplomats and ribbon-chasing brass hats, termed "the moronic little king."

Nor has this policy in Greece been made popular by our Spanish policy. Granting that most Americans have been profoundly moved by the Loyalist cause, especially as depicted in Ernest Hemingway's novel and the motion picture that was made from it, and that, in the South especially, valiant lost causes are held especially dear, the fact remains that Americans do know about Spain. They know that Spain was conquered by Italian and German troops loaned to Franco by Mussolini and Hitler. They know that even the most conservative of French leaders have urged that something be done to eradicate this Fascist menace to Europe's peace. They want to know why our attitude remains one of support for Franco.

Our Argentine policy has not been popular. Peron is no more a hero to Americans than was Machado, and they are apprehensive that the acceptance of the military clique in Argentina means a return to that "dollar diplomacy" that was abandoned in 1933.

These doubts and criticisms do not mean that Americans disapprove of opposition to Russian expansion and to Russia's use of Communist parties as fifth columns in that imperialistic advance. On the contrary, on the Pacific Coast, which is more aware of Asia than the rest of the country, there was a demand for a more vigorous and more intelligent policy in China, a policy that would replace the corrupt clique now in authority with a democratic government and thereby check Communistic advances.

But Americans disapprove of imperialism and totalitarianism everywhere. Wiser than their career diplomats, and the increasing numbers of senile military men who retire from active duty to enter the foreign service, the people are realistic rather than "practical," and desire an American policy that helps democracy grow. They know that democracy is a competing form of social and economic life; like all good merchandise, it can be effectively sold only on its own merit and not upon the want of merit of its competitors.

The American people want an American foreign policy based on right. They believe that democracy is a preventive of war. They do not wish to aid any form of authoritarian government; they wish to aid democratic governments wherever they exist.

Their attitude toward national security is a sensible one. While they believe that most of the men in our military establishment are honorable public servants, they were distressed by the efforts of some of the military hierarchy and monopolists to control governmental policies. They are in favor of a comprehensive reform of the entire system.

The people are in favor of universal public service in the event of war. They are not opposed to training, although they look with skepticism upon any program that devotes too much emphasis to outmoded ground techniques or that might be the vehicle for nothing more than an indoctrination in mechanical obedience. They believe that universal training should be both universal within the age group affected and training for real usefulness in emergency.

They are insistent that any training program leave education completely in the hands of civilians. Indeed, throughout America, there is a demand for more civilian control over the military, especially in two particulars: in the matter of discipline, so that the citizen-soldier will not be at the mercy of the professional; and in the matter of procurement, where the professionals have demonstrated a gross incompetence.

A well-organized militia is a necessary defense for free people. The centralization of direction of the military forces, except in time of actual war, is always a potential menace to democracy and to peace. The citizen-soldier has won America's wars.

Policies must be made by the people, through representative processes. No policy ever should be formulated by a bureaucracy; and of all bureaucracies, the military one is the most dangerous and the most objectionable. The time has not come to convert the United States into a military republic, dominated by some man on horseback; that time never will come.

The acceptance of political posts by professional soldiers is greatly to be deplored. General William T. Sherman, who is not especially popular in my native Georgia because he disclosed a somewhat incendiary disposition on the occasion of one of his visits, set the pattern for the honorable soldier, when he refused not only the Presidency but every civilian post in the government. General Dwight Eisenhower, with dignity, followed that honorable precedent.

There is a well-established rule of government that the armed forces are a subordinate part of the machinery of diplomacy; their leaders await direction from the proper civilian authorities responsible for foreign policy: the armed forces exist to maintain the foreign policy, but under no circumstances are policies determined by the convenience, the proposed strategy, or the exigencies of the military.

If this rule is broken, even in the very slightest degree, in the interest of expediency, the inevitable dissolution of free government is near. Those conservatives who called upon Sulla to preserve law and order in the Roman Republic invited the subsequent government of their land by the officers of the Praetorians. The members of the Directory called in a slight, paunchy Corsican artillery officer, and soon discovered that France was a country ruled by an Emperor and his Marshals.

Wherever the General Staff has been permitted to intermeddle in the making of foreign or domestic policies, as in Germany, Italy and France within the past thirty years, not only was war inevitable, but defeat was inevitable.

The foreign policy of the United States must not be dictated by monopolists who control copper holdings in Chile and sugar plantations in Cuba and oil in the Near East; neither must it be directed by military leaders, who, if honest, must think exclusively in terms of security, and who, if dishonest, ineluctably will think in terms of obtaining greater power over the nation's life.

The American people want to direct their own foreign policy. They demand open agreements, public discussions, and complete information. They want a policy that means that America will embark on no new imperialism itself, that America will combat imperialism wherever found, and that America will give support to democratic governments everywhere in the world.

The people want adequate defensive forces, and whatever is required in the way of armaments for national security, but they want assurances that control shall rest completely in the hands of the civil government, which is responsible to them.

4: Roofs over their heads

In the columns of a Los Angeles newspaper that I picked up on a trip to the Pacific Coast, there were actually more columns of advertisements seeking a place to live than there were single advertisements offering apartments. An Atlanta newspaper of September 25, 1947, offered for rent two unfurnished rooms and one five-room house; the house was several miles from Atlanta on an unpaved road. In every section of the nation, the housing shortage is acute.

It is not surprising. There are thirteen million more Americans to be housed than there were in 1940, and there are perhaps a million and a quarter fewer housing units of all types available. Statistically that provides a picture of approximately five million American families with no place to live; but the statistics are faulty on housing, precisely as Senator Flanders of Vermont discovered them to be on nutrition. The statistics do not take population shifts into account, nor do they take into account certain psychological factors such as the unwillingness of a tenant-farmer to return to a substandard house that has disintegrated still further since he left it for the shipyards or the airplane plant or the armed services.

The housing problem is not one problem, but three. There is the problem of the urban family that should and could purchase or build a house and can neither buy nor build at a reasonable price. There is the problem of the urban family that, for reasons associated with employment, ought not to own a house, but must be provided with a suitable place to live at a reasonable rental. There is the problem of the substandard rural dwellings, especially in the South and New England, which need replacement.

To assume that one phase of the general problem can be approached satisfactorily without reference to the other two is folly. A program of low-rental public housing, unrelated to any other program, will result in additional shifts of population from rural areas. Plans to finance urban home building and buying, unrelated to other aspects of the housing problem, will result in the creation of class hates, in economic chaos attendant upon purchases of homes by people who do not need them permanently but who must make any sacrifice to obtain a place to live, and in a resultant collapse of real estate prices. The rural problem is even more complex, since rural housing can not be separated from acquisition of farmland.

It is necessary that all three aspects of the problem be attacked vigorously and immediately.

The people of America want homes. They want comfortable housing, and they want durable housing.

In the rental field, as even such conservatives as Senator Taft recognize, direct intervention by the Federal government is necessary. That does not imply subsidized housing, except for a relatively few Americans; it does mean cheap housing for many, because the Federal government can afford a longer amortization on its facilities than can independent investors.

In the home-owning field, the builder and seller have been the object of some unfair attacks. Homes do cost too much, and there have been many contributing factors: monopolistic practices, a shortage of skilled workers, shortsighted municipal planning which resulted in too few available sites for homes, diversion of relatively scarce materials into unnecessary building projects, and the entry into the building field of individuals who were utterly inexperienced. Some of these factors can be eliminated and some can be avoided by the application of mass-production methods to house-building, without sacrificing the individuality that the family desires.

Home financing, however, requires a new approach. A liberalization of terms, with requirements as to down payments definitely liberalized, would make it possible for more homes to be built. There is no reason why payments upon homes should not be stretched out over a period of twenty-five years for all applicants, and why home-building credit should not be liberalized. Again, that does not necessitate a subsidy to anyone; the use of Federal guarantees on home mortgages in the past has brought no danger of socialism, even in its mildest form; the expansion of those guarantees would be equally valuable in solving a vital problem. Private financial institutions and governmental agencies can make this possible.

In the instance of some rural homes, the same general statement is true. But in some sections, more must be done. In the rural South, for example, a housing program can not be separated from a program to end tenancy and finance yeoman-farmers in establishing themselves. In those cases, the money and facilities to push such a program must be provided.

The Americans with whom I talked want roofs over their heads, and fireplaces to sit by, and kitchens in which to prepare their meals. They want homes for themselves and their children now, not a decade from now; and they expect their government, which is an agency that they have established to carry out their collective endeavors, to deal with the matter effectively and promptly.

5: SOMETHING REALISTIC SHOULD BE DONE

The tax system of the country needs a thorough overhauling. The Federal government has expanded the zone of its taxation to take in many sources of revenue from which the States derived their money. The States have invaded those fields usually left to local units of government. The present tax system does not take too much money out of circulation, if you think in terms of statistics; but it takes too much money from certain income groups, and it is changing the habits of America by heavy excises upon articles classified as luxuries but deemed necessities, or at most petty comforts, in the America of abundance that we have always talked about.

The people want a tax system that encourages thrift, that stimulates incentive, that does not protect monopoly, that does not oppress those least able to pay, and that supports their public services adequately.

This will necessitate a comprehensive revision of the tax laws of the nation. Wartime excises should be eliminated; throughout the country there is opposition to taxes on shaving lotion, lipstick, purses, and other items that someone in Congress decided were luxuries. Many other excises should be removed or reduced, especially since the products carrying the tax also carry State taxes in many instances.

Something realistic should be done about the income tax laws. The present system that taxes earned income at a far higher level than speculative profits is essentially wrong. Short-term capital gains should be subject to normal income taxes, and there should be prompt reduction in the tax rates on incomes.

The tax rate on corporate earnings should be reduced very sharply, but the reduction should be attached to a drastic undistributed-profits measure that will prevent accumulation of enormous surpluses.

Lower taxes on corporate incomes and individual-earned incomes would be offset in part by the increased taxation on capital gains, and would be the increase incidental to distributing corporate profits to stockholders. Lower taxes would create a greater incentive for all those, in every income bracket, whose incomes are earned. Eventually lower taxes would produce more money for the Federal Treasury. Although an ultimate stabilization of the tax structure is not only desirable, but essential, experimentation in the tax field must be undertaken to provide an efficient and equitable system to replace the present hodge-podge of revenue measures.

Except in the utility fields, where special provisions possibly should be made, corporations should be required to pay to their stockholders their earnings. The transition from private ownership-management to private bureaucracy-management has gone dangerously far in America; the owners of the major corporations are now regarded, publicly as well as privately, as "investors." As such, they should be paid their share of the earnings. There is nothing to prevent them from reinvesting those earnings in the corporation, if they wish; but they should be free to use them for other investments or for the purchase of consumer goods.

State and local governments should operate upon balanced budgets, because of their limited sovereignty; they should accumulate neither deficits nor surpluses, except within a very narrow range. Obviously, this is not applicable to the Federal government. But gradual retirement of the existing public debt is necessary, and the revenues of the Federal government should be maintained at a level that will permit such a reduction as will extinguish the debt within the next three decades.

Attention should be given to the inheritance tax law. Probably the exemption should be increased, as an incentive to thrift. On the other hand, the loopholes should be stopped, so that so-called charitable, educational, and philanthropic foundations may not be used as private holding companies to defeat the purposes of taxation and to rob the government of revenue.

As a public official and in my trips around the country, I discovered that the people were willing to pay taxes, if they were certain of two things: that the services supplied were in proportion to the taxes paid, and that the tax system was equitable and was fairly enforced. They want their money's worth, and they want tax favoritism ended.

I discovered likewise that most of the municipalities and counties in the nation, and at least half of the States, needed more money and need a revision of tax methods, but could not undertake any reform because of the chaos of the Federal system.

The people want a fair tax system of reasonable stability, flexible enough to provide for the needs of public services in the event of economic changes, but durable enough to permit them to make plans for their individual futures.

6: The slack in the nation's economy

Americans desire economic security, and the people want this to be provided through a program of full employment. Sanely, they recognize the possibility of ups and downs in the business cycle, and they expect their government to assume the responsibility of cushioning the shocks.

Unemployment compensation is a palliative, not a cure. It is an excellent thing to cover emergencies within limited fields. It is not designed to cope with conditions arising from drastic economic changes.

Employment may remain at a high level for a good many years, without any intervention from government. World-market conditions and technological changes and the redistribution of industry about the country may lead to some type of recession, just as faulty economic policies on the part of the government paralleling those of the twenties will lead to a depression.

There is ample room for public enterprise and for private enterprise in this country. There are dams to be built, schoolhouses to be erected, public institutions to be enlarged. Sometimes, of course, these projects represent emergency operations; but, in general, they can be planned for and utilized to take up the slack in the nation's economy. Whenever it is possible to avoid it, public enterprise should not compete with private enterprise; this is especially essential in employment and in purchases of materials.

If we are to maintain employment at a level of approximately sixty-five million persons, which is necessary to sustain the American standard of living, we must have a permanent and integrated program of public works.

In general, only the Federal government can finance such a program. But there is no reason why the program should be inflexible, centralized, and removed from popular control.

The depression of 1920 struck the South first and hardest. The depression of 1929 began in the grain States and spread to the urban industrial centers, which were in acute distress before the Southeast felt the impact of the crash.

If there had been an intelligently planned public works system, operating upon a regional basis, a construction program could have been initiated in the South in the winter of 1920, or in the grain States in 1927, when the depression usually associated with the 1929 market crash actually began.

It was the exodus from the South of many workers that swelled industrial ranks unwholesomely in Ohio, Michigan and New York after World War One, thereby contributing to the acuteness of the relief problem a decade later. It was the complete destruction of the buying power of the Middle West, followed by an inevitable industrial recession when inventories became dangerously swollen, that precipitated the collapse of 1929.

In a measure, this is an oversimplification. Other factors existed, such as the inability of the Southern farmer to turn to crops other than cotton because of internal tariff barriers, in 1920; and, of course, the elements of speculation, dishonesty, and a vicious and immoral foreign policy throughout the twenties that culminated in the Stock Exchange collapse.

However, the maintenance of buying power throughout the country is an essential for industrial stability, since America's biggest market for consumer-goods is America.

Emphasis must be placed upon the necessity for regionalizing any system of public works. This is imperative, because decentralization is a safeguard against totalitarian planning. It is also imperative because speed is one of the essentials in making a public works system effective as an averter of depression.

Throughout America, the average citizen feels that he has a right to use his government as an agency to guarantee that employment shall be available to all those who want jobs. He points out, with a grasp of the essentials of history that some of his representatives in public office lack, that this has been the American policy since 1789.

Indeed, the disagreement between the Hamiltonians and Jefferson's followers was partly over the methods to be utilized. Essentially, the Hamilton group wished to use public funds for internal improvements within the areas already settled and under centralized control, compatible with their semi-totalitarian ideology; while Jefferson wished, as part of his program for decentralization, the rapid settlement of the western lands and their admission to the Union as States instead of their retention as colonies.

The Whig party, that most disingenuous of American hybrids, had other tenets than unfaltering worship of the Bank of the United States and unwavering hate for Masons and Catholics. Its tariff planks were expressly predicated upon the need for full employment and upon recognition that the Federal government was responsible for assuring it.

The Republican platforms of the sixties and seventies contained land-settlement planks that had the ostensible purpose of providing full employment. It is true that the inner circle of boodlers, who came to dominate Congress in the Grant Administration and who gave away the public domain lavishly for a price, used these planks to justify their grants to the railroads. But their abuse of a policy does not condemn the policy, nor does it obliterate the recorded approval of nationally supported full employment.

The Democratic party, while insisting that Federal guarantees of employment should not be made the mechanism for an increased centralization of government or for a process of class stratification, also has recognized the right of the people to mutual guarantees of jobs.

And precisely that is what the people want.

7: The principal menace to America's future

Americans always have opposed monopoly. The more experienced among the Founders had observed its evil effects abroad, and sought to safeguard the infant Republic against it. They pointed out that England, although retaining monopolies in colonial trade, was scrapping the system at home, far in advance of the era when free competition and free trade would be the doctrines of the Manchester school of economists. They pointed to the disaster that monopoly had brought upon France, where living standards were depressed, taxes were unbearable, and trade was hampered by a multiplicity of restrictions.

Jefferson was not alone in his opposition to monopoly, although his proposed amendment that would have prohibited any form of monopoly in America, was somehow not adopted with the rest of the Bill of Rights. Franklin, Samuel Adams, Willie Jones, Madison, and Monroe, among the liberals, and John Adams, Charles Carroll, John Rutledge, and George Mason, among the conservatives, were strong opponents of monopoly. The failure, perhaps chargeable to the bluntness and political ineptitude of John Adams, was an American economic tragedy. Despite his personal contempt for Hamilton and all that he stood for in an alliance between government and exploitation, Adams was not strong enough with his party to prevent establishment of monopoly in the country. The Bank of the United States was chartered.

Since that day, the fight between the exploiting monopolists and the people of the United States has continued. The people have won most of the wars, and lost all of the peace treaties. Assisted by the brilliant judgment of Roger B. Taney, the political astuteness of Amos Kendall, the trenchant pen of Francis P. Blair, and the forensic eloquence of Thomas Hart Benton and John Forsyth, it was possible for President Andrew Jackson to overthrow the monopoly of the Bank of the United States.

Monopoly did not make another frontal attack upon the government of the United States thereafter until nearly the close of the century.

Already many of the great monopolies had been engineered and were on the planning boards, but the engine was missing. Coöperation of the Federal government was essential. The monopolists, with the accidental coöperation of conservative banking interests, had provoked a panic during the second Cleveland Administration. The West was in revolt, and honest conservatives were as concerned about the situation as were liberals.

The test came in the Republican convention of 1896. In 1876, the responsible elements in the Republican party had made themselves heard. They had been victorious again in 1888 in the convention, with Senator Benjamin Harrison, who defeated Cleveland although he ran behind him in popular votes.

Responsibility in 1896 could hardly have chosen an abler public servant nor a less magnetic personality than Thomas B. Reed. Irresponsibility could not have selected a more adroit manipulator than Mark Hanna, nor a more perfect candidate than William McKinley. Hanna's was the voice of speculative finance and management; McKinley's voice was that of a beautifully tuned robot, repeating what he was told; most frequently he seems to have been told to tell them to "see Mr. Hanna."

Between 1800 and 1928, the years of the Democratic candidacies of Thomas Jefferson and Alfred E. Smith, there was no campaign as disgraceful in the misuse of money, power, and propaganda as in 1896. Irresponsibility went into office, and the era of monopoly in earnest began.

Theodore Roosevelt was something of a gadfly to certain monopolists; Woodrow Wilson annoyed them with the Clayton Act; Franklin D. Roosevelt gave them considerable trouble. But they were strong enough to endure, and to make America's preparations for war inadequate, and to make the cost of the war perhaps seventy billion dollars more than it otherwise would have been.

Today, more entrenched than ever, monopoly presents the principal menace to America's future, politically and economically.

During the war years more than five hundred thousand small business concerns were eliminated. By the end of the war, the holdings of two hundred fifty corporations in the manufacturing field exceeded all manufacturing facilities in the nation in 1939.

We have chalked up some gains, if we can retain them. The monopoly in aluminum may be broken, unless the monopolists can win the active coöperation of the Federal government to destroy their competition. But patent pools dominate the fields of synthetic rubber, chemicals, and radio. Shoes must pay tribute to a monopoly. The transportation monopoly remain unbroken, and its questionable rate-making during the war remains largely uninvestigated.

The public may not be aware of every instance of the growth of monopoly, but the average American appreciates the menace deeply enough to demand tough and effective enforcement of the anti-trust and conspiracy laws.

The people do not want to see the emergency war plants closed down by monopolists. They want them utilized to increase competition. It would be a sound rule for the Federal government to decline to lease or sell any war plant to any concern that, occupying a monopoly or dominant position in the production of any essential, permitted a shortage to develop.

The people want real penalties applied when conspiracies in restraint of trade are proved or where defendants plead guilty. Fines of thirty-five thousand dollars in the fertilizer trust case, and of fifty thousand dollars in the chemical and petroleum case, are ridiculous. They constitute an affront to every American's sense of proportion. Thirty million American farmers can not produce without fertilizer, yet those who conspire against thirty million people are assessed roughly one mill for each person against whose welfare they plotted.

It can be recognized that the stockholders of the corporations, now treated as investors instead of owners, are not largely to blame; the guilt is that of an irresponsible management. But corporations twice violating the anti-trust laws should be liquidated for the benefit of the shareholders and creditors. This would not reduce facilities, nor decrease any actual values; but it would protect the public against dangerous enemies. The penalties should be severe enough to require compliance with the anti-trust statutes.

The most effective method by which monopoly thrives in this country, however, is not through financial power, but through control over patents. Provisions that any patent may be utilized by any manufacturer upon the payment of a royalty have been suggested. Personally, I regard this as both drastic and unnecessary. However, patents upon which production has not begun should be opened to public use after three years, and patents generally should be usable after seven years upon the payment of a royalty. This preserves the bargaining power of the individual inventor on the one hand, and the incentive of the initial investor to take a chance on a new method or new product. It is assumed, of course, that in any revision of the anti-trust laws, patents involved in conspiracies in restraint of trade shall pass into the public domain at once.

Everywhere that I went in America, I found a detestation of monopoly and a strong faith in "little business." Although the war closed many enterprises, a half-million in all, 340,000 new ones had replaced them by the start of 1946, and by the end of 1947 the number of small manufacturing plants of all kinds undoubtedly exceeded the 1941 total. This was an expression of faith by hundreds of thousands of average Americans, in small and medium-sized cities throughout the nation, that their government intended to enforce the laws on the statute books and actually make free enterprise free.

Not every American would employ Wendell Berge's language; but he expressed their thoughts when he said:

> "It is sheer delusion to believe that we can tolerate regimentation by monopoly without in time necessitating regimentation by government. If we forsake the principles upon which economic freedom rests by failing to apply them, freedom will forsake us. There is no question as to which way freedom lies. The danger is that in the affairs of men it is always later than we think."

8: Only production is the solution

The upward spiral of the cost of living is a matter of concern throughout the country. Statistics do not reflect conditions adequately, as the surprised language of Senator Ralph Flanders revealed when his committee reported its findings of a study of actual cases about the country.

Some of the rising prices have reflected unavoidable shortages and mounting costs. Some have been the result of deliberate gouges from monopolies, and a few have been a result of gouges by unscrupulous individual merchants. The breakdown of the nation's transportation system has contributed its share, as, I believe, has the ineptitude with which surplus war commodities have been distributed. The hostility of reactionary politicians to any plan to finance small business in resuming operations has been a factor not to be overlooked, especially since many governmental measures favor large corporations.

Agricultural shortages unquestionably will continue for several years, but it is doubtful that agricultural profits will remain at their present level. Throughout the nation, farmers told me that the 1947 crop was more expensive to produce than that of any recent year. Most of them, livestock producers excepted, regarded 1944 and 1945 as their best years in history. In the South, undoubtedly, production costs are rising, in spite of the increase in mechanization, and these increasing costs can not be attributed wholly to the inflated prices on consumer goods.

Financial regulations can not halt rising prices. Wage adjustments can not solve the problem. Only production is the solution.

Production can be speeded up partly by prudent tax revision in the interest of smaller manufacturers, partly by utilization to their full capacity of plants built by the Federal government during the war, and partly by a more realistic approach to the problems of distribution.

Although most of the Americans I talked with about the country were worried about inflation, there were many who feared even more the deflation that they thought inevitable. While the volume of debt for consumer-purchases has been held low, there has been an appreciable decrease in the savings of many workers. A sudden break in buying, and a depression would be on the way.

When European production is restored, there will be no need for extensive agricultural shipments abroad, and these will revert to prewar levels.

Imperative as is the need for ending the inflationary spiral, in the long run it is even more imperative to be prepared to avoid the calamities of a sudden deflation.

The reserves in the hands of low- and medium-income groups, which are now dwindling, represented almost wholly deferred purchases of durable consumer items. If these reserves are expended for current needs, a breakdown of the national economy could occur. The generation that went through the depression of 1929 thinks that it sees the same symptoms in our economy and hears the same kind of foolish prattle from conservative politicians. A ruinous depression is one luxury the people can ill afford.

9: An intelligent and informed citizenship

The passion that Americans have for education is evidence of their optimism. They want education for themselves and for their children.

In the early twenties when everyone knew that prosperity was here to stay through a process of plucking bare the geese that laid the golden eggs, it was fashionable to make fun, good-humoredly of course, of the American delight in self-improvement.

No doubt some of the more prominent and sophisticated hucksters made capital of the naiveté that accompanies the search for knowledge, and urged Americans to achieve a university education in thirteen minutes a day. No doubt some of the women who joined discussion clubs were as stupid as the Carol Kennicott whom Sinclair Lewis made the doubtful heroine of *Main Street*.

Nevertheless, Americans are better informed than they themselves suspect, and have more respect for knowledge than do those who see in their quest for learning something very funny indeed.

In Georgia, in 1940, the year preceding the advent of that State Administration that endeavored unsuccessfully to wreck the University System and destroy freedom and education, there were 13,736 students enrolled in the sixteen colleges operated by the State. In 1945, a war year, there were 11,498. In September 1947, there were 25,210.

A large number of them are there under the GI Bill of Rights? Yes, 12,058; so what? Featherbedding, did you say? Try and make ends meet in Athens or Atlanta or Macon on that income. Or, for that matter, try to do so in Ann Arbor, Lewisburg, St. Louis, Chapel Hill, or Denver.

A larger percentage of young people are going to college than ever before, and a larger percentage are completing high school than in the past. And each group constitutes a problem.

There is the problem of juvenile delinquency, for example. In 1945 it was fashionable for youngsters, who read much about the subject, to refer to each other as "JDs." As the father of two juveniles, whom I had not regarded heretofore as detectably delinquent, I had disregarded the extent of this problem until I came across a most serious magazine article. It revealed for me the dangers of the situation, in language that was direct and with reasoning that was cogent. Not only did it point out the ill-effects of the war upon Young America, but it developed a powerful indictment against the teen-age terrors, whose reprehensibility it exposed relentlessly in the following vivid phrasing:

> "Where does the real fault appear to lie. To one who views the panorama of Society from the peak of middle age . . . all around him is a vividly colored throng of restless, excited, noisy human beings, exhibiting little grace and less elegance, possessing no mystery, no romance, making no appeal to the poetic fancy. They trot like foxes, limp like lame ducks, one-step like cripples, and all to the barbaric yawp of strange instruments which transform the whole scene into a moving-picture of a fancy ball in Bedlam. . . . In observing the giddy whirl at their revels, he is sufficiently old-fashioned to find himself watching the 'cheek-to-cheek' dancing with his grey hairs standing on end.
>
> "It is not necessary to review in detail the astonishing facts that are brought up for discussion nowadays among little groups of outraged—but intensely interested, mothers . . . we have heard them: the perfect freedom of intercourse between the sexes, the unchaperoned motor-flights at night, the intimacies of modern dancing, the scantiness of modern dress, and the frankness of conversation between young men and girls. There are even whispers concerning the sharing of the smuggled bottle . . ." *

The Atlantic, because of the durability of its format, must share responsibility with the professional man in whose office I discovered

---

* The quotation is from an article by Mr. Grundy, which appeared in *The Atlantic Monthly* in its issue of May 1920.

this masterly study of youthful behavior while waiting to have an ailing bicuspid filled; it is most embarrassing to discover that I am a full twenty-seven years behind, and that the wild youngsters are not members of the present generation but their parents.

I do not believe that juvenile delinquency is a serious menace to the country today; I rather doubt that it constituted a serious menace in 1920; I am somewhat inclined to doubt that it will constitute a serious menace twenty-seven years from now, unless there is meantime a complete breakdown of our economy and of our social order. Misconduct is a human tendency, not confined to any age group; delinquency very definitely is not a juvenile characteristic. The offenses committed by young people arise sometimes from a maladjustment of society, but far more often from the distortion of the virtues of courage, loyalty and generosity.

Most young Americans are busy with the serious matter of getting an education and are taking the matter seriously themselves. The range of their interests is wide and sincere.

Examine the record of Georgia's 1947 Youth Assembly. When the Georgia State Committee of the Young Men's Christian Associations undertook the organization of the first assembly in my native State, during my governorship, I delivered a formal message to the representatives on the condition of the Commonwealth and the legislative problems that required solution. I found that year that the young men and young women who made up the assembly knew what they wanted in a place to live, in public services, and in administrative methods. When I looked over their 1947 agenda of measures, introduced by young folks all over the State, my belief in their sincerity and seriousness was confirmed.

Here were measures to improve school administration, to provide adequate salaries for teachers, and to encourage outstanding students to enter the teaching profession. Here were measures to provide for public health, including a bill to provide for premarital health examinations. A whole series of measures dealt with an intelligent program of public parks and recreation. A carefully drawn and very sensible home rule law for counties and municipalities was presented.

Political issues received attention. Measures were introduced to provide for a legislative drafting and information service, and to secure uniform literacy tests for voters. And there was a bill to provide for more adequate instruction in government in the high schools.

What do the people want from education? The answer is the same, all over the United States; they want the schools and colleges to provide what the young people need in today's world.

The program of the Georgia Youth Assembly in my native State is the basis of a sound educational program.

We need decently paid, decently treated, teachers in our public schools. Until decentralization shall have readjusted the economy of the country, it is almost imperative that the Federal government provide an equalization fund to aid economically depressed areas and States in providing good schools.

Federal aid to education should not be limited to the common schools, although the most acute crisis is that existing in the low-income States in their operations of grade and high schools on limited budgets. Federal assistance should extend to the colleges.

In those instances, it should be upon a basis of assistance to the student himself, so as to leave the student free in the selection, within reasonable limits of accreditment to the institution, of the college of his choice. To exclude the private colleges and denominational schools of the country from any participation in this program would be undesirable and uneconomical; to base the aid upon the needs of actual students rather than upon some arbitrary abstract calculation is desirable.

We need a realistically devised educational program. The war demonstrated the need for technological and vocational skills, and for scientific training. But it also demonstrated that vocational skill in most fields can be acquired very rapidly through intensive courses.

What is needed in all our institutions are more courses designed to fit citizens for life in our times. There has been an unfortunate trend away from history, government, language, and logic in the curricula of all our educational institutions, both secondary schools and colleges. We face the danger of training too many experts who lack a background in the humanities and whose general knowledge is too limited to make them effective as citizens. Lawyers unschooled in semantics and history, atomic-energy scientists untrained in politics, and engineers unschooled in economics hold a menace for a democracy.

For the democratic ideal requires an intelligent and informed citizenship to be effective. The individual intelligence is adequate to make decisions, but it is the responsibility of society to see that the education is available.

10: THEY HAVE A RIGHT TO THIS

The fear of an expensive illness is more widespread among the middle-income groups than among any others. The menace of inadequate medical services reaches into more than half the rural homes in the nation.

The bureaucrats, those detestable individuals whom the citizens hire at inadequate salaries to look after their business for them, have all but wiped out some of the worst plagues in the nation. Georgia pioneered in the South in the fight on diphtheria and on pellagra. The former was the most dreaded malady of childhood; the latter was the most dangerous American diet-deficiency disease. Despite the victory that the public health workers won over those two forms of illness, it was a long time before Georgia provided adequately for its health service. One of the final acts of my Administration as Governor was the acquisition of a 2,500-bed hospital for tuberculars; the previous facilities, for a State of more than three million population, had been six hundred beds.

Today there are disputes in Congress over a broad program of medical care for all the people. A start has been made toward a rural hospital program, which is badly needed. The same people who see no harm in a program of subsidy to one group, however, see immeasurable dangers in letting all the people provide for themselves in a nation-wide and completely adequate program for everybody. I am so glad to see something done in an obvious emergency that I find it difficult to criticize subsidizing housing for low-income groups condemned to slums. It is obvious that some political leaders who scream "socialism" about any form of public enterprise, except a direct subsidy to some favored vested interest such as the transportation monopoly, do not find it impossible to accept the basic tenet of totalitarianism—that the submerged must be quieted down by a few concessions now and then.

At the present time only the very lowest income group, who live precariously day by day, and the rich can afford to be sick. The white-collar worker and the skilled industrial worker and the average yeoman-farmer are in the same boat together on medical costs. A serious illness can be entirely ruinous. These three groups of Americans want some form of publicly operated fund to provide mutual insurance against that kind of disaster.

They have a right to this kind of legislation. They have a right to merge it with other forms of social security, if they think it wise. After listening to some hundreds of Americans discuss the question with the common sense that the average citizen brings to bear upon problems that experts sometimes fail to comprehend, I am not now convinced that it would be undesirable to consolidate the collection of funds for and the administration of benefits in the fields of retirement insurance, death benefits to widows and orphans, unemployment compensation, compensation for illness and medical care. I am thoroughly convinced that all social security benefits should be made available to all citizens, regardless of the nature of employment.

But even more serious than the matter of payment for illness is the problem of medical care, due to the shortage of physicians, dentists, nurses, technicians and laboratory workers. There is one American State in which thirty-two counties have no dentist. Sixty-eight thousand more physicians are desperately needed today in the United States. Although the East has more physicians and dentists proportionately than the South and the West, the problem is not a regional one; it is more nearly a rural-urban problem, although even the cities need more general practitioners.

There are two necessary actions toward a solution of the problem.

One is the immediate expansion of the medical schools, to provide more graduates. Utilizing what was learned of speed-up methods during the war, the medical schools should provide as many trained men as rapidly as they can. More medical schools must be provided and those now in existence must be enlarged where possible.

The other solution is that of finding a way to assist young practitioners, medical or dental, who elect to serve in rural areas. In part this can be done by providing them with facilities; but some direct subsidy may be necessary until some sections of the nation find a way to increase rural incomes.

To suggest that, when the health of the people is at stake, they can find no way to help themselves through the government that belongs to them is to admit an impotence in society that does not exist.

11: THE SUCKERS ARE NOT AS NUMEROUS

In every part of America, there was deep concern over those aspects of individual freedom that deal with civil liberties and political rights.

Racial and religious intolerance is unquestionably widespread in the nation. Minority groups such as the Mexican of the Southwest, the Japanese of the Pacific Coast, the Negro in the South, in Detroit and Chicago, and the Jew in New England are definitely concerned over invasions of their civil and political rights. Such minority groups are displaying an increasing sensitiveness in many instances.

Some years ago I expressed regret over that sensitiveness, which has driven from the stage the comic Irishman, Jew and German that delighted generations of Americans, and which has made interpretation of the Negro in American fiction a matter of earnest ponderousness devoid of laughter. But many members of minority groups in America have little to laugh about.

There is irony, but little humor, in the plight of the American soldier, of Japanese extraction, who returns to the Pacific Coast. There is more of pathos than of laughter in the lives of citizens of Mexican descent. Although the Southern Negro is properly prideful over gaining his political rights as a citizen, the economic condition of members of that race, throughout the nation, is not a cause for jubilation. Anti-Semitism remains the stock in trade of hate-mongers everywhere, and it is not easy for an American Jew to laugh with the memory of the German concentration and murder camps still fresh in the mind.

The attack on basic civil rights is also serious. Proposals to prohibit certain political parties, Congressional investigations that are conducted with all the juridical fairness of a witch trial and with all the dignity of a fishwives' brawl, private raids upon gatherings of legitimate and legal political groups, and the efforts to deny political rights to many Americans upon racial grounds are serious.

But there are credit entries upon the ledger, also. The leading spokesman of intolerance nominally classified as a Democrat in the House was overwhelmingly rejected by the citizens of Mississippi when he tried to move over to the United States Senate. In many States, charters of hate organizations have been revoked, as Georgia revoked the charters of the Klan and the Columbians. The right to vote is not being denied many literates in the United States, in spite of poll-tax requirements in some States and the adoption of legislative subterfuges in South Carolina.

There have been few serious attacks upon freedom of education in the postwar period, in contrast to the condition that followed World War One. Educators are relatively free from pressure, and the distortion of textbooks, a commonplace in the early twenties, is now infrequent.

Book and motion picture censorship raises its head often, however. But examination of reported instances does not disclose any very serious condition. There is nothing to compare with the foolish book-suppressions of two decades ago, and the movie censorship cases, which usually boil down to a local juvenile delinquency scare or the excessive zeal of some individual, are few. Of course, the efforts of J. Parnell Thomas and his fellows to impose Rightest propaganda upon the motion picture industry could be serious ultimately, but it is extremely doubtful that the producers of Hollywood will be impressed by the saleability of the kind of movies desired by the Thomas-Hoffman-Rankin-O'Konski school of thought.

Despite the fact that civil liberties have undergone no such assault as followed the era of Mitchell Palmer in the Department of Justice, there was a growing concern about the matter throughout America. It is a healthy sign. It is a recognition that political freedom depends upon freedom of discussion, and that any limitation upon freedom of speech impairs every citizen's liberty. If our democratic institutions are so weak and tottering that they can not withstand criticism, if we can protect our country only by adopting some form of semi-totalitarianism, we are indeed ill-equipped for the crises into which we are moving.

The hate-merchants, who flourished from the early twenties until the onset of the war, are still maintaining their shops. They assert that their following is increasing; but this assertion does not agree with the facts. Their waning is due, I believe, to their sources of cash being reduced. There are fewer industrialists than in the twenties who believe in dishing out money to such frauds, and, of course, there were many of them who were subsidized, directly or indirectly, by German or Japanese agents in the five years that preceded Pearl Harbor. With financial support withdrawn, only the trickle of money that comes from suckers ready to part with Klatockens in return for mumbo-jumbo remains. The suckers are not as numerous as once they were, and the hate-merchants are having to peddle their wares at definitely reduced prices.

Civil liberties present a serious challenge to States' rights. The protection of the security of the citizen in his home, in his rights to exercise his franchise, in his rights to freedom of speech, assembly, and worship, and from injustice in the courts or extra-legal discipline always has been associated with State government in the United States. The earliest statement of the doctrine of the rights and responsibilities of State government was that embodied in the Kentucky Resolutions, which protested against the iniquitous Alien and Sedition Laws.

If the States eliminate themselves from the field of enforcement of civil rights, as they have eliminated themselves from so many other aspects of government, they will continue a process that is inherently dangerous. Yet it is obvious that, unless the States act, the Federal government will be called upon to act.

It is undesirable for the civil liberties of our people to be guarded exclusively by agencies in Washington. An elaborate technique of legal sophistry is necessary to provide Federal jurisdiction in most instances.

But unless States determine upon a "get tough" policy with those who conspire against the civil liberties of their fellow-citizens, it is almost inevitable that there will be a public demand for the Federal government to assume the obligation. This represents still another move toward centralization, less dangerous fundamentally than that in the field of economics, but dangerous nonetheless.

The basis of our concept of dual sovereignty was an extension of our checks-and-balances system. The States were left with very real powers, so that they could perform many services and protect their citizens in many ways. It was even assumed that States' rights meant the right of each State to protect its individual citizens against invasions of their liberties by Federal authority, just as it was assumed that the Federal government would protect a citizen of any State against State invasion of his rights. Each government was conceived to be a servant of every citizen, intent upon preservation of each citizen's liberty. It was never the concept of the Founders that either State or Federal government had any right of itself. Certainly it was never assumed that States' rights implied the right to do nothing instead of doing something.

In Georgia, we reasserted the old doctrine of States' rights to bring action against the transportation monopoly and to cancel the charter of the Knights of the Ku Klux Klan, Incorporated. It was a limited and tentative beginning, but it points the way toward an avoidance of relying exclusively upon the central government for things that can be done by the States. It is the direction that we must take, if we are to preserve the civil liberties of our people.

There is no idea so dangerous as the suppression of its expression.

12: THE NEED FOR FREE TRADE

The problem of decentralization has been discussed by thousands of Americans, and from many points of view.

One of them is a concern over national defense. Not an enormous ground force, nor even an alert naval and air fleet, can defend a nation today. Defense is a matter of industrial production. The concentration of the productive capacity of the United States within a small and very vulnerable area is our greatest strategic weakness, recognized by almost all experts.

When the Federal government was compelled, because of the inadequate manufacturing facilities in many fields, to set up plants during the war, some thought was given to this problem. Many of the war-built installations are in areas hitherto denied manufactures. However, this was done according to no definite plan, and, in general, the sections of the country most needing industries were awarded only plants of a short-lived type: shipyards and assembly facilities.

Decentralization also is made essential by rising costs in the field of transportation. While I concur with Robert R. Young that much could be done toward making the rail lines efficient, transportation costs will be higher in the future than in prewar America under any circumstances.

Likewise, it is necessary to reverse the trend toward political and economic centralization. One accompanies the other. If we permit economic imperialism in America, we shall have political imperialism in America, with an accompanying loss of liberty.

All these are subsidiary arguments, however. National defense, industrial efficiency, and political safety argue less strongly for a decentralization of the country's industry than does justice.

One of the fundamental arguments for a national Union between the thirteen independent States, loosely confederated into a Congress, was the need for free trade between them. One of the safeguards in the constitution deals with the surrender by the States of the right to erect trade barriers against their fellow-Americans.

What the national government is not permitted to do, and what State governments are forbidden to do, is permitted today to the men who control transportation and to the cartel-organizers of the major monopolies. To permit them to continue is to surrender government into private hands.

Nowhere I travelled in the United States did I find citizens unwilling to see the economy of the entire nation developed. The sense of justice of the average American is sincere; he asks no more for his section of the nation than he is willing to grant to every other. He wants a truly free economy, with opportunity for every citizen of every section.

Transportation rate differentials, wage differentials between sections, and artificial trade barriers and restrictions of any kind have no place in the United States.

13: They believe in their vision

Everywhere I went in America, I found evidence that its people wanted one common country, with opportunity for every citizen and every section, with justice for all, with security for all, and with freedom to do, freedom to think, freedom to experiment with life, freedom to dream.

They wanted no Utopia, with a ready-made happiness devised on mass production lines and sold, cheaply enough, at the price of freedom. They wanted to make their own dreams, as different as they pleased from those dreamed by their neighbors.

It was no impossible vision, unattainable and unreal. It is a vision as durable as the granite of Vermont, as real as the golden valleys of California, as commonplace as the Court House square in New-nan, as imaginatively bold as Manhattan's skyline. It is a changeless vision, that their fathers and mothers before them saw as they wan-dered across the continent, felling the forests, breaking the prairies with their plows, taming the rivers, overthrowing the mountains.

Today, as then, they believe in their vision and in themselves. They know that in any test, free men shall stand.

Not only do they believe that freedom can be maintained and made complete in America, but they believe that they can have a free America in a free world. They do not believe that democracy must go upon the defensive, must contract its orbit, must make com-promises.

When I went into a schoolhouse in Maumee, Ohio, to make a talk, I stopped briefly in a classroom. Obviously, it had last been occupied by a group studying American literature, for there, chalked upon the blackboard in a round, schoolgirlish hand, were two lines from James Russell Lowell's "The Present Crisis":

> "List the ominous stern whisper from the Delphic caves
>   within
> 'They enslave their children's children who make com-
>   promise with sin.' "

Democracy is not an outworn creed. It is a practical way of life. It is the way of life that Americans chose voluntarily. There is no reason why they should retreat from it. There is every reason why they should encourage its development elsewhere; for a democratic world will be a world at peace. Free men do not seek to enslave their fellows; they are too occupied by their conquest of the twin worlds of things and thoughts to desire other empires.

The ideal of the brotherhood of all men is not to be cast aside. It is forgotten only by those who have forgotten that Man is the miracle of the Universe and that Earth is distinguished by Man's occupancy from the other thirty billion stars that travel their orbits through space. There is room for all things in that Universe except forgetfulness of the dignity of Man and of the realization that nowhere in all the world can any man be free until everywhere all men are free.

14: FREE INSTITUTIONS NEED FREE MEN

I was in Baltimore, Maryland, when my secretary, Grace Cannington, called and gave me the message that the Supreme Court of Georgia had announced its decision in the controversy over Georgia's Governorship. So great had been the indignation of the citizens at the seizure by force of the State Capitol, so strong was the prestige of the courts that had been established to provide justice, that the Young Pretender and his aides did not await the formal transmission of the decision to the lower tribunal for judgment. Quietly they slipped from the Capitol. Legal government had been restored.

Free institutions need nothing for their defense except free men. And free men shall stand . . . .